D0378853

AMAZING
PACE

AMAZING
PACE

THE STORY OF OLYMPIC CHAMPION
MICHAEL PHELPS
FROM SYDNEY TO ATHENS TO BEIJING

PAUL McMULLEN

RODALE

Rodale books may be purchased for business or promotional use or special sales. For information, please write to: Special Markets Department, Rodale, Inc., 733 Third Avenue, New York, NY 10017

Printed in the United States of America

Rodale Inc. makes every effort to use acid-free ∞, recycled paper ♻.

Book design by Tara Long

Library of Congress Cataloging-in-Publication Data

McMullen, Paul, date
    Amazing pace : the story of Olympic champion Michael Phelps from Sydney to Athens to Beijing / Paul McMullen.
        p.   cm.
    Includes bibliographical references and index.
    ISBN-13 978–1–59486–326–4 hardcover
    ISBN-10 1–59486–326–1 hardcover
    1. Phelps, Michael, date   2. Swimmers—United States—Biography.   I. Title.
GV838.P54M35 2006
797.2'1092—dc22
    [B]   2006011627

Distributed to the book trade by Holtzbrinck Publishers

2   4   6   8   10   9   7   5   3   1   hardcover

We inspire and enable people to improve their lives and the world around them
For more of our products visit rodalestore.com or call 800-848-4735

To Wendy, Kate, and Don
My own world-class kids

AUTHOR'S NOTE

I first interviewed Michael Phelps in June 2000, when he was an awkward but self-assured boy of 14 who had never been overseas. Three months later, the swimmer became America's youngest male Olympian in 52 years, then nearly won a medal at the Games in Sydney, Australia. As a reporter for *The Baltimore Sun,* I covered Michael in Sydney and then around the world over the 13-month buildup to the 2004 Olympics. *Amazing Pace* follows that road to Athens, Greece, exploring the institutions, issues, people, and times that shaped an athlete who was still a teen when he placed his name in the Olympic pantheon.

In Athens, Michael gained distinction among the nearly 120,000 men and women who have competed in the modern Olympics, as he became the first to win eight medals in a Games that were not devalued by a boycott. Most applauded his ambition and courage, but at one point in Athens, Michael was seen by some as a failure for not clearing the outrageously high bar that he had willingly set for himself. After 3 days of competition, with five events to go, his total included two bronze medals, which meant that he had no chance to match the record seven golds that American swimmer Mark Spitz had won in 1972. The world press moved on to other athletes and sports, just as Michael's story was about to become even more intriguing.

En route to bettering Spitz's medal total, Michael became the first male Olympic swimmer to medal in five individual events. The last of those came in a remarkable come-from-behind victory over world record holder Ian Crocker and granted Michael the right to represent the United States in the climactic event of Olympic swimming, the men's medley relay. His ambition and single-mindedness had been construed as selfishness, but Michael, amid a jumble of jubilation, relief, and vindication, set aside his own interests and considered the welfare of Crocker, the vanquished American teammate who had been his primary source of inspiration. Michael, who had found success and even solace in the water, stepped aside and let Crocker take his place in the medley relay, the Olympic final he had talked about the most.

Michael earned six gold medals in Athens. Three men and one woman have each won nine gold medals in the history of the world's largest and most enduring sports event. At the 2008 Olympics, he intends to establish a new mark for gold medals in a career. Michael has motivated men around the world, who will try to gain their own acclaim by beating the most versatile swimmer ever.

In the aftermath of the 2004 Olympics, an injury threatened Michael's livelihood, and bad judgment brought him embarrassment. What lessons does he carry from those experiences? Will Michael, now a student at the University of Michigan and living on his own, be able to regain his focus and continue to make the sacrifices that he did between the Sydney and Athens Olympics? After nearly a decade of wear and tear under the same demanding coach, will Michael's body, as well as his spirit, hold up against the fatigue that will crop up on those cold, dark Ann Arbor mornings?

Michael will be just 23 years old when the 2008 Olympics are held in Beijing, China. His journey, his *Amazing Pace,* figures to remain as compelling as his achievements and that destination.

PAUL McMULLEN
JANUARY 2006

CONTENTS

PREFACE

SYDNEY, SEPTEMBER 2000

Is he the next Tom Malchow, the next Tom Dolan, or the next Mark Spitz?

That was the pertinent question on the night of September 19, 2000, after Michael Phelps finished fifth in swimming's 200-meter butterfly at the Sydney Olympics. Tardy for his sophomore year at a suburban Baltimore high school, Michael missed medaling in the world's biggest sporting event by less than four-tenths of a second. He was still only 15 years old, America's youngest male Olympian in two generations and its youngest swimmer at the Games since the Great Depression. All arms and ears, he shuffled onto the deck with a gawky gait. At the start of the race, he seemed out of his league against older, stronger men, but his still-developing body settled into the proper rhythm of the butterfly's windmill stroke and remained steady. He maintained his pace while the competition slowed, and covered the last 50 faster than anyone else in the Olympic final.

That youth and potential led to sky's-the-limit speculation about his future, and comparisons to some of his American predecessors. Malchow, a graduate of the University of Michigan, won the 200 butterfly in Sydney. He was the world record holder and had been inspired by the work ethic of Dolan, another Michigan man who stamped himself as the best all-around swimmer of his generation with a repeat victory in the 400 individual medley. Spitz, of course, held the standard not just for swimmers but for all Olympians. No man or woman had come close to duplicating the seven gold medals he had won in as many events at Munich in 1972.

After Malchow discussed his performance in a spacious pressroom to print and electronic reporters from around the world, Michael was ushered into a smaller interview room at the Sydney International Aquatic Center. He wore the same dog-eared Michigan baseball cap that had been on his head for much of the year, and it was clear that the Wolverines' program was the early front-runner in what figured to be the most fevered recruiting fight ever for an American swimmer. Asked if he was a Michigan fan, the boy nodded yes. He said that he had just had a dream come true, but that there was much work to do, particularly on his starts and turns.

Michael did not revel for long. The next morning, he was back at the Olympic pool, training. Bob Bowman, the coach who mapped Michael's progress with assurance and precision, handed him a piece of paper that described the details of the workout. The margin included the note "Austin WR." His next major meet was the 2001 Spring Nationals at the University of Texas in Austin, and it wasn't too soon to begin mounting an assault on Malchow's world record.

Bowman wasn't on the U.S. coaching staff, and he relied on others to supervise Michael at the Olympic Village. The coach didn't have quarters or dining privileges there, let alone a per diem, and when a newspaper reporter from Michael's hometown invited Bowman to dinner, he jumped at the offer. At the end of a long day, one that began with that purposeful morning practice, Bowman took the train from the Olympic Park to central Sydney and walked a few blocks to a hotel on the outskirts of Chinatown. It's always deadline for someone at the Olympics, and the Café Nine at Arons, a media hotel, never closed during the Games. Bowman's work in Sydney was done, and there was no rush after he finished his steak and mashed potatoes. Another round of beers was ordered.

The discussion ranged from the rabid Australian swim fans to that ragged Michigan cap on Michael's head and his long-range plans. The teen was scheduled to graduate from high school in 2003, so his freshman year of college would coincide with the buildup to the Athens Olympics. Bowman's demanding boss back at the North Baltimore Aquatic Club would surely contend that a hard college season and the distractions of campus life were not the way to prepare for Greece, where Michael would be expected to do more than just make a final. Assorted scenarios crystallized into an epiphany and a few pointed questions for Bowman.

Michael is never going to swim in college, is he?

To best prepare for Athens, he's going to remain with you at your club during that crucial pre-Olympic year, right?

Is the kid thinking about turning professional?

Bowman reacted with the aplomb of a cool murder suspect who had been confronted with damning circumstantial evidence. He averted his eyes, assumed a poker face, and took another draw from his bottle of Crown Lager. After a pregnant pause, he drew a breath and switched topics.

ROOTS

INDIANAPOLIS, APRIL 2003

At first glance, the 17-year-old appeared indistinguishable from millions of American boys. Raised in the suburbs, he got a vicarious thrill listening to rap music, had little interest in books or schoolwork, was fiercely protective of his single mother, and tried to impress the girls with a hot set of wheels, in his case a Cadillac sport-utility vehicle. A baseball cap usually covered his unruly dark hair, a defense left over from adolescence, when oversized ears had made him a target of derision. He had a pleasant, goofy grin but wore a scowl when he was introduced to a sport that wasn't his first choice. That aversion became an avocation, and was now his vocation, but it still seemed preposterous, the astonishing things the boy could do in a pool. He was among a select group who had become world-class athletes before having had a chance to grow up, but calling him world-class damned him with faint praise.

Michael Phelps manipulated water like no man since Moses.

Swimming had never seen anything like him.

He stood 6 foot 4 inches but had a wingspan that spread to nearly 6 foot 7. A struggle to keep his weight at 190 pounds had led to guilt-free gorging and 4,000-calorie breakfasts, the ritual refueling that followed draining morning practices. The Sabbath carries little weight in the cult of athletics, and Michael found no rest on the seventh day. Eleven times a week, he dove into his work in Baltimore, Maryland, sharpening his strokes and physiology in a training session that lasted two or three hours. His form had been torn down and improved by a coach who had done everything but dance when he grasped the full measure of the boy's gifts. Years of training had expanded Michael's lung capacity and widened his shoulders. His elbows and ankles were double-jointed, which allowed him to reach angles that other swimmers could not. His most dominant feature was an abnormally long torso, which led the sailor who ran his club team to make the point that the boat with the largest wet surface moved the fastest.

Not yet physically mature, Michael moved on land with the grace of a large-breed puppy, but in his element, he had the self-awareness that comes with being on the cusp of something extraordinary. The matter wasn't as weighty in Olympic circles as the threat of terrorism or rooting out drug cheats, but predicting what he would do next was about to become swimming's main talking point. He was the world record holder in the 400-meter individual medley (IM); in order, the butterfly, backstroke, breaststroke, and freestyle. What the decathlon is to track and field, the individual medley is to swimming: a test of endurance and proficiency in multiple disciplines. The holder of the 400 IM world record could claim to be the best all-around swimmer on the planet, but Michael was also without peer in the two butterfly events and was on the verge of national titles in the backstroke and freestyle. Whatever program he chose, it was apparent that, in another 16 months, he had the potential to achieve something marvelous at the 2004 Olympics in Athens, Greece.

Those Games were already being forecast as the defining moment of a career that had first gained international notice with a series of precocious milestones. In October 2001, Michael became the youngest American male swimmer ever to turn professional. In March of that year, he became the youngest man ever to set a world record in one of the stopwatch sports that had formed the foundation of the Summer Olympics. Neither of those distinctions came as a surprise to anyone who had seen

Michael in 2000—six weeks past his 15th birthday and too young to drive a car—swim fast enough to qualify for the Sydney Olympics.

That giddy accomplishment came in Indianapolis, at one of America's most storied pools, where Michael was now making his first return appearance. The occasion was the 2003 Duel in the Pool, which matched the United States against Australia, the powerhouses of international swimming. Given enough recovery time, Michael's range was so vast that he could beat all but those two nations in a hypothetical dual meet. Now even the other Americans and the Aussies were about to be overshadowed by the breadth of his skill, which had as much to do with nature as it did nurture.

On the first Sunday in April of the pre-Olympic year, as Michael prepared for another eventful competition, spectators found their seats. The Duel in the Pool crowd included his parents and sisters, the people who had brought him into the world and plunged him, sometimes screaming, into his sport. Perhaps the only thing that fully united them was that they all wanted the best for Michael. They understood that dreams don't always come true. The truth was, no family in America was better equipped to explain both the joy and the heartache that could be found at that pool in Indianapolis.

The three men who have won nine gold medals in the Summer Olympics were shaped by their relationships with their father. Bill Lewis, who grew up in Alabama when racism remained highly institutionalized in the South, told his son Carl, "Don't get mad, get even." Arnold Spitz drilled into his son, Mark, that only one lane in a pool could produce the winner. Losing his father at age 12 likely had something do to with hardening the chilly demeanor of Paavo Nurmi.

Michael's father, Fred Phelps, received similarly devastating news on Lincoln's Birthday in 1959. A blood clot had ruptured in his father's brain, killing him suddenly and unexpectedly. Fred was 8 years old, and the loss of his father shook his idyllic life in the Tri-Towns, a collection of burgs in a remote valley in the Appalachian Mountains where the Potomac River separates Maryland and West Virginia. The Tri-Towns still share a variety of social clubs, a little league, and a paper-processing plant that pollutes the Potomac. It has been linked to an abnormally high rate of cancer in the area but has provided employment for thousands. The plant dominated the view off the back porch at Fred's childhood home on a hillside in Luke, near where the Savage River, site of the 1988 U.S. Olympic Trials in whitewater canoeing, feeds the Potomac. On the West Virginia bank, just downstream, sits Piedmont. A mile to the north is Westernport, the hometown of Debbie Davisson Phelps.

An hour's drive to the north, on nearly the same longitudinal line as the Tri-Towns, sits Windber, Pennsylvania. It was the birthplace of Johnny Weissmuller, who didn't win nine gold medals but became more famous than the men who did. The great Olympic swimmer became Tarzan in the movies, the Arnold Schwarzenegger and Bruce Willis of his day. Like hundreds of communities in the Appalachian Mountains, the simple life was the only life in Windber and the Tri-Towns, not a reality television show. With pride and self-deprecation, Fred describes himself as a hillbilly. As a doe and her fawn bolted past the concrete foundation amid the ruins of his Grant Street home one recent autumn, he reminisced about what he called the three seasons in the Tri-Towns: hunting, fishing, and football.

"I didn't know what a lock was," Fred said. "You can still do a contract on a handshake in Tri-Towns. They don't care about fashion. They don't care about keeping up with the Joneses. They don't know who the Joneses are. I had the same teacher for my first three grades of school. Luke used to have 250 people, but it's down to 80 now. Somebody dies, the plant buys the house. Eventually, they'll buy up everything, and the town will stop being incorporated. Then they won't have to pay taxes."

Ancestors from Great Britain dominate the family trees of Debbie and Fred. In 1857, her maternal great-grandfather had emigrated from Wales to a settlement north of the Tri-Towns. Fred's maternal grandparents were born in that same county, Allegany, in the 19th century. Debbie's father was a home-improvement contractor for the Sears Roebuck Company. Fred's was a chemical engineer at the Westvaco paper mill, which employed 2,500 in the 1960s. Now its payroll was closer to 1,300. Like many mill towns in Maryland, Pennsylvania, and West Virginia, the Tri-Towns were depleted by a reverse migration. Instead of continuing west in search of a new start, men before and after World War II headed back to the East Coast and found work there in smokestack industries. Later generations knew that stable employment could be had there, in classrooms. In the suburbs of Baltimore and Washington, D.C., thousands of schoolteachers shared roots in mountain towns, where fond memories didn't put food on the table. Teaching was a sensible career choice for some of the best and brightest from Luke and Westernport, who went to Bruce High School.

Fred played football, basketball, and baseball there. Title IX came too late for Debbie, as Allegany County was among the Maryland jurisdictions that waited until the 1970s to offer interscholastic sports for girls. The only uniform she wore at Bruce High was a cheerleader's, as girls in her era had to slake their competitive thirst in the neighborhood. Debbie spent many hours at the municipal pool in Westernport, but swimming was a country club sport, and kids went there not to train but to frolic and flirt. She could walk, down one hill and up another, from the pool to her home at the corner of Rock and Hammond. In the 1968 Bruce High yearbook, seniors were asked the location where they would most likely be found. Fred listed the street Debbie lived on.

That fall, he went to Fairmont State College in West Virginia. Debbie joined him there in 1970, after a year at Allegany Community College. Fred weighed 165 pounds in high school but filled out to 195 in college. A cornerback on the football team, he was fierce enough to knock bigger linemen off their stance but employed enough finesse to set a Fairmont State record for interceptions in a year. A football assistant doubled as the track and field coach. In need of bodies, he recruited Fred, who established another school record in the triple jump: 43 feet, 11 inches. Debbie and Fred both studied education at Fairmont State. They earned teaching certificates and married in May 1973, agreeing that they would move east to one of the suburban counties surrounding Baltimore, wherever one of them could land a good job.

Debbie's older sister taught in Harford County, northeast of Baltimore. That's where Debbie found her first job in education, teaching home economics to middle schoolers in Havre de Grace, where the Susquehanna River becomes the Chesapeake Bay. Fred's shot at professional football went no further than a cattle call for the Washington Redskins. After a year of substitute teaching, some flag football teammates encouraged him to apply for a position with the Maryland State Police. He was working a blue-collar job at a General Motors plant in Baltimore when he was accepted into the state police academy, and he was commissioned in October 1975.

Their first child, Hilary, was born in 1978, on St. Patrick's Day. Whitney, another active, adorable girl, came along on April 15, 1980. Fred and Debbie purchased 5 acres of land near the Pennsylvania state line, in Whiteford, not far from where the Boy Scouts of America still operate a large reserve of land, and designed and built a custom home. There were children under foot and deer drinking from the stream behind their property, but the harmony was short-lived. A decade after leaving the Tri-Towns to pursue their future together, Debbie and Fred separated.

On the rebound, they had a third child, a son. Michael Fred Phelps II was born on June 30, 1985.

The family's growth coincided with the cable television boom, and Debbie and Fred, determined to provide more healthy diversions, became typical American parents on the go. The girls were signed up for Brownies and ballet, and Hilary played baseball with the boys one spring, when there weren't enough girls in the community for organized softball. Charles Wax, the family pediatrician, touted the benefits of swimming, so the Phelps family joined the North Harford Swim Club. Sans goggles and cap, in a department store suit with a floral print, lace frills, and one shoulder strap, Hilary had a third-place finish in a 1986 meet and vowed to get the biggest trophy the next time. The only girls she couldn't beat wore Speedo suits and practiced year-round. Around Michael's first birthday, the girls advanced to a more ambitious club, in the Harford County seat of Bel Air. The move represented a greater commitment and more travel. A snapshot from that time shows Michael with scabbed knees, crawling on a wooden deck. His strongest memory of the home in Whiteford is a long driveway, perhaps because he was constantly being bundled into and out of a car or van. Debbie remembers driving an hour to a swim meet at a college on Baltimore's west side and changing Michael out of his sleeper pajama and into a playsuit.

Michael was 3 in 1988, when Debbie approached Tom Himes, an

assistant coach at the North Baltimore Aquatic Club (NBAC), about moving the Phelps girls to that club. The NBAC did its summer training in Baltimore City, and the round trip from Whiteford to its pool at Meadowbrook was more than 70 miles, much of it on two-lane roads. As Michael wandered the Meadowbrook picnic grove, mooching from friendly tables and playing under them with his Matchbox cars, his parents tried to adjust to the commitment they had made to the NBAC.

"We had built a brand-new home on 5 acres," Debbie said, "but we were never there. We were never all home at one time in that house. I remember sitting at a desk at Loyola High School, before or after an indoor practice there, one girl eating pizza, another doing homework. You hear about ice skaters relocating or kids moving in with coaches, but they were not going to move without us."

Fred liked the country life, but Debbie yearned for the suburbs and a shorter commute to the pools where the girls were thriving. In 1990, when Michael was 5, the family sold the Whiteford home and bought another inside the Baltimore Beltway, in Towson, only a 15-minute drive to Meadowbrook. The move made it easier for the girls to develop as swimmers but did not improve the widening rift between Debbie and Fred. Despite the reconciliation that had produced Michael, their marriage was back on the rocks. What little time they had away from their careers and swimming was not spent together. Debbie described a marriage that over two decades went from "storybook" to "growing apart." Fred moved out for good in 1993. Their divorce was complete in 1994, and the dissolution of their bond did not occur quietly. Whitney saw the pool as a haven from the bickering, a place where she could release her pent-up anger and frustration. If Michael has any impressions of the tension that accompanied his parents' breakup, he has repressed them but doesn't consider it a coincidence that he developed a lasting friendship with Matt Townsend, who was 5 years old when his father died.

"Matt was raised by a single mom," Michael said. "That's why we're so close."

Michael appears sanguine on a starting block at an international meet, but his formal introduction to swimming was chaotic. In 1992, the year he turned 7, he was enrolled in a stroke clinic taught by Cathy Lears, a close friend of Debbie's. As the other children learned how to breathe properly, Michael refused to take direction. He did not like putting his face underwater, and Lears accommodated his obstinacy with the proviso that he could use the backstroke if he wanted, but he was going to finish every item on the practice plan.

"I complained, I whined," Michael recalled in 2005. "I was a brat. I'm still a brat sometimes."

Diagnosed with attention-deficit/hyperactivity disorder (ADHD), Michael was hard to get started some days, but on most, swimming was a welcomed outlet for his energy and one where his aptitude was apparent. In retrospect, Debbie felt that Hilary had moved up through the NBAC ranks too fast, and she worried that Michael was getting too much too soon. Placed in more advanced training groups with older children, he was labeled "Little Phelps" by Troy Pusateri, one of the club's older boys. Siblings can shift easily between affection and animosity, and Whitney and Hilary bristled when Michael cramped their style. He formed an alliance with Erin Lears, Cathy's youngest, who also had to deal with being the runt in the family and the practice group. Erin recalls a boy who was constantly being picked on, a high-maintenance prospect who went into a crying jag at the slightest upset. That was what Himes, the same coach who had helped the Phelps girls join the NBAC in 1988, found when Michael entered his training group in 1995.

"He was just like any other little kid," Himes said. "When he got tired, little things became big issues. When I'd get on him about doing something that he wasn't doing the right way, his defense was tears. If his sisters had not been swimming, he wouldn't have been swimming. I'm relatively sure Fred had no interest in swimming. He would rather have seen his son in a contact sport. . . . The structure of the family was the structure of swimming. This is the way the Phelps family was run."

Fred says that he would have supported his son in whatever he pursued.

"No matter what it was, I would have been behind him 100 percent," Fred said. "If it had been band or football or baseball, I would have supported it. The only thing I wouldn't have supported was him lying around playing video games."

Hilary Phelps grew into a fine distance swimmer and set records at the University of Richmond. Whitney became the next in a line of succession at the NBAC, which had produced female gold medalists at the 1984 and 1992 Olympics. In August 1994, four months past her 14th birthday, Whitney won the 200 butterfly at USA Swimming's Summer Nationals, with a time that no American woman bettered in the run up to the 1996 Trials. A berth at the Atlanta Olympics became dinner table conversation. Fred got an early Father's Day gift, a commemorative brick bearing his name at Centennial Park in Atlanta.

Debbie figured that Whitney was a shoo-in to get there, but the U.S. team is selected through production in a pressure-packed meet, not personal bests, and Whitney was far from peak form when she went to the Trials. She battled with bulimia, a common malady among young female athletes, to the extent that her coach wouldn't let her practice until he saw her finish a bagel and cream cheese. There had been an ominous practice in 1995, when she tried on a new training apparatus that triggered back pain. Heading to the 1996 Trials, she was slowed by two bulging discs along her spine and a pair of stress fractures, which affected her confidence, form, and training.

"I just pounded through it," Whitney said. "I didn't want to be a wimp. I wouldn't get out of the pool, even though I was injured. It came to the point where I didn't want to think about the fact that I was injured."

Two teammates from the NBAC qualified for the U.S. Olympic team in 1996, but Whitney limped in sixth in her 200 butterfly final at the Trials, more than 2 seconds behind the winner. Her personal best would have won by more than a second, and Debbie used the most tragic analogy possible to describe the aftermath of Whitney's brush with an Olympic berth.

"I didn't know what to say to her," Debbie recalled. "The Christmas before, my brother B.J. gave Whitney a 1996 Atlanta mug. She said, 'I'm going to be there.' I thought she was going to be there, too. She should have been there, but she was injured and wasn't telling anybody. When it happened, people were sending cards to the house. It was like someone had passed away."

Debbie prides herself on discussing life's choices and consequences with her children, but for years, the 1996 Trials were too painful to relive. It became the elephant in her home, a topic too sensitive to discuss.

"Don't feel sorry for me," Whitney said. "Just understand. I don't think she (her mother) understands the pain. I don't think she understands how much that injury hurt, emotionally and physically."

Michael, 10 years old and a fifth-grade student at the time, accompanied his mother to the 1996 Trials. He would matter-of-factly describe the meet as leaving a "scar on our family," but his sister's disappointment apparently steeled his resolve. Already the holder of a national age-group record, Michael was known for winning five or six events at a meet and reacting to his rare losses with emotional outbursts that could quickly spiral into goggle-throwing tantrums. A month after witnessing Whitney's setback, Michael digested a close call of his own and made an internal course correction. The Eastern Zones' age-group championships at Princeton University became a showdown between two of the best 10-year-olds in the nation. Delaware's Rory Connell had more than a 3-second lead on Michael at the midpoint of their first race, the 200-yard freestyle. Already identified by his ability to close a race, Michael narrowed the gap at the end to one-tenth of a second, pushing Connell to within five-hundredths of the NAG record.

"I can almost pinpoint that race as the moment when Michael stepped up," Himes said. "He didn't cry. He didn't throw his goggles or have a fit. It's like he said to himself, 'I'm going to get this guy next time.' Michael had five more events at that meet, and didn't lose. He tied a national age-group record, came close to another, and won the 200 individual medley by 5 or 6 seconds."

Whitney was 15 when she faced the defining moment of her swim career. Michael was the same age 4 years later but was faced with radically lower expectations when he went to the 2000 Trials. Whitney had been touted as an Olympic hopeful for 2 years, while Michael had figured in Trials speculation for all of 4 months. The meet's location was one of the few commonalities in their Trials experience.

USA Swimming had conducted the nation's Trials in four of the last five Olympiads at the Indiana University Natatorium, the Latin name for a pool. The facility was not on the main IU campus in Bloomington, but in Indianapolis. The ceremonial flourish that freshly minted Olympians most anticipated was seeing their name being painted in blue, on a white wall behind the diving platform. The oldest names on the wall went to Los Angeles for the 1984 Olympics. The youngest went all the way around the world, to Sydney, Australia, in 2000. Until a wrecking ball knocks it down or USA Swimming reverses its policy and returns the Trials to a venue that small, Michael will always be the youngest male on that wall.

By 2000, Debbie had moved farther south to a town house in Rodgers Forge, leaving a commute of less than 10 minutes to the pools where Michael trained. She had taken her master's degree in education and shifted from the classroom to a series of administrative posts in the Baltimore County public school system. Fred had moonlighted on tactical SWAT teams but spent most of his career with the Maryland State Police inspecting commercial vehicles on the interstate highway system. He does not have a politically correct bone in his body and feels that his unwillingness to be a yes-man may have cost him a promotion or two. Fred took his son fishing and to ball games and taught him to look a stranger in the eye and shake his hand firmly. Whatever sport Michael tried, Fred instructed, "Take no prisoners." He went to his son's swim meets but moved to the other side of Baltimore and did not let age-group swimming dictate his life. An abundance of Debbie's free time, conversely, was spent supporting Michael's swimming. She admits that her son became the only male in her life.

Both of Michael's parents attended the 2000 Trials in Indianapolis. Debbie went to the Sydney Olympics, accompanied by her sister, Amy; brother, B.J.; his wife, Krista; and Hilary. Fred made his own arrangements and went Down Under with Jackie, his new partner. On the night that Michael advanced out of the semifinals of the 200 butterfly at the Sydney Olympics, the proud father talked his way down to the concourse that separated the practice and competition pools, congratulated Michael, and gave him a pep talk. When they met again a few days later, Fred informed Michael that he had remarried. Jackie wasn't just a woman he was interested in; she was his wife. Father and son had not lived under the same roof for 7 years, but Michael did not take the news well. There was a gulf between the two, and it was about to widen.

When Michael set his first world record, in March 2001, he did not recall his father making a congratulatory telephone call. Fred said that some of his attempts to reach out and maintain a normal father-son relationship were rejected.

Uneasiness ran through the family. Whitney was studying at the University of Nevada, Las Vegas, and trying to revive her swim career when she attended the 2000 Trials at the IU Natatorium. She did not go to the Sydney Olympics, but now she again set aside her own comfort to watch Michael at the 2003 Duel in the Pool.

"I don't enjoy being around the pool," Whitney said of the emotional anguish she put herself through to be a spectator at the IU Natatorium. "I don't enjoy watching swimming. I enjoy watching my brother compete, but if I could have watched him swim and then left, that would have been fine. I really didn't want to sit there for the entire meet. It's frustrating to think, if I could have trained, how fast I could have gone. That's one of the reasons that I don't like to go to meets. I don't like to discuss swimming with him. I look at Michael as my little brother, someone I used to wake up in the morning, fix him breakfast, get him off the school bus. We did kid stuff. I see more to him than just Olympic star. Fame doesn't make him who he is."

The Duel in the Pool piggybacked on USA Swimming's Spring National championships, where Michael became the first man to win titles in three of the four strokes at a national championship meet. He beat Olympic champion Lenny Krayzelburg, one of his role models, in the 200 backstroke; topped Klete Keller, an Olympic bronze medalist, in the 200 freestyle; and took the 100 butterfly with a time that was one-hundredth of a second off of his own American record. That was all a prelude to the performance he put on before a Sunday matinee crowd at the Duel in the Pool. Whitney took her seat, alongside Fred and Jackie. In the same row, at the opposite end, sat Debbie and Hilary. Only Michael's mother had witnessed one of his three world record performances. On this day, in the span of 41 minutes, they saw him nearly get two.

Under his own world-record pace at every turn, Michael won the 400 individual medley by 6 seconds, lowering his standard to 4 minutes, 10.73 seconds. He pointed to Debbie in the stands and dove into the adjacent practice pool to keep loose. It was already a happy 38th birthday for his personal coach, Bob Bowman, whose exhilaration grew when Michael dominated the 100 butterfly on 40 minutes' rest. The 4-year-old world record was 51.81. Michael touched in 51.84, studied the time on the scoreboard, grinned, and brought his hands to his head. By four-hundredths of a second, the length of a fingernail, he had missed becoming the first swimmer to lower world records in different events in the same day.

The crowd was drained, but Michael couldn't slack off, as he prepared for the 200 butterfly. The event was his family's legacy, the one that had frustrated Whitney in 1996 and sent him to the 2000 Olympics. The competition was Tom Malchow, who had surrendered his world record to Michael but was still the reigning Olympic champion. Coming off the final turn, Malchow had a lead of .73 seconds, but no deficit seemed too large for Michael, especially in this pool. At the 2000 Trials, he had been fourth with 50 meters remaining, but rallied to claim his spot in Sydney. Now Michael gauged Malchow, with a glance to his right off of the final turn. As they neared the final wall, Michael caught him with one last windmill stroke to claim his third win at the Duel in the Pool, all in a little over two hours. Australia's men combined for four all day.

Michael wasn't done. University of Texas junior Ian Crocker was capable of handling the butterfly leg in the finale, the medley relay, but Michael owned the fastest relay split ever, and the American coaches decided that even fatigued, he represented their best shot at a world record. Physically spent, Michael went a half-second slower than his record split, but the Americans nonetheless won with history's third-fastest time. Over five days, he had repelled world-class fields in three different strokes, over as many distances. Michael was clearly the hottest swimmer on the planet, but his reach was met with skepticism from an expert on the outer limits of a swimmer's capabilities.

Speaking for his side after the Duel in the Pool, Australian Grant Hackett, the Olympic champion in the 1,500 freestyle, advised the young American not to spread himself so thin. Michael was oblivious, already thinking of how to spend the $25,000 bonus he earned from USA Swimming for his world record in the 400 individual medley. A representative from Mutual of Omaha, the meet's title sponsor, thanked Michael for his performance, telling him that it would surely boost the play that *USA Today* would give the Duel in the Pool. One of swimming's finest individual shows, however, merited only a few hundred words, buried on an inside page, in the nation's newspaper the next morning.

Michael was among the last arrivals at a postmeet reception in a downtown ballroom. To Fred's chagrin, he heeded a lesson from his father. Years earlier, when a pitcher from the Baltimore Orioles had refused Michael's autograph request, Fred admonished the professional that he should know better than to brush off a little kid. Now father and son were visiting, when Michael turned to acknowledge a fan. Fred took exception to the interruption and walked away.

At one point in the evening, Michael embraced Whitney, who had tears in her eyes and confusion on her face. The best day of Michael's career had just come in the same arena that had produced her worst. Catching up with former international teammates, Whitney heard the talk about her baby brother's grand prospects. Grown men who were no kin got misty-eyed describing what they had seen Michael do that afternoon, and what he might be capable of at the Athens Olympics.

The possibilities were greater than even the people who believed in him the most could imagine.

COACH

BARCELONA, JULY 2003

Michael climbed out of a temporary practice pool, shoulders sagging from the exertion of five hard days of racing and disbelief at what had just occurred. He plopped into a plastic chair, leaned forward, and heaved his chest. As his heart rate slowed, he took in the counsel of Bob Bowman. The coach took a knee and placed his mouth a foot from Michael's left ear. For the next 5 minutes, Bowman deconstructed a surprising twist of events and the positive effect it could have on the next 13 months. He wore glasses to correct an astigmatism and was not accustomed to being compared to movie idols, but Bowman evoked a sappy Robert Redford film, *The Horse Whisperer.* He placed a positive spin on the evening's upheaval in Michael's mind, then chided himself for letting it occur in the first place.

"I feel I could have done more to keep him mentally sharp," Bowman said. "He was a little too loose when he got to the pool, signing autographs, playing with the Australians, talking to his friends on the deck. Every other race, he was totally focused. This time, he was focused maybe 98 percent, and that 2 percent would have made the difference. I sensed that he was a little bit further from total concentration. If only I had put my foot down. The next time, he'll know to wait until after the final swim to relax."

Over the previous four nights, Michael had established himself as the star of the 2003 World Championships. A spectacular run peaked on Friday, July 25, when Michael got the unprecedented double that had eluded him at the Duel in the Pool. He followed a world record in the 100 butterfly semifinals with another in the 200 IM, becoming the first swimmer to establish world records in different events in the same day. One more and he would become the first to notch five in one meet. Victory seemed certain in the finals of Saturday's 100 butterfly and Sunday's 400 IM, the events he had used to scare history at the Duel in the Pool. Surely Michael would be the first to win four titles at a world championship meet, and perhaps the first to set five world records in one meet.

His timing was elegant. This was the last major international competition before the Athens Olympics, and Michael's prospects caused a buzz at the Palau Sant Jordi in Barcelona, Spain, where FINA, swimming's international governing body, had brought its premier event. Advertisers had their antennae out for the next big thing, and the media rushed to frame Michael's story. A headline in *Mundo Deportivo*, a Spanish sports daily, neatly summed up the new world order: "Phelps, El Nuevo Spitz." He was entering territory that had been explored only by Mark Spitz, who had won seven gold medals at the 1972 Olympics.

Twenty-four hours later, the Sunday headline read "Phelps est Humano." The New Spitz was human after all. For the second straight day, Michael blew away the world record in the 100 butterfly but could have gone faster had he not lowered his guard. Now Ian Crocker had torn into that opening, dropped the world record to an unfathomable level, and taken Michael's spot on the American medley relay.

The sudden turn of events would reverberate clear to the 2004 Olympics. Instead of staggering him, the blow cleared his head and became 55 weeks' worth of motivation. He went from feeling like the king of the Catalan Province to being more receptive than ever to the cajoling, cursing, pulling, and pleading of his coach. Michael set the highest standards for himself. During his own coming of age, Bowman had been even harder to satisfy.

Other than finding purpose and stability at the North Baltimore Aquatic Club, Bowman and Michael had little in common.

Michael, profoundly efficient with his strokes, gave little thought to the science involved, the angles and levers that needed to be so precise. Bowman, the assertive mentor who refined that economy of motion, had been a hesitant mess during his own competitive days. Michael squirmed in a classroom. A voracious reader, Bowman was obsessed with cause and effect, in an esoteric range of subjects. Michael's energy led desperate teachers to plead with his mother to medicate him. At the same age, Bowman's gift for mathematics had him reading sheet music. Michael saw the sequels to *Star Wars* and wanted to be Luke Skywalker. When Bowman was 11, he studied the credits of the original and wanted to become a composer like John Williams, who scored the movie. Michael was well-versed in pop culture and fluent in ESPN. Bowman took 3 years of high school French, the language of diplomacy and the Olympics. Michael came from a broken home, was doted on by his mother and two sisters, and was extremely at ease around girls. Bowman didn't have time for women and was reared in a genteel Southern household, which wouldn't have aired its dirty laundry had there been any.

The NBAC was the only swim team Michael had ever represented. Bowman's insistence that his way was the only way had turned him into a vagabond. He had burned bridges on both coasts, expecting parents to leave the details to him, and their children to bring the same commitment he had taken to Florida State University (FSU). As a Seminole junior, Bowman qualified for the 1985 Spring Nationals in the 100 butterfly, while training with the distance swimmers. Back home, in Columbia, South Carolina, Bowman had been an accomplished artist and musician and was president of his high school's National Honor Society. Swimming captivated him because, unlike everything else he tried, it did not come easy. His effort outdistanced his talent in a pool, where Bowman became a victim of what he diagnosed as paralysis by analysis.

"I didn't have a perspective on failure," he said. "My expectations weren't very realistic. I overdid the whole cognitive analysis thing, and that hurt my swimming. I should have trained as a sprinter when I got to college, but I insisted on working with the milers. More work means better, right?"

As he completed his undergraduate work at FSU, Bowman took a coaching job with a local swim club. The World Wide Web was still a theory, and research was done the old-fashioned way. His boss handed Bowman a stack of reading: magazines and mimeographed articles on an assortment of pertinent topics. Bowman was expected to hold on to the reading for a month. He did an all-nighter, returned the materials the next day, and asked for more.

"Beware of Bob" read a sign in his modest NBAC office, but the kids there knew a kinder, gentler Bowman than the one who hadn't been able to last more than two winters in any of his previous coaching jobs. Bowman had taken his impatience and a degree in developmental psychology to Ohio, Nevada, back to Ohio, California, Maryland, Alabama, and again to California before he finally stayed put in Baltimore. As a young coach, Bowman didn't realize "that parents were part of the equation and that I wasn't the sole owner of knowledge in the universe." That approach twice got him fired by the Cincinnati Marlins, but each dismissal led to an important influence.

Bowman was 23 in 1988, the first time he got the ax, but got a break from David Marsh, a young entrepreneur whose club team, the Las Vegas Gold, thought big, with a budget to match and talent like Olympians Rowdy Gaines and Melvin Stewart. In 1991, when Bowman's second gig in Cincinnati ended as badly as his first, he joined Paul Bergen's staff at the Napa Valley Swim Club, north of San Francisco. Because there is a lot of Bergen in Bowman, there is a lot of Tracy Caulkins in Michael.

In Barcelona, Michael became the fifth swimmer to win three individual events at a world championship meet. Two women have pulled off that hat trick, and Bergen coached both, Inge de Bruijn of the Netherlands, in 2001, and Caulkins, in 1978. Before Michael was born, Caulkins was considered the best female swimmer ever. She was the first woman to win both individual medleys at the Olympics, in 1984, when she was 21. A boycott kept the United States out of the 1980 Olympics, where she could have won four individual events. She is the only swimmer ever to hold American records in all four strokes, and she retired with a record 48 national titles. She was hardened in Nashville, Tennessee, by Bergen.

"He's one of those guys who would not hesitate to repeat an entire practice if the last stroke was not efficient," Bowman said.

Was Bowman like that when he went to work for Bergen?

"Oh yeah," Bowman said. "He just intensified it."

Two men immersed in one of the slowest forms of mammalian racing found a diversion in one of its fastest. Bergen grew up on a Wisconsin farm. At Kent State, he aspired to represent the United States in the Modern Pentathlon at the 1960 Olympics. Its five disciplines are equestrian, fencing, swimming, shooting, and running. In 1988, Bergen took over the Napa Valley club team in California, in part because its pools were situated alongside stables. Bergen and Bowman bought an interest in a few thoroughbreds, and cross-pollinated training theories. Their horses swam to build endurance. Another of Bergen's methods left Bowman with a right hand that can't hit the high notes on a piano. As Bergen drove a Jeep around a Napa Valley dirt road at a good clip, Bowman sat on the tailgate, his hands on the reins leading a filly, and his head ringing with his boss's cardinal rule.

"If a horse gets scared and breaks away, don't come back without something," Bergen said. "I want a hunk of hair, or bridle, in your hand. You better come back with something other than a shit-eating grin on your face."

The Jeep hit a bump, the filly bolted, and Bowman went flying. He returned to Bergen without the horse, but did have the stopper, a part of the bridle, along with a snapped ligament in his hand. The incident did not dampen his enthusiasm for the sport of kings. Before he was selected by the United States to coach at an international meet, he had incorporated Bowman Thoroughbreds LLC, which breeds, sells, and trains horses. His direction of Michael is peppered with terms from the thoroughbred business. Having seen Michael sleep on the floor of a jet crossing the Pacific, Bowman likens him to a horse that "travels well." A few days before a race, horses are put through what their trainers call a "last fast work," usually a furlong in a target time. Four days before the start of a meet, Bowman liked to have Michael pop a fast 100 in a specific stroke.

Bergen maintains that their experience with four-legged athletes gave them an advantage.

"Bob and I are better observers of swimmers because we had to be observant of horses," Bergen says. "Horses can't talk, and you have to be observant of their body language. You have to watch their eyes, their ears, their gait, day in and day out."

Bowman and Michael communicate wordlessly in practice or at a meet. The swimmer will stop at a wall and find his coach on the pool deck. Bowman will tilt his head or make a hand movement, and Michael will nod. In the heat of a race, coaches whistle to their swimmers, and Michael came to recognize Bowman's pitch. That level of communication was years in the making and was the result of sheer coincidence. When Bowman went to Baltimore, it wasn't with the intention of coaching Michael. He was actually searching for a way out of the business.

Bergen and Bowman had left Napa Valley in 1996 and headed east, where both stumbled upon male prodigies. The mentor moved to the Solotar Swim Club in northern Virginia, where he came upon an apt but undersized pupil. As good as the boy looked in a pool, he was even more fluid when cross-training introduced him to running, so Bergen encouraged him to join his high school cross-country team. That boy was Alan Webb, who in 2001 broke the American high school record for the mile that had stood since 1965.

Bowman, meanwhile, pondered an offer from Marsh to become a graduate assistant at Auburn University and enroll in its farm management school. The job paid just $10,000, but it would move him closer to becoming a full-time breeder and trainer. Bowman called his contact at the North Baltimore Aquatic Club, where he had babysat a training group during the 1992 Olympics. Instead of advice, he got an invitation to join the NBAC staff, at a starting annual salary of $35,000. He accepted and began to explore Baltimore's graduate school options. On June 30, 1996, Michael Phelps turned 11. The next day, Bowman was introduced as the NBAC's newest assistant. He knew of Michael only in the context of Whitney, but a year later, a staff shakeup placed Bowman in charge of Level VI, the group just below the club's elite performers. It ranged from high school seniors to Michael.

On September 5, 1997, Athens was awarded the Games of the XXVIII

Olympiad. Within a month, Bowman called for a meeting with Michael's parents, and it wasn't to discuss their 12-year-old's problematic behavior. The boy was gifted and had no anxiety about performing under pressure. It was 18 months after the U.S. Trials had devastated Whitney, and Bowman raised big-picture scenarios that had the potential to similarly backfire and burn. Like a New Testament parable, the details of the story vary with its narrator, but the message was clear. Bowman raised the 2004 Olympics as a near certainty for Michael. He also issued a warning to be ready in the event that he developed in time for the Sydney Olympics, a bold vision for a boy.

"I told them that things are going to change, and they'll never be the same," Bowman said. "I wanted everyone to be ready for 2000. Debbie said, 'Oh, no, not Michael, he's too young.' But I told her, 'What are we going to do to stop it? When he's ready to go, he's got to let it go.'"

Michael had already produced national age-group records, despite cutting corners. His butterfly was efficient only when he put real effort into it. Similarly, his turns rated average only when he exerted considerable energy. He would win a race, lower his personal best, and respond to Bowman's critique with a quizzical look that said, "How can you complain about that?"

Bowman came to the NBAC with multiple American Swim Coaches Association awards for teaching stroke technique. In 1989, he won three of the available six in two age groups, and entered an elevator in Pittsburgh proudly clutching his hardware. The only other passenger nodded. It was George Haines, who had made the Santa Clara Swim Club the best in the world. Haines stepped off the elevator, congratulated Bowman, and said, "If you work harder, maybe you'll win all of those awards next year." Bowman was a perfectionist before that encounter. Haines toyed with him the same way Bowman toyed with his swimmers. Asked if Michael had ever seen a sports psychologist, Bowman replied, "every day."

They clashed immediately. In that summer of 1997, Bowman began to alter all of Michael's strokes, reshaping some and refining others. His first task was to change Michael's rudimentary alternate kicking motion to the more advanced six-beat kick. Each day for a week, Michael went a little longer using the more efficient method but eventually lapsed into old habits and got kicked out of practice. He waited impatiently in the pool lobby for his mother. Debbie took her son's phone calls but firmly said no, she couldn't leave work early, that he would have to wait until the scheduled end of practice for his ride home.

"I was being denied something I wanted to do," Michael said.

"The thing that got Michael the most, and still does, is to take swimming away from him," Bowman said. "He hated to be excused early. He considered that an embarrassment. He knew practice was important; he was raised on that concept. Because of his ADHD, it was one thing that came naturally and felt good. It probably calmed him down. He always left practice in a better state than when he arrived."

Debbie approved of the way the horseman broke her stallion, but Bowman incurred her wrath on at least two occasions: when Whitney tattled about his foul language, and the time he allowed Michael to play hooky from Towson High School for an afternoon at Laurel Race Track. Pimlico, the site of the Preakness, the middle jewel in the Triple Crown, is a 5-minute drive from the Meadowbrook pools where Bowman spent 8 years. All but the first year of that tenure was spent directing Michael. When Bowman finally felt secure enough to purchase a home, he bought one a street over from where Debbie and Michael lived. He winced at the suggestion that he had become the boy's father figure, but by the time they got to Barcelona, Bowman had been the major male influence in Michael's life for more than 2,000 days.

His abilities to gauge Michael's progress and anticipate his production were remarkable, but there were times when even Bowman was caught off guard. Three weeks before the opening of the 2003 World Championships, they went to California for the Santa Clara International Invitational. At an outdoor pool made choppy by the wind, and on his last day as a 17-year-old, Michael lowered the oldest men's world record on the books, Jani Sievinen's mark in the 200 individual medley, which had stood since 1994. Until Michael went 1 minute, 57.94 seconds, only two other men had gone under 1:59 in the 200 IM. Considering the conditions and the fact that Michael was not primed for Santa Clara, it was a shocking performance. It had been 36 years since any male—Spitz, of course, had been the last—had set a world record without shaving his body hair to reduce friction and tapering his training to build energy.

Santa Clara made Michael the world record holder in three events. He was prepared to do very big things at the world championships in Barcelona and emerge as the front-runner in the hype for Athens. The other swimmers up for that role included fellow American Natalie Coughlin, the first to win five individual events at a national championship meet since Caulkins, and Ian Thorpe, a brilliant Australian who had won six gold medals at the 2002 Commonwealth Games. In Barcelona, Thorpe entered seven events, Spitz's magic number, including a much-anticipated meeting with the new world record holder in the 200 IM. Michael's schedule was slightly less daunting, as he also entered four individual events but just two of the three relays.

Doubters stirred the muggy Mediterranean air.

"We've got Ian Thorpe, and they're trying to say they've got someone even better," Australian coaching giant Don Talbot responded to Michael's latest world record. "In the major international meets, Phelps has done nothing yet."

Bowman printed out the article that contained that quote and handed it to Michael, but the encounter with Thorpe had to wait. The boy a local newscaster described as being from "Baltimoro" opened his world championship program with the 200 butterfly and promptly dropped his 2-year-old world record to 1:53.93 in the semifinals. A day later, when Michael won the final with the second-fastest time ever, the crowd had little reaction. Less than 45 minutes after that, Michael set an American record in the 200 freestyle, leading off an 800 freestyle relay that eventually finished second to Australia and Thorpe. After his first two nights of racing, spontaneous applause greeted Michael when he entered the dining room at the Hotel Fira Palace, where the U.S. team was being housed. When he walked in Thursday evening, after setting another world record in the semifinals of the 200 IM, his teammates barely looked up from their pasta.

The blasé pose was dropped on Friday, July 25.

Michael's need to nap in the middle of the day seemed odd in North America, but he felt at home in a city where shops close for the afternoon siesta. As Michael rested, Bowman's mind raced over the evening's stakes. In less than 50 minutes, Michael faced the semifinals of the 100 butterfly and a final in the 200 IM. The first race was a matter of advancing, but there was a primed field waiting for him in the second. Bowman fretted over the scenario and its ramifications for the coming Olympic year. The four individual events Michael was attempting in Barcelona were the ones he wanted to try in Athens. He was considering more, but if he couldn't deal with a crowded schedule at the world championships, how could he be expected to handle a more daunting one under the pressure of the Olympics?

Michael went to Barcelona as the second-fastest man ever in the 100 butterfly, and watched Andriy Serdinov of Ukraine lower a soft, 5-year-old world record in the first semifinal. As a television crew interviewed Serdinov, Michael readied for the second semi and flashed a knowing smile at Bowman, who peered down from a ramp. The slowest of all 16 semifinalists at the turn, Michael closed with his customary purpose and commandeered his semifinal, bettering Serdinov's 51.76 with a 51.47. Michael now owned the world records in both butterflys and both IMs and was just the third man ever to hold world records simultaneously in four events. The others had been Spitz and Michael Gross, the German known as the "Albatross" for his 6-foot-11 wingspan.

There was no time to celebrate or even to swim down in the main practice pool. Michael instead walked a few meters outside to a smaller one and stayed limber with 15 minutes of medley swimming, alternating his strokes. He moved to a massage table, where Brian Campbell, a masseuse hired by USA Swimming, kept Michael loose with his hands and manner. Waiting inside was that fresh field in the 200 IM final. It included Sievinen, the former record holder; reigning Olympic champion Massi Rosolino of Italy; and Thorpe. Michael promptly assumed a record pace, led at every turn, and lowered the world mark for the third time in 27 days, all the way down to 1:56.04. Thorpe, the runner-up, became the fifth-fastest man ever but was still more than 3½ seconds back. Horsemen like Bowman considered the 1973 Belmont Stakes the yardstick for thoroughbreds. Secretariat won the 1½-mile race by 31 lengths. Michael won that 200 individual medley by three lengths. Extrapolate that to the Belmont distance, and he would have beaten Thorpe by 36 lengths.

Technically, Michael was not the first to achieve world records in different events in the same day, but symbolic asterisks accompanied his predecessor. At the 1976 Olympics, Kornelia Ender, a product of the systematic doping used by East Germany, bettered her own world record in the 200 freestyle, then tied her standard in the 100 butterfly.

At the conclusion of the 200 IM medal ceremony, a woman in a green outfit introduced herself to Debbie Phelps.

"What's this," she said, "about a rivalry between our boys?"

It was Margaret Thorpe, Ian's mom. Two women who shared a rare perspective had a pleasant exchange.

A British Airways strike had made for some tense delays, but Debbie had gotten to Barcelona, accompanied by her brother, B.J., and his wife, Krista; their cousin Darlene Blaney; Michael's sister Hilary; and Gerry Brewster, one of Michael's high school teachers. Fred did not make the trip, as the rift between father and son had worsened. At Michael's graduation party in June 2003, Fred reacted angrily when he learned that Debbie and Hilary would be Michael's guests, courtesy of Speedo, in Barcelona. Fred had been under the impression that one of those spots had been reserved for him. Michael said that his father hadn't been around. Fred mentioned the games they had attended together, the times he had gotten Michael special treatment in the Baltimore Orioles locker room. Michael reiterated his position, that his father hadn't been around. Fred reminded his son that he had paid child support. Michael mocked that $800 a month as "chump change," and a testosterone-charged confrontation nearly turned physical.

In Barcelona, Michael seemed oblivious to that tension and assumed a mindset that Bowman didn't dare disrupt. Before a race, Michael donned headphones and listened to angry, loud rap music. In the pressroom after his big double at the 2003 World Championships, he was asked what was coming through his headphones. It was a track from one of his favorite rappers, off *The Eminem Show,* "Till I Collapse."

In 1992, the Palau Sant Jordi had been a basketball venue during the Barcelona Olympics. Eleven years after Larry Bird, Magic Johnson, and Michael Jordan had been dispatched to prove the superiority of the American game and win converts, the arena had a new Dream Team, and its roster consisted of one name. Was there anything Michael Phelps couldn't do?

In his last 10 races, Michael had set five world records and an American record. Two years after Thorpe had become the second man to win three events at the world championships, Michael was now favored to surpass that standard. Saturday figured to be his easiest day of the meet, since he had only the final of the 100 butterfly. Bowman felt so confident he gave him the morning off. Michael went to have lunch with his mother, but she had left her hotel to do some early Christmas shopping. He was mildly disappointed, but had no idea how unsettling his day was about to become.

Crocker's career had been stuck in neutral since 2000, when he won the 100 butterfly at the U.S. Olympic Trials and had an American record and fourth-place finish in Sydney. While Serdinov and then Michael busted down the world record in the semifinals of the world championships, Crocker continued to blend into the background, matching his personal best, 52.21, which suddenly seemed pedestrian. Before the final, as Michael and Crocker entered the ready room where swimmers were held before a race, head U.S. coach David Marsh, the same man who had given Bowman one of his first breaks, held up a piece of paper that read "50." Who would be the first man under 51? Surely, the visual was meant for Michael.

In the ready room, his iPod malfunctioned, an omen to go along with the crossed signals that kept him from having lunch with Debbie. Michael matched Crocker's reaction time off the blocks but fell six-tenths of a second behind at the turn. He never panicked, maintained his stroke, and improved on his day-old world record, dropping from 51.47 to 51.10. There was, however, one very big catch. Crocker never relented, and went below not just the 52-second barrier but all the way down to 50.98. Crocker removed his goggles, studied the scoreboard that read "WR" alongside his time, and shrugged his shoulders with an expression that said, "Where did that come from?"

Three racers did not take turns lowering a world record over two days. It just didn't happen. When Michael said that he wanted to change his sport, he didn't envision that occurring overnight. It had taken professional golfers years of conditioning to turn themselves into better athletes and close the gap that Tiger Woods had established in the late 1990s. It took Michael 25 hours to remake his sport, as his tide of excellence had raised another boat, one that was rather ominous. Crocker's emergence cost Michael more than another gold medal. The fastest American in the 100 butterfly earned a spot in the final of the medley relay, and No. 2 headed to the preliminary.

The pressroom moderator added to a surreal night and introduced Michael as the gold medalist. Even Crocker acknowledged the pecking order: "I had a lot of confidence in myself, but deep down, you say, 'It's Michael Phelps.'" To that point, Michael had been bland and noncommittal with his comments. This time, he opened his heart and echoed the words that Bowman had just whispered in his ear on the deck of the temporary practice pool.

"I'm going to do everything I can to be on that nighttime relay in Athens," Michael said. "It's better for me to have this experience here rather than next summer."

Bowman was more expansive than that.

"What kind of person is the media going to remember?" he said a day later, when asked what he told Michael. "Let the loss go, but remember how ridiculously high the standard is to win four individual events, when every event has people sitting around for two days, waiting for the chance to beat you. Every event has fresh horses. That's why the Triple Crown doesn't get won very often and why people don't win seven gold medals every Olympics. I had been walking on air all week. It's healthy to come back to the reality of the situation. It's not a fairy tale. It's a reminder of my job and how I need to go about it. Getting beat is tough for someone who seldom gets beat, but I feel I could have done more to keep him mentally sharp. I call it being in total lockdown. It's a big one-tenth of a second, because that relay is a slam dunk."

Wasn't Bowman being harsh? Michael had to swim the preliminary, but wouldn't he get a gold medal just the same if the United States, with Crocker, won the final of the medley relay?

"I don't think of that as a medal," Bowman insisted. "It will always be a morning relay."

Thirty-six hours after the best session any swimmer had ever enjoyed outside the Olympics, Michael faced the roughest morning of his career. On the final day of the world championships, he had a preliminary not just in the 400 individual medley, as he had anticipated, but the medley relay. He pleaded with Bowman, an assistant on the American coaching staff, to find someone, anyone—Crocker even—to take his place on the butterfly leg, but learned at "a meet like that, it's not about you." Michael got through both races, and that night, in the 400 IM final, found two more reminders that the swimming world wouldn't stop while he posed with his medals. Michael became the first man to break 4:10 with a 4:09.09, but Hungarian Laszlo Cseh followed in 4:10.79, what would have been a world record at the start of the year. Cseh was 17, younger even than Michael. Another teenager, Tunisia's Ous Mellouli, took the bronze.

Michael leaned back against the pool wall and used his right hand to steady himself on the deck. He pointed to Debbie in the stands and raised his left index finger, to signify who's No. 1. The other 1,065 men and women, from 150 countries, combined for nine world records at the 2003 World Championships. Michael recorded five by himself, but that was not the memory he took home from Barcelona. Moments after he accepted his third individual gold, four other Americans took the top step on the medal podium. The third man, the one who helped the Americans to a world record in the medley relay, was Crocker, not Michael.

CLUB VERSUS COLLEGE

COLLEGE PARK, AUGUST 2003

By the thousands, high school seniors from mid-Atlantic states collect their diplomas, then charge like lemmings to the Maryland resort of Ocean City, an 8-mile strip of overcrowded beach, neon, and high-rise condominiums. "Junebugs," who party too much and tip too little, begin to arrive around Memorial Day, but Michael didn't join his friends from the Towson High School Class of 2003 in that bacchanal. It conflicted with an intense period of training, but once his work at the world championships was done, he thought of play.

"Bob actually said I could take a break," a dripping Michael said moments after the 400 IM in Barcelona. "Maybe go down the ocean."

Fat chance.

The next morning, Michael and nine other elite Americans boarded a jet, not for home but to do reconnaissance work in Athens, where the 2004 Olympics would begin in 382 days. They saw the aquatic center that was behind schedule, toured the site of the Olympic Village, strolled through the Plaka, gaped up at the Acropolis, and got a feel for heat and humidity that was every bit as sapping as Barcelona's. Michael returned home on the last day of July, and USA Swimming's Summer Nationals opened five days later. The meet was of little consequence to a world champion, let alone an athlete of Michael's status, but instead of a well-deserved vacation, he dove back into competition. Besides reiterating the obvious, that he wasn't an average swimmer, the Summer Nationals revealed that he wasn't affiliated with an average club.

The meet was held at the University of Maryland, in College Park. Michael competed in the Summer Nationals not because it was an hour's drive from his home, but because Murray Stephens had supported the event and the venue. Since 1997, Michael had taken orders from Bob Bowman. Since 1996, Bowman had gotten his from Stephens, the cofounder of the North Baltimore Aquatic Club, whose influence on Michael's career cannot be overestimated. Without Stephens, Michael would not have been exposed to the mores of swimming in a demanding atmosphere or enjoyed the convenience of doing his double practices 10 minutes from his back door. The indoor pool where he trained in the winter was completed the year he turned 10. The NBAC had turned out an Olympic gold medalist before Michael had even been conceived. It was the only team he had ever represented, and no elite swimmer had lasted his 12 years in a club that at its highest levels assumed the mindset of a paramilitary organization.

As Stephens made the rounds in College Park, another man who would soon have a hand in Michael's Olympic fate maintained a lower profile. Eddie Reese had already been named the head coach of the U.S. Olympic men's team for Athens, where maybe his most important duty would be determining the American relay lineups. Reese had his own swimming empire at the University of Texas, where his athletes included Ian Crocker and Aaron Peirsol, the only men who would beat Michael in 2003. Like two-thirds of the American team that had gone to the world championships, Crocker and Peirsol passed on the Summer Nationals. Granted, older swimmers didn't recover as quickly, but during his heavy training phases, Michael logged 50 percent more mileage than did the men from Austin. While Michael chafed under the tight rein applied by Bowman at the NBAC, the collegians had their studies and all that the cultural capital of the Southwest offered. Crocker, however, knew that the transition from an overly structured adolescence to the freedom that came in college held hazards of its own.

Most children must be pushed or pulled out of their comfort zone to accomplish great things, and it is fitting that the acronym for a national age group record is NAG. That dynamic is described in "A Few Suggestions on How to Be a Better Swimming Parent," which could be found on the NBAC's Web site.

> "Failure isn't such an evil thing that parents should try to shield their kids from it. Allow them to fail, then teach them to get up off the canvas and try harder to succeed the next time. . . . If you try to temper your child's dreams, if you teach her to settle for the ordinary, you may indeed save her from many a heartache and many a failure. But you also rob her of the opportunity of achieving great things. . . . If 'fun' means mindless entertainment and sensory bombardment, then wasting hours playing Nintendo is loads of fun and swimming is by definition 'not fun.' If 'fun' means working hard and challenging yourself, taking pride in accomplishing difficult goals, and discovering talents you didn't know you had, then swimming is fun and Nintendo by definition is 'not fun.' . . . If a work ethic is not created and cultivated when a swimmer is young, it very likely will never appear. It is so rare as not to be an option that a kid who is a slacker from ages seven to fourteen will suddenly change his spots and become a hard worker. . . . Discipline and commitment are good things, not things we should downplay, hide, apologize for, or (worst of all) stop demanding because it may be unpopular."

Michael Brooks completed that manifesto in July 2002, when he was an assistant coach at the North Baltimore Aquatic Club. It was proofread by Stephens, who cultivates self-sufficiency. Some clubs have a parent take the hand of an 8-year-old and escort him to the starting block. The NBAC's kids show up on time, ready to race, without Mommy. In 1990, Debbie Phelps kissed her daughters good-bye and shipped them off to a meet in Atlanta. They were 11 and 9.

Two years later, their brother joined them at an institution that exemplified the side of Baltimore that had little in common with the one portrayed on American television. The city had some of the nation's highest rates for drug addiction, murder, and teen pregnancy, which provided graphic plotlines for series like *Homicide, The Corner,* and *The Wire.* The Meadowbrook Aquatic and Fitness Center, where the NBAC has been based since 1986, was less than 2 miles from some troubled neighborhoods, but figuratively, it was light-years from the social ills that created the city's seedier side.

There has been a Meadowbrook pool in Mount Washington, a redeveloped mill town on Baltimore's north side, since 1930. Its compound is flanked on the west by Interstate 83 and on the east by the Jones Falls, the stream that bisects the city. It is usually innocuous, but in 1916, 12-year-old Harold Murray Stephens nearly drowned in it. Four decades later, he determined that his only child needed to know how to swim.

The pool where a young Murray Stephens was taken for lessons now sits empty in the basement of the Baltimore School for the Arts, where one of Michael's favorite artists, the late rapper Tupac Shakur, was once a student. The Knights of Columbus, a fraternal organization for Catholic men, ran that pool in the 1950s, and one of that faith's most vigilant orders shaped the ethos that Michael absorbed at the NBAC. In the 1960s, Tim Pierce and then Stephens graduated from Baltimore's Loyola High School, where the alumni include Jim McKay, the longtime ABC Sports announcer, and Tom Clancy, the best-selling author of military techno-thrillers. Both Pierce and Stephens then went to Baltimore's Loyola College. Both the high school and college were operated by the Jesuits, the order of priests who call themselves God's Soldiers.

Stephens won some conference freestyle titles as a Loyola College senior in 1967. The next winter, he assisted Pierce, the head coach of the swim team at their prep alma mater. In the spring of 1968, they gathered some ambitious boys and formed the North Baltimore Aquatic Club. That summer, the NBAC sent Bobby Gavin to the U.S. Olympic Trials. In a sequence that would be repeated by Michael, Gavin qualified for the Trials in the 200 butterfly and went on to the University of Michigan. Stephens heard Lefty Driesell, the new basketball coach at the University of Maryland, boast in 1969 that he was going to make the Terps "the UCLA of the East," and drew a parallel to another West Coast dynasty. The world's best swim team was in Santa Clara, California, where

George Haines was a Pied Piper, attracting talent like Don Schollander and Mark Spitz. California and other Sun Belt states traditionally turned out most of America's best swimmers, but Stephens wondered if a decaying industrial city in the Northeast could do the same.

He devoted his free time to the NBAC and carved out a niche in a previously untapped market. Stephens took two girls to the 1972 U.S. Olympic Trials. Four years later, one of them reached a Trials final. In 1980, two NBAC females placed fifth at the Trials. One of them, Theresa Andrews, took a sabbatical from college and returned to the NBAC to improve her shot at the 1984 Olympics, where she won gold in the 100 backstroke. Initially, Andrews had moved from Annapolis to Baltimore to join the NBAC. Other elite young swimmers in the mid-Atlantic region similarly reordered their lives. A girl from Pennsylvania who had been born during the 1976 Olympics and was baptized Nadia Anita Louise Nall, in honor of Romanian gymnast Nadia Comaneci, moved south and became America's best breaststroker in 1991. A few days past her 16th birthday, Anita Nall took silver in the 100 breaststroke, bronze in the 200 breaststroke, and gold in the medley relay at the Barcelona Olympics.

Pierce had retired from coaching and the club in 1984. Autonomy was vital to Stephens, who ran the NBAC by personal mandate rather than by committee. Emboldened by the success of Andrews, Stephens inspected the fixer-upper that Meadowbrook, which he had been renting, had become. Its pool was in disrepair, but it was 200 feet long and 110 feet wide, a bulkhead away from being converted into an Olympic-size, 50-meter facility. Borrowing $5,000 from his mother for a down payment, Stephens began to renovate the property and became the owner of Meadowbrook in 1987. The NBAC remained at the mercy of Loyola High's six-lane indoor pool and other rental facilities during the cold weather months, so Stephens started construction on an indoor pool at Meadowbrook. It was completed in 1995, the year Michael set his first national age-group record.

In 1996, when Bowman sought advice from Stephens about the Auburn assistant's position, he instead got a job offer. Bowman was single and single-minded, the way Stephens preferred his assistants. He was 42 when he started a family. Besides his wife, Patty, Stephens employed seven assistant coaches in the winter of 2003–04. None were married. He owns a 65-foot sailboat and devoured Patrick O'Brian's series of books that dropped Jack Aubrey, a fictional British naval commander, into the Napoleonic wars. Some of Stephens's swimmers and English students were more likely to compare him to Captain Bligh. There was a reason Bowman described nonswimmers as civilians and why two NBAC products were tough enough to become Navy Seals. Before former NBAC swimmer Jason Roberts became the oldest man to graduate in his commando class, he returned to Meadowbrook to harden his body and mind.

"When I decided to pursue the Seals," Roberts said, "I went back to Meadowbrook to train, just to be in that environment. It was the best possible preparation I could think of for Seal training, where you're cold, wet, and tired for nine months."

Stephens's swimmers received more than expert instruction. He was fascinated with the Arthurian legend, and his pep talks would mix the teachings of George Haines with lessons more apt to come from Joseph Campbell, the scholar who explained the power of myth. One afternoon in 1997, while Stephens went on about some guy who held his breath underwater for 45 minutes in order to slay a monster's mother, a restless 12-year-old fidgeted. The Beowulf legend includes archetypes that resonate in Michael Phelps, but the lesson went over his head.

In some respects, Michael had not been the most peculiar American swimmer at the 2000 Olympics. He was from an age-group team that was second to none, one that enjoyed the luxury of two 50-meter pools. The state of Maine, conversely, did not hold a single Olympic-size pool, which made for a humble introduction to the sport for a boy from Portland. Crocker spent his early years training in a facility that was also used to provide physical therapy for the mentally handicapped. Sometimes, their diapers didn't do the job.

"My age-group background was a four-lane, 25-yard pool," Crocker said. "It was attached to an elementary school. Most of the time, the water was kept at 85 degrees, because the handicapped didn't want to swim in cold water. There were fecal contaminations about every other week."

Like Michael, Crocker had been diagnosed with a learning disability, attention-deficit disorder (ADD), but the East Coast phenoms were markedly different in other ways. Crocker took guitar lessons, was introspective, and did not define his life through swimming. At the 1998 Summer Nationals, he became the first 15-year-old American to break 1:50 in the 200 freestyle. Crocker was so uncomfortable with his sudden notoriety, his parents had to coax him into competing at the 1999 Pan Pacific Championships, even though it meant a trip to Australia. Crocker won the 100 butterfly at the 2000 U.S. Olympic Trials. At the Sydney Olympics, he came within 22-hundredths of a second of the bronze medal and swam the final of the medley relay, where the United States won gold and set a world record.

Fresh out of high school, Crocker was late for the start of his freshman year at the University of Texas. Austin is home to one of the nation's largest universities and a renowned athletic department. The capital of Texas smelled of power, oil, and freedom, and its music scene had been a launching pad for artists like Willie Nelson and Stevie Ray Vaughan. If a coach couldn't recruit athletes to UT, then he could not recruit. If a young man couldn't be happy in Austin, then something was wrong.

Reese's first teaching and coaching jobs had come in Roswell, New Mexico, the UFO capital of the world, and he had worked with his share of space cadets. When Reese recruited Crocker, he sensed that the tall, quiet boy was a special case who might require extra care, and warning signs mounted as his prize freshman struggled to adjust to college life. Self-esteem is not usually an issue for an Olympic gold medalist and an American record holder, but Crocker had little. He liked to tinker on a 1971 Buick Riviera, but when it broke down, that hobby became just another torment. Crocker drank too much, became reclusive, and floundered through his first two years of college. He was a fan of Pink Floyd, but there was nothing comfortable about his numbness. He contemplated transferring to another college or quitting the sport altogether. On a visit to Austin, Gail Crocker, a registered nurse, saw that her son was not well. Before an Austin doctor diagnosed Crocker with clinical depression, an on-line screening pointed to that illness.

"The best description I've heard of depression is that it strangles your ability to appreciate the joy in life," Crocker said. "The things you enjoy doing, you don't want to do. I didn't want to leave the house for things that were fun, let alone a morning training session or three hours' worth of classes. I wanted to sleep all day, and I couldn't sleep at night. I didn't look at the challenge of training in a healthy way, I looked at it as a burden. I had gone through a nasty breakup with a girlfriend and was dealing with a lot of different growing-up things, events that you can't escape, regardless of where you're living."

In the summer of 2002, Crocker was prescribed Zoloft, an antidepressant. After spending two summers as the top American in the 100 butterfly, July brought a wake-up call from Michael, who lowered Crocker's American record and beat him at the 2002 Summer Nationals. The nation's best went directly from that meet to the Pan Pacific Championships in Japan. It was all he could do to make that trip, but after Crocker returned to Austin for his junior year of college, he resumed getting his life back in order. He stopped drinking beer, dropped Pink Floyd's shade of lyrical introspection for Bob Dylan's, and embraced training like he never had before.

The American men's swim team at the 2000 Olympics included nine past, present, or future Longhorns. Crocker's recruiting class included Brendan Hansen, who was growing into America's best in the breaststroke. When Crocker returned to Austin at the end of that pivotal summer of 2002, the freshmen included Peirsol, already a world champion. Longhorn Aquatics, the club team that trained at UT, included steady influences like Neil Walker. Kris Kubik, Reese's assistant coach, aided Crocker's reemergence out of his darkness, and training became enjoyable again. For the first time, Crocker was motivated to do endurance work in the pool and hit the weight room at Darrell Royal Stadium, a key element in Reese's training philosophy. Because his body and mind had found peace, Crocker was able to deliver an effort in Barcelona that was truly Beamonesque, the overworked adjective that is used to describe big and unexpected breakthroughs. (The origin of the term was Bob Beamon's long jump at the 1968 Olympics, when he improved the world record from 27 feet, 4¾ inches to 29 feet 2½.)

After kicking his medication cold turkey and embracing training, Crocker still remained fuzzy about the best way to beat Michael. He gained that final bit of clarity on the eve of the 2003 World Championships in Barcelona, where Reese laid down an aggressive plan of attack.

"There's nobody on this earth who can beat Michael in the last 50," Reese recalled months after the 2003 Worlds. "If you go out with him, you are conceding the race. You've got to forget all of your fears, all of your pain, and take it out, don't wait to sprint coming off the turn. When Ian beat Michael in Barcelona, he was the most surprised guy in the pool. I was second most, and Michael was third."

Reese had been on every American Olympic coaching staff since 1988. Stephens, who had no weight room but gave his NBAC swimmers a sturdy aerobic base, got his sole Olympic assistant assignment in 1996, when the U.S. women's team included two of his swimmers. Whitney Metzler made the Olympic final in the 400 IM. Beth Botsford was 14 when she qualified for the U.S. team, and her four-month wait between the Trials and Olympics ended anxiously. Arriving at a U.S. training camp, Botsford didn't even get out of the airport in one piece, as she aggravated tendinitis in a shoulder while lifting a piece of luggage. Botsford experienced her first menstrual cycle in Atlanta but held up well enough to win the gold medal in the 100 backstroke.

Whitney Phelps's absence, of course, is what Michael and his family remembered from 1996.

Stephens was at a crossroads after the Atlanta Olympics. He had gone from gadfly to positions of authority in USA Swimming. Few age-group coaches had produced three gold medalists. Business was booming at Meadowbrook, where the cash flow from family memberships dwarfed the dues paid by his NBAC swimmers. Stephens had young children of his own and sought a successor to oversee North Baltimore. Cathy Lears and Julie Gorman had taught Michael the basics. Keith Schertle and Tom Himes continued his development and provided calm during his parents' breakup and divorce. In 1997, Stephens placed Bowman in charge of one of the club's top groups, with specific orders to make over its youngest member. To this day, Michael remains incredulous that other parents complained and a few left the NBAC over what they perceived as preferential treatment for him.

"How is that possible?" Michael said. "If you swam well for Bob, you got praise. If you swam poorly, you got yelled at. Bob spent time on the people who cared the most, the ones who wanted to get better. At one point, he had to change the attitude of the group. That was easier after 2000, when they saw what I had done. I never trained against people in workouts. I trained against the clock. I used to try to lap as many people as I could in a set. Don't like it? Swim faster. That's how I grew up."

In its initial heyday, Meadowbrook had weathered fire, flood, and complaints about the Big Band noise coming from its dance pavilion. Into the 1960s, blacks and Jews protested over its discriminatory policies. After Stephens became its owner, Meadowbrook came to be viewed as elitist for other reasons.

"People call our swim school," Bowman said, "and say, 'I don't want my kid to be like Michael Phelps, but I want him to learn how to swim.' Murray said he's like a character in the Harry Potter books, 'He whose name cannot be spoken.' Michael brought some kids in, but now it's viewed as a place where the standards are so high."

Nearly all of the 220 on the North Baltimore roster were age-group swimmers. Once they reached 18 and graduated from high school, they went to college, which, to Stephens, was the place where a swimmer's work ethic went to die. Postcollegians might contaminate the cocoon he had constructed, but as Michael finished high school and his contemporaries headed to college, adjustments had to be made.

The occasional guest had alleviated Michael's frustration over a lack of training peers. Sabir Muhammad, one of America's best sprinters, stayed at the Phelps's home in Rodgers Forge before a World Cup meet in December 1999 and asked his host for a ride to practice one day. Michael was 14. British butterflyer James Hickman was among those who came to train at Meadowbrook. Michael was committed to the NBAC at least through the Athens Olympics and needed more permanent influences, so Stephens granted Bowman's request to add some maturity to the training group. Before the men in their 20s were allowed in, they were read the riot act. Jamie Barone played high school ice hockey in Connecticut, walked on to the Loyola College swim team, and found the religion of swimming during his junior season. Barone asked to join Bowman's group in April 2001 and was told not to sully the air around Michael.

"Bob warned me," Barone said. "He was adamant, that 'you will not bring any of your college lifestyle to this atmosphere.' I remember walking out of my first practice, wondering what in the hell I had gotten myself into. In my first three years of college, I probably partied three or four nights a week, so when I joined North Baltimore, I went from one end of the abuse spectrum to another, too much beer to too much physical and mental torture."

Barone earned the Rookie of the Meet award at the 2002 Summer Nationals and cleared a path for others. In May 2003, two months after Kevin Clements had completed his eligibility at Auburn University, he moved into the vacant bedroom across from Michael's. At the world championships in Barcelona, Clements finished seventh in the 200 IM. He listed his affiliation as his hometown club in California but was a de facto member of the NBAC.

The North Baltimore roster remained in flux at the 2003 Summer Nationals. Clements wore an NBAC cap for the first time in competition. Emily Goetsch, who was delaying her freshman year at the University of Southern California to remain with the NBAC and prepare for the 2004 U.S. Olympic Trials, got her first national title in the women's 100 butterfly. Like Michael, she needed a training partner, and plans were firming up for Marianne Limpert, a silver medalist, to make Baltimore the base for her bid to become Canada's first four-time Olympic swimmer. Paul Yetter coached a solid group of girls at the NBAC's satellite operation in Harford County. Courtney Kalisz, the most promising, had struck up a friendship with a rival from a club in Virginia. Now that girl's family was preparing to relocate from Williamsburg, so that she could train under Yetter. There were smiles all around the NBAC staff as that girl, 14-year-old Katie Hoff, placed fourth in the 200 IM in College Park.

On August 6, a mere 10 days after he had concluded his historic run in Barcelona, Michael started his Summer Nationals program with a pair of titles. The day's double gave credence to the speculation that if he could handle six events at the world championships, he was capable of more at the Athens Olympics. Michael became the third-fastest man ever in the 200 backstroke, an event he insisted "I don't know how to swim," but that was not his most important performance of the night. Wearing a full-body Speedo for the first time, Michael dominated the 100 freestyle, dropping his personal best nearly 3 seconds, all the way down to

49.19. The performance carried great significance. Only one American had gone faster in the pre-Olympic year. Michael wasn't a threat to medal in the Athens 100 freestyle, but suddenly he was among the pool of candidates for the American 400 freestyle relay. Just like that, Mark Spitz's seven gold medals weren't so untouchable. Reese, the man who would have the final say on those relay decisions, stated the obvious.

"Very simply, we know he's that fast, and we know he'll be faster next year," Reese said. "The goal is to win relays, and we'll take whoever can help us. The Olympic schedule is going to be very interesting for Michael and Bob Bowman."

Michael expanded his options the next evening, when he became the first American to break 1:46 in the 200 freestyle. Friday night brought another American record in the 400 freestyle, the first time since Spitz that one man had simultaneously held five. A spreadsheet was required to comprehend what Michael was doing. There are 13 individual events in Olympic swimming. Over the course of 18 days, he had set world records in four and won national titles in four entirely different events. In that span, Michael had posted personal bests in all eight, fairly common for a novice but unheard of for a world champion. It was as if the Atlanta Falcons had decided to have quarterback Michael Vick go both ways, except that instead of playing cornerback on defense, he would assume a four-point stance and plug gaps at nose tackle, *and* handle all of the kicking responsibilities.

Was there nothing Michael couldn't do in a pool?

The meet illustrated his ability to find motivation where there should have been none, and to blot out distractions. Michael knew that his father wasn't going to Barcelona, but College Park was less than 30 miles from Fred's home. When Fred did not make an appearance at the Summer Nationals, Michael was nonplussed.

"This is his world, and I'm just watching him travel through it," Fred said of their estranged relationship. "People ask me how he's doing, where he's swimming next, and it's hard to say that I don't know."

Debbie was still trying to process what her son had done at the world championships when she took her seat at the final session of the Summer Nationals. The season had been long, hard, and fulfilling, and Michael wanted to withdraw from his final event, the 200 individual medley.

One more title, however, would make him the first man to win five individual events at a national championship meet. In order, Johnny Weissmuller, Spitz, and Tom Dolan had claimed four titles in one meet. Michael's arms and legs had all the snap of soggy spaghetti. He told Nick Wooters, a friend from the Loyola College swim team, that it was safe to head back to Baltimore, since he would be lucky to break 2 minutes. Stretching for a way to end the summer in style, Bowman announced that if Michael broke his world record from Barcelona *and* the 1:56 barrier, he would shave his head.

Michael led Clements by a second after the butterfly, and by nearly two after the backstroke. The sellout crowd realized that they might witness the first world record ever in Maryland, and roared at Michael to move faster. Clements had a breakthrough performance, as he became the second-fastest American ever, faster even than the great Dolan. Far ahead was Michael, who somehow located the composure and strength to touch in 1:55.94.

"My hair's not that long," Bowman shrugged. "I might look better."

It was Michael's seventh world record in 41 days and his best according to the computerized scoring system that FINA uses to rate times against history. In Barcelona, the premier performance had been Michael's world record in the 200 IM. He needed just 15 days to top himself and cap the best non-Olympic summer ever by a swimmer.

ROLE MODEL TO RIVAL

AUSTRALIA, NOVEMBER 2003

Michael Phelps was gifted with good genes and chromosomes, steered to the proper club, and placed under the right coach, a fortuitous blend of heredity and environment. He had moved beyond the phenom stage to comparisons with the all-time greats. The year's run had its ground-breaking in Indianapolis, gained steam in Santa Clara, grew to audacious proportion in Barcelona, and somehow sustained itself through College Park. For all of his accomplishments and the promise of even greater things to come, however, there was one place where Michael was a bit of an arriviste.

Hadn't Australia already hatched the greatest swimmer of the millennium?

The Summer Nationals in College Park were followed by a 109-day break from competition, which ended with a pair of meets in Australia's largest cities. The first marked Michael's return to the pool where he had made his international debut at the 2000 Olympics—a cute story in Baltimore, a brief note elsewhere in the United States, and of no consequence in Australia. That nation had Ian Thorpe, then still a teenager himself, whose elegant strokes in the pool and sense of style out of it were noticed before he delivered what may have been his nation's finest Olympic hour. In the entire history of the Games, has a host city ever produced a bigger local hero?

From 1998 to 2002, *Swimming World* magazine had named Thorpe the best in the world four times, but things were turned upside down when Michael returned Down Under in November 2003. Over five days, starting with the Qantas Skins in Sydney and moving on to a FINA World Cup meet in Melbourne, Michael dominated and Thorpe was reduced to a bit player. From Asia to Europe, the two had been gracious to each other on medal podiums, in press conferences, and on shuttle buses, but theirs was an uneasy changing of the guard.

Eric Clapton was God until Jimi Hendrix landed in London, but at least the Yank died young. Arnie's Army, the devout fans of Arnold Palmer, did not take kindly to Jack Nicklaus ruining their march, and Australians had to stomach Michael just after Thorpe had redefined the zenith of swimming, seemingly once and for all. Michael should have been as welcome as the architect who finds fault in the design of the Sydney Opera House, but the warm reception he received from swim fans there was testament to Australia's appreciation of the sport.

Michael was no longer in awe of what Thorpe could do, but he did envy his status in a country that embraced and respected the water like no other. A poster of Ian Crocker was taped to a window in Michael's bedroom, a constant reminder of what had happened in Barcelona, but the five years prior to the 2003 World Championships had been spent chasing the other Ian.

The beat of rap music pounded in Michael's head before big international races. Afterward, he usually stood atop a medal podium and mouthed the words of a song that had been written some 10 miles south of where he trained. Baltimore's Fort McHenry was under bombardment in 1814 when Maryland native Francis Scott Key, a prisoner of war on a British ship, penned the words to the National Anthem. South of where that ship anchored, the Patapsco River feeds into the Chesapeake Bay, the largest estuary in the United States. An advertising copywriter once described the region as the Land of Pleasant Living. The first white man to explore it was more effusive in his sales pitch to prospective settlers. Captain John Smith, who sailed up the Chesapeake in 1607, described the bay and its surroundings as "a country that may have the prerogative over the most pleasant places known, for large and pleasant navigable rivers, heaven and earth never agreed better to frame a place for man's habitation."

An 18th-century British seaman made a similar assessment of a Southern Hemisphere locale. Combining an extraordinary solution to prison overcrowding with standard colonial-era expansion, 11 ships—the majority bearing convicts—had completed a journey from England to Australia in 1778. Having found Botany Bay on the Tasman Sea too harsh for settlement, Captain Arthur Phillip sailed north, steering east between a treacherous straight and into a long, stunning harbor. He exceeded Smith's hyperbole with this description: "The finest harbour in the world, in which a thousand sail of the line may ride in the most perfect security."

The tourists who make Sydney the world's premier destination agree.

Kangaroos, Paul Hogan's *Crocodile Dundee* character, and the Outback Steakhouse chain form the typical American's knowledge of Australia, but dust is not a major issue for the overwhelming majority on the world's largest island, since 90 percent of the population lives within 6 miles of surf. Americans flock to the beach on the Fourth of July, but the seasons are reversed in the Southern Hemisphere, where Christmas is the most crowded beach day of the year. New Yorker Woody Allen once joked that the only reason to swim was to avoid drowning, and Australian parents who don't teach their tots how to are considered negligent. Water is treated like a deity, to be feared and worshipped. Nets on cove beaches keep weak swimmers in and sharks out. One of the short ferries from Sydney's Circular Quay goes to Manly Beach, where children by the dozen take lessons in surfing, scuba diving, or kayaking. Manly's promenade includes war memorials and monuments to surfers. A T-shirt reads "Australian Surf-Rowers League." A sign hints at the origin of that pursuit: "No Swimming Due to Surf."

The first swim meet in America was conducted in 1877. Sydney Harbor had served as the site of races in 1846, more than three decades earlier.

Earlier authors had described the art itself, but a man who emigrated to Australia from England published the first book about competitive swimming in 1867. Bondi Beach has Speedo's Cafe, maybe the only restaurant on earth dedicated to a brand of swimwear. At the Paris Olympics in 1924, 16-year-old Andrew "Boy" Charlton won the first of the nation's eight gold medals in the longest race in Olympic swimming. America has its home-run champion, Australia its gold medalists in the 1,500 freestyle. The nation's stranglehold on that macho event, most recently extended by Kieren Perkins and Grant Hackett, epitomizes the can-do vitality of Australia, where the Summer Olympics have been held twice. Thanks to the pioneering use of interval training that its coaches borrowed from track, the country won every event in freestyle—a stroke once known as the "Australian crawl"—at the Melbourne Games in 1956. That year, the nation toasted 17-year-old Murray Rose, who won the 400 and 1,500 freestyles. Five decades later, Australia's strength in the sport hasn't lessened. At the 2003 World Championships, the United States collected 28 medals to Australia's 22. On a per capita basis, Australia handily won that medal race. It had fewer than 21 million people, compared with more than 290 million in the United States.

At the 2000 Olympics in Sydney, Australia produced another 17-year-old prodigy, one who bore the weight of considerably more expectation and scrutiny than Charlton and Rose. Three years older than Michael, Thorpe had a head start similar to the one Australia had on the United States in swimming, but the parallels between the two were eerie. Both were the sons of schoolteacher moms. They swam because their big sisters did. Both Whitney Phelps and Christina Thorpe raced at the 1995 Pan Pacific Championships, then failed to achieve Olympic berths the following year. Both had shaky introductions to the sport, as Thorpe was thought to be allergic to chlorine at one point, and Michael had an initial aversion to putting his face into the water. Once immersed in swimming, however, both prospered like no boy who had come before.

Thorpe was 12—the same age at which Michael was placed under the charge of Bob Bowman—when Doug Frost became his coach, and all of 14 when he began his international career at the 1997 Pan Pacific Championships. Michael was the youngest male ever to set a world record, but

Thorpe remains the youngest world champion ever, as he was three months past his 15th birthday in January 1998 when he won the 400 freestyle in Perth, Australia. The 1999 Pan Pacifics, a competition that usually includes Australia, Canada, China, Japan, the United States, and other Pacific Rim nations, served as a test run for the Sydney International Aquatic Centre, a 17,500-seat venue built for the 2000 Olympics. Still only 16, Thorpe marked the occasion with his first world records, in the 400 and 200 freestyles. The boy from the Sydney suburb of Milperra donated his $25,000 (Australian) check for the first world record in the facility to cancer research.

Thorpe grew to 6 feet 4 inches and a sculpted 200-plus pounds. The feet that required size-17 shoes served as giant flippers in a freestyle that combined economy and power. Beyond his racing record, he had a distinctive nickname—"The Thorpedo"—and panache that the pop culture labeled "metrosexual." Whether his light brown hair was slicked back or meticulously disheveled, his physique was always accentuated by a black bodysuit that adidas designed to his specifications. Thorpe made his way around a deck the way James Bond did a casino and worked a press conference like Jay Leno, hitting rehearsed lines in his opening monologue and meeting the rare fresh query with a glib ad-lib. Craig Lord of *The Times* of London remembers Thorpe at 16, offering not just an opinion about his favorite book but also his favorite painting. Thorpe did and said all the right things, had appeal that ranged from his home to clear around the globe, and seemed destined to become a lead figure at the Sydney Olympics.

Bowman acquired the videotaped highlights of the 1998 World Championships, which included Thorpe overtaking Hackett in the 400 freestyle and then coolly dealing with a television interviewer. Over the next year, once or twice a week, Michael studied that grainy VHS tape for a technique or quality that contributed to Thorpe's success. Like Alexander Popov, a Russian who was the top sprinter at the 1992 and 1996 Olympics, Thorpe had a stroke that appeared effortless. Michael took note of his revolutionary use of the dolphin kick off turns. The young American studied the Australian's mannerisms and speech habits. Bowman described that video as a major step in Michael "getting serious."

That tape came in handy at a time when Bowman was attempting to increase Michael's workload. The coach had already succeeded in winnowing other diversions. In the spring of 1997, just before Bowman became his coach, Michael played organized baseball and lacrosse for the last time. Two years later, he was angered when Nick Williams, who would go on to play college football and lacrosse for Division I Towson University, was named the top student-athlete in Dumbarton Middle School's Class of 1999. Later that year, when Michael was just another freshman at Towson High, he desperately wanted to fit in with his football-playing friends. Michael heard a solicitation for players for the school's golf team and cited its noncontact nature in another appeal to Debbie. She explained that there were no guarantees, that he would have to try out, and gently reminded him that golf practice would conflict with afternoon training at Meadowbrook. Her son was too young and living too much in the moment to fully grasp his potential.

At the start of 2000, Michael's fastest 200 butterfly had been 2:04.68, but he was near the end of a growth spurt that boosted his confidence, increased the length of his stroke, and made him more amenable to the increased demands of Bowman. In March, they took an open mind and few expectations to a Seattle suburb for USA Swimming's Summer Nationals. On the morning of March 30, Michael went under 2 minutes in the preliminary, a major breakthrough. Whitney, competing for the University of Nevada, Las Vegas, informed Michael of the moment's gravitas, and Bowman pondered a new reality. If he didn't screw things up, Michael could go to the Olympics *that* year. In the final, Tom Malchow and Great Britain's Stephen Parry announced themselves as Olympic medal contenders, with the world's fastest times of the year to date. Michael followed in 1:59.02, just a half-second behind the year's second-fastest American. He was only 14, but was firmly in the hunt for a berth in the Sydney Olympics.

In May 2000, at a meet at the University of Michigan, Michael made the Trials qualifying standard in all five events he entered. "He'll probably make the Olympic team," said Jon Urbanchek, the host coach, "but nobody knows about him." That was still the case in August, when the U.S. Trials went to Indianapolis. Dara Torres's bid to become the first swimmer to medal in four Olympics was a major story. She had made her Olympic debut in 1984, the year before Michael was born. On the eve of the meet, Malchow remarked that "a kid that young is probably naïve about what's at stake, and that might be a good thing for him."

Four years after watching Whitney fall short in the same pool, Michael seemed oblivious to pressure. He lowered his personal best in the preliminaries and did so again that night, when he won his semifinal. A day later, the final unfolded poorly. He dawdled removing his warm-up jacket, was rushed onto the blocks, and had a lousy turn at 100 meters. When Michael was fourth off the final wall, more than a second out of second place and a spot in the Olympics, Bowman began to rehearse his "We still love you" speech. The other contenders decelerated, however, while Michael came back with a fourth 50 that was faster than his third, and faster than anyone's in the field. He passed Steve Brown, then Jeff Somensatto with 20 meters left. Had it been a 210-meter race, he might have even caught Malchow. The world record holder won, but Michael touched second in 1:57.48, making him the fourth-fastest American ever.

"I may have to retire sooner than I thought," Malchow said. "He doesn't know how much his life is going to change, but it's going to change real soon."

Michael was about to learn the folly of blowing spending money on a sweat suit. NBAC teammate and 1992 gold medalist Anita Nall knew that Michael was primed to make the Olympic team and become awash in keepsake shirts, suits, and backpacks, let alone warm-ups, but she did not want to mess with karma a few days before his final and let him spend away.

"I didn't want to jinx him," she said. "I knew he was going to be getting all the Olympic gear he wanted, but I didn't want him getting ahead of himself."

Two months past his 15th birthday, Michael was anonymous in that downtown Indianapolis mall. On the other side of the world, a young man two months shy of turning 18 could not walk two blocks in the business and shopping districts of his hometown of Sydney without encountering his own image in a storefront or on a billboard. Thorpe had endorsement deals with an airline, a bank, a breakfast cereal, and a telecommunications company. He was sold as the smiling face of what would be the perfect Olympics.

After even the International Olympic Committee had branded the 1996 Games in Atlanta as an aesthetic and logistical failure, Sydney easily came up with something better. The 2000 Games were efficiently organized, albeit somewhat antiseptic, as the main Olympic Park was built on reclaimed industrial wasteland in Homebush Bay, 12 miles to the west and a half-hour train ride from the city center. There was no language barrier to slow English-speaking visitors, but Australia's mania over swimming would have been understood in any language.

The opening ceremony featured men on horseback, psychedelic color and light, and symbols of atonement in a land where women and the native people had been subjugated. Cathy Freeman, an Aborigine who would win track's 400 meters, lit the Olympic Flame, and Thorpe ignited another patriotic frenzy the very next night. For the third time in 13 months, all in his new favorite pool, he lowered the world record in the 400 freestyle. His time, 3:40.59, would have placed him fifth in the inaugural 400 freestyle *relay*, in 1964. An hour later, Thorpe was assigned the anchor in that relay, which the Americans had never lost at the Olympics. He was matched against Gary Hall Jr., who owned history's fastest relay split. Hall taunted the Aussies with the boast that the Americans would "smash them like guitars," but the home quartet made sweet music. Michael Klim staked the Australians to a substantial lead on the opening leg with a world record. The Americans narrowed the gap, and Thorpe had only a slight lead at the final exchange. Hall moved ahead in their first 50, but Thorpe drew even coming off the final wall and rode the emotion of what had to be the loudest man-made sound ever heard at a pool. He touched a fifth of a second in front of Hall. Klim strummed an air guitar, and all of Sydney seemed to pulsate.

The reign of Australia and Thorpe atop Mount Olympus did not last long. The next night, Pieter van den Hoogenband of the Netherlands, another nation with a healthy respect for the water, lowered Thorpe's world record in the first semifinal of the 200 freestyle. In the second, Thorpe went two-hundredths of a second slower, then gave a wave and a nod to the crowd as if to say, I'll take care of business tomorrow. Australians remember that 200 final on September 18 for the wrong reasons, and few noticed something equally ominous: Michael's Olympic debut.

A callow youth who had just had the braces removed from his teeth, Michael blended in on an American squad that was an anomaly, as the women's roster was older than the men's for the first time in Olympic history. Malchow had been the only teen on the American men's team in Atlanta, but there were eight in Sydney. Crocker, Klete Keller, and Erik Vendt were 18. Aaron Peirsol, who qualified a month past his 17th birthday, roomed with Michael and seemed like a veteran by comparison. Michael was the youngest member of the entire American contingent and its youngest male Olympian since 1952. He was the nation's youngest male Olympic swimmer since 13-year-old Ralph Flanagan had made the team in 1932, during the height of the Great Depression, when able-bodied men had more serious matters to tend to, like supporting a family.

His age required some adjustments from the Olympic staff, which did not include Bowman. Susan Teeter, the longtime Princeton women's coach, was the assistant manager on the Olympic team and served as Bowman's eyes and ears. When Michael blew off training camp curfew and goofed off in a hallway, she placed a call to Bowman, who gave him a long-distance scolding over the phone. The people who ran Australian swimming provided Bowman with daily deck passes, but he had no access to the Olympic Village, where Margaret Mead could have added to her observations of mating rituals. The Sydney organizers distributed 80,000 condoms, and not all were tossed in kit bags for use back home. The adult activity concerned Bowman more than Michael's swimming.

Michael won his first Olympic race, beating a preliminary field that included Russia's Denis Pankratov, the defending champion. An atrocious start in his semifinal buried Michael in last place, but he surged to third and a place in the final. Lenny Krayzelburg, fresh from victory in the 100 backstroke, high-fived the rookie. Mark Schubert, Krayzelburg's coach and the head of the U.S. men's team, dropped his customary reserve.

"How do you stand this?" Schubert asked Bowman. "I have never seen anyone his age like him. You look at the Olympic Trials, the most pressure-packed meet in the world, and now the Olympics. He is truly phenomenal."

It was only minutes later that Thorpe and van den Hoogenband were even off the final turn in the 200 freestyle. The Dutchman pulled away and won by a half-second. A crowd of nearly 18,000 was in shock, and found little solace in their favorite phrase. In America, Shit Happens. In Australia, there are No Worries, and disconsolate fans put up a brave front, analyzed a great race, and filed out of the Olympic pool.

A day later, as Michael prepared to board a shuttle bus that would take him to his 200 butterfly final, he glanced at the credential around his neck and saw that it was Peirsol's. Like travelers without a passport, Olympians are naked without the official photo identification that gets them through security checkpoints at the Village, bus stops, and competition sites. In a panic, Michael returned to his room, where he found his own credential and Peirsol napping. The misstep cost Michael a half hour of warm-up time, but Bowman improvised and prepared him as best he could. Malchow won. Denis Sylant'yev of Ukraine took silver. Justin Norris delighted the Australians with a bronze-medal performance. Michael finished fifth, 33-hundredths of a second out of the medals, with a time of 1:56.50 that would have won every previous Olympic final. It was his sixth straight personal best in the event, as Michael improved in all three rounds at both the Trials and the Olympics. It was not the time to grouse about what went wrong, and as Thorpe and the Australians bounced back with a runaway gold medal in the 800 freestyle relay, Bowman never let on about the hasty preparation.

"Michael has the most important thing an athlete needs: the ability to focus and relax," Bowman said. "All of the great champions have that. It's Thorpe's greatest asset. I have never seen Michael get rattled in a competition."

Michael returned the next morning, where Bowman's workout sheet included the notation, "Austin WR," an overt reminder that the world record could be his in another six months. Bowman promised that if they got to Athens in 2004, Michael could do anything he wanted once he was done competing, but as soon as swimming concluded in Sydney, they were on one of the first flights back to the States. The 2000 Olympics were still being conducted when Michael returned to Towson High, nearly a month tardy for his sophomore curriculum but with an excused absence. On September 30, as Michael dozed through Sunday morning in his own bed for the first time in months, one of the largest fireworks displays the world has ever seen illuminated the Australian night and the closing ceremony to the Sydney Olympics.

It included Thorpe bearing the flag of his country.

As predicted, Michael made history at the 2001 Spring Nationals. At the University of Texas in Austin, he beat Malchow in the 200 butterfly, as a clocking of 1:54.92 made a boy the first under 1:55. At 15 years and 9 months, this was the race that made Michael the youngest male ever to set a world record.

The title sent him to the 2001 World Championships in Fukuoka, Japan. As Michael shared a lane with Inge de Bruijn and lazily warmed up for his 200 butterfly final, a third figure flew into the pool and blew by both. Michael lost his rhythm and nearly stopped to watch as Thorpe made up 20 meters on him in two strokes.

Michael got his first world title and lowered his world record to 1:54.58 that night, but was among those obscured by the finest performance the world championships had seen to that point. In Fukuoka, Thorpe won the 200, 400, and 800 freestyles, all in world record time, finished fourth in the 100 freestyle, and anchored the Australians to victory in all three relays. Most satisfying had been the 200 freestyle, where Thorpe avenged his Olympic loss to van den Hoogenband. Most inconsequential was the 800 freestyle, a non-Olympic event. At one of his press conferences, Thorpe mentioned that perhaps he would fill that opening in his Olympic program with the 200 butterfly. His three world records had come in four days, and his six gold medals in seven events had been international swimming's biggest haul by a man since Mark Spitz at the 1972 Olympics.

Michael described two memories of Fukuoka as "awesome": his bathroom at the Grand Hyatt, which had a bidet and a TV, and Thorpe. He was studying Thorpe at close range instead of on grainy videotape. Some American athletes wore gaudy jewelry with the acronym WWJD, What Would Jesus Do? Michael's motto could have been WWID, What Would Ian Do? Bowman picked Frost's brain, and Michael became a mimic.

Asked how he passed the laps in practice, Thorpe said, "I sing whatever was on the radio in the car on the way to training, and the last song I hear is what I sing." Thorpe's stock response to questions about attention was that he didn't view it as pressure, but support. Nearly verbatim, Michael echoed those lines.

The 2002 Pan Pacifics took them back to Japan. Michael landed in Yokohama fresh off a world record in the 400 individual medley and got Thorpe's attention on the third leg of the 800 freestyle relay, where he gave the Americans their first lead over the Australians since the 1996 Olympics. Thorpe restored order by anchoring another Aussie victory. On the meet's final day, Michael won the 200 IM and turned in the fastest butterfly split ever in helping the Americans to a world record in the medley relay. The athletes faced a lengthy commute back to their hotel, and one night when they were the only ones on the last bus, Michael chatted up Thorpe about training, the flip side of celebrity, and the adulation of the Japanese. Thorpe said that if Michael was ever in Sydney, to drop by and work out with him. Michael said likewise, in the event Thorpe ever got to Baltimore.

Thorpe was probably just making conversation, but Michael took the invitation seriously. When Bowman lined up a speaking engagement on the Gold Coast of Australia in April 2003, arrangements were made for Michael to train with Thorpe in Sydney. Several nights before they left, Bowman received an e-mail from David Flaskas, Thorpe's agent, with regrets that Ian would be out of town, accompanying *his* coach to a clinic. Michael seethed over what he perceived as a slight, and instead hooked up with Hackett on the Gold Coast.

Michael was the most versatile swimmer in the world but wondered what would happen if he dropped his primary events and went after history's fastest middle distance freestyler. Thorpe had tested Michael in the 200 individual medley at the 2003 World Championships, where Bowman continued his observation of the Australian. In Barcelona, Thorpe cited the aftereffects of taking ill in January 2003, when he headlined FINA's World Cup swing through Europe. As Bowman plotted Michael's path to Athens, he factored in Thorpe's reaction to a winter tour of Europe and ruled out trains, planes, and automobiles to cold-weather destinations. Every meet Michael entered in the fall and winter of 2003–04 took him someplace warmer than Baltimore. The only one that took him out of the United States held the promise of an encounter with Thorpe.

Jamie Barone, Kevin Clements, Emily Goetsch, and Marianne Limpert were the other members of the NBAC traveling party that went to Australia in November 2003. En route, they stopped in New Zealand, where Speedo had rented one of the world's most accurate flumes, at the University of Otago, to measure Michael's specifications for the suits he would wear at the Athens Olympics. On November 24, three camera crews greeted Michael upon his arrival in Sydney, where the previous day's *Sun-Herald* supplied another hint that he wasn't in Baltimore anymore. A readers poll of their most-wanted Christmas guest had Russell Crowe in fourth, one place behind Nicole Kidman. The runner-up was Prime Minister John Howard. The winner was Thorpe, who arrived on the morning of the Qantas Skins from altitude training at the University of New Mexico.

"Ian's identity was low key," Tracey Menzies, who had replaced Frost as Thorpe's coach, said of their trip to the States. "The image Ian has here is extraordinary, the same as when he goes to Japan. It's very flattering to walk down the street. With that comes a price tag. His life has to be governed in a certain way. He can't go and be a normal 21-year-old. I suppose there's a price tag for anything. Movie stars and people like that have a very sheltered life, in a lot of regards."

Thorpe's popularity was all the more remarkable, since he wasn't performing in a vacuum. Sydney was getting over rugby's World Cup, in which Great Britain subdued Australia in the final at a packed Olympic stadium. The FINA World Cup in Melbourne was overshadowed by the biggest event in team tennis, as the Aussies beat Spain in the Davis Cup final. Melbourne's locals making good included Andrew Bogut, who had taken his basketball career to the University of Utah.

The Qantas Skins drew more than 6,000, the largest crowd at the Aquatics Centre since the 2000 Olympics, but it couldn't sell out a venue that had been reconfigured to 8,000 seats. Thorpe's same-day arrival displayed his regard for the event. Qantas paid Michael's expenses, but he earned his keep by becoming the first man in the Skins' brief history to win two individual events, including a distance freestyle series that totaled 400 meters and nearly put Hackett in the hospital. At the 11th hour, the organizers added a medley relay that matched Michael against Thorpe on the anchor. Even with the Australian begging out with jet lag, the Americans and a wobbly Michael got whipped.

Michael traveled on Thanksgiving Day to Melbourne, in search of his first world records in the short-course format (25-meter pool), where the faults in his turns were magnified. He opened with an American record in the 200 butterfly. On day two, he came within .43 seconds combined of the all-time bests in the 200 backstroke and 200 IM. On day three, Thorpe finally made a token appearance, in the 50-meter freestyle. Michael won all six of his events at the meet. Petria Thomas was the only other swimmer to win as many as three.

Michael was among the guests at the Australian Swimmer of the Year Awards that followed the World Cup meet in Melbourne. Asked about Spitz's seven gold medals, Thorpe replied, "I think it is unattainable for me, and unattainable for anyone."

Michael returned to Sydney, where he trained in Manly and took in a 50 Cent concert at the Superdome. Michael slept and Bowman watched *Seabiscuit* on the 14-hour flight to Los Angeles. Michael had a brief layover to plug the 2004 U.S. Olympic Trials in Long Beach. Handed a piece of chalk, he wrote his 400 individual medley world record on the parking lot where a temporary pool was to be constructed.

Two months later, Thorpe dropped the 200 IM from his Olympic program.

PROS AND CONS

BALTIMORE, DECEMBER 2003

For one night's work in Sydney and the long weekend in Melbourne, Michael earned approximately $20,000. Qantas, the nation's largest airline, sponsored the first meet, and telecommunications giant Telstra branded the second. Spectators paid admission fees, purchased slick glossy programs, and watched fine athletes from several continents in meets that were televised. Michael had a driver waiting, a custom-tailored tuxedo hanging in his hotel closet, knowledgeable fans in the stands, and the warmth of spring.

A week later, Michael tumbled out of his own bed, climbed into his SUV, and cruised down snow-dusted Charles Street for three days of racing that were more training and family get-together than high-level athletic competition. The 30th annual North Baltimore Aquatic Club Christmas Meet had no title sponsor. It was conducted less than 3 miles south of Michael's home, at Loyola College, not among the most glamorous stops on what the NBAC had dubbed the "2003–04 World Tour." A full-page ad in a stock paper program displayed its particulars over a map of Earth—the final stop, of course, was Athens—and announced "Congratulations & Good Luck!!! Bob, Emily, Jamie, Kevin, Marianne, and Michael. Best wishes." Boys under 10 far outnumbered the handful aiming for the 2004 Olympics, symbolizing the chasm that elite swimming faced as it haltingly struggled to transform itself from an amateur to a professional sport.

The turnaround from Australia to Baltimore exemplified Michael's good fortune of being in the right place at the right time. He came of age in an era when swimmers and other Olympians could finally play for pay, and his own club provided a cautionary tale from swimming's first tentative forays into professionalism. Michael was barely 16 when he signed an endorsement contract with Speedo that made him the youngest American male swimmer ever to turn professional, a decision that had more to do with continuity than economics. Bowman always knew that Michael's freshman year of college would coincide with the run-up to Athens, a turn of the calendar that became paramount in their master plan. Two years in advance, the decision was made to have Michael spend the 2003–04 school year at home, continue to train under Bowman at the NBAC, and let Speedo and other sponsors foot the bill. Forfeiting his college eligibility for that first modest deal was a calculated risk. Scholarships had supplied the means for all but a few American swimmers, but rather than balance the demands of a new campus and coach in September 2003, Michael remained at home and adopted the lifestyle of a full-time, professional athlete.

The pace and stakes of the pre-Olympic year had already been raised by innovative endorsement deals and marketing strategies that centered on Michael's potential to duplicate the greatest feat in the history of the Games. Three decades earlier, that same kind of radical deal-making essentially ended the career of the man who provided the most compelling—and profitable—reference point to Michael's story. The boy from Baltimore had been born the same year that FINA voted to permit national federations to compensate their swimmers. Mark Spitz's legend had been forged in 1972, at the last Games in which the word *amateur* appeared in the International Olympic Committee (IOC) charter.

There is no Greek word for *amateur*. Winners at Olympia, the site of the ancient Games, were presented only an olive wreath, but the best prospects were paid to train and rewarded handsomely upon returning to their homeland. Those men would have been puzzled by the modern Games, as the IOC wrestled with the issue of professionalism nearly all of its first century. The 19th-century revival of the Olympics adopted an eligibility code that had been promoted by the British aristocracy, which had the leisure time to dabble in what Americans call track and field. The common man who needed financial assistance to train was considered a professional and was about as welcome at the 1896 Olympics as women (who did not compete). Who had the time and money to go to Athens that year? One of track and field's first double-gold medalists won the shot put and discus. Robert Garrett was a scion of a banking and rail dynasty that placed the family name on Maryland's westernmost county. He had been raised at Evergreen, one of Baltimore's great estates, just south of the pool that was the site of the 2003 NBAC Christmas Meet.

In 1912, Jim Thorpe won both the decathlon and pentathlon at the Stockholm Olympics. Six months later, Thorpe was stripped of his medals, as he had been paid to play minor league baseball. Other legends were limited by Rule 26 in the Olympic charter. Johnny Weissmuller could have made it three straight gold medals in the 100 freestyle at Los Angeles in 1932, but he had surrendered his amateur status to become a model for the BVD underwear company. Paavo Nurmi was primed for the 10,000 meters and the marathon in Los Angeles, but track and field officials ruled that he had accepted payments beyond his expenses during an exhibition tour, and banned the "Flying Finn" days before the start of the 1932 Olympics. His total of career gold medals would remain, forever, at nine.

Ways around Rule 26 were found. Promoters doubled as bagmen, paying athletes under the table or inflating their expenses. Adolf Hitler used the 1936 Olympics in Berlin as a platform to display the Third Reich's link between a sound mind and a sound body. During the Cold War, athletic potential in the Soviet Union often meant a commission in the armed forces. Before the Free World carped about that Iron Curtain method, the Brits criticized the American concept of a college athletic scholarship. Generations have trained on campus without having to worry about paying tuition or room and board. Once that 4 or 5 years ended, however, many quit at the ripe old age of 22 or 23, walking away from their most promising years. That reality confronted Spitz, who within hours of completing the single greatest achievement in Olympic history, ended a career that was both splendid and circuitous.

Whereas Michael had trained under Bowman uninterrupted since 1997, Spitz had been shaped by three of his era's greatest coaches. Born in California, Spitz spent part of his childhood in Hawaii before his family returned to the mainland. He was taught by Sherm Chavoor, a two-time head coach of the U.S. women at the Olympics, and moved on to Santa Clara, where George Haines had a spot on every American Olympic coaching staff from 1960 to 1984. Spitz was 17 in 1967, when he won five gold medals at the Pan American Games and boldly predicted that he would win six at the Mexico City Olympics. His only gold medals in 1968, however, came in two relays, where the United States was unbeatable. His last individual event was the 200 butterfly, but the world record holder finished dead last in the final. Shaken, Spitz altered his college plans and headed to Indiana University. When IU hired Bobby Knight for basketball in 1971, it already had a resident coaching genius, as James E. "Doc" Counsilman and the Spitz-led Hoosiers were in the midst of six straight NCAA team titles. War hero and three-time Olympic coach, Counsilman monitored both the physical and psychological needs of his athletes.

"You want to stay away from people who have everything going for them," Counsilman said in a 1971 speech in Montreal to swim coaches. "I've yet to have a good swimmer who was talented physically and also well-adjusted. A person can have all the physical and mental attributes and not do well, because the person with everything going for him does not have a strong ego drive."

Michael absorbed the fallout from his sister Whitney's close brush with the Olympics. Spitz headed to Munich in 1972 needing to fill the holes in his own record. On swimming's opening day, he enjoyed a cathartic 2-second victory over Gary Hall Sr. in the 200 butterfly, his biggest flop in Mexico City, and anchored the victorious 400 freestyle relay. A day later, after another lopsided win in the 200 freestyle, Spitz became a tempest in the amateur teapot. Rushed barefoot from signing autographs to the medal podium, he waved to fans while holding a pair of tennis shoes, which led to accusations that he was endorsing a product, in violation of Rule 26. Hustled in front of a panel of IOC Pooh-Bahs, Spitz had some explaining to do.

"The head of FINA told me to wave to the crowd," Spitz recalled in 2004. "I've got a (medal) box in one hand, a towel over my shoulders, shoes in hand. The shoes weren't free (ones) from the village. They were old, good-luck shoes, but I got called into a hearing with Avery Brundage."

The amateur code had been the raison d'être for Brundage, the president of the IOC, who once went as far as to compare professional athletes to trained seals. The IOC admonished Spitz but didn't ban him, and he returned to the Schwimhalle the next day and got two more gold medals, in the 100 butterfly and 800 freestyle relay. His sixth gold came in the 100 freestyle, and he finished with the butterfly leg on the winning medley relay. Spitz produced gold medals and world records in all seven of his events. Between the U.S. Trials and the Olympics, he posted nine world records in his four individual events. His repertoire didn't include the 400 freestyle, the event that had brought him his first international acclaim. He was at the peak of his powers, but his career was over.

Spitz had been accepted into the dental school at Indiana University, but Munich meant that he would never have to return to a classroom or stick his hands in a patient's mouth. Days after earning his seventh gold medal, Spitz sat for a photo session arranged by a German magazine. It produced 1.2 million posters of Spitz, posing in his Speedo Stars and Stripes tank suit and with his seven gold medals. As Lisa Dillman of the *Los Angeles Times* noted, what Farrah Fawcett of *Charlie's Angels* was to cheesecake in the 1970s, the mustached Spitz was to beefcake. In an era when NFL linemen were making $40,000 a year, he made a quick $1 million off his Olympic fame, but was Spitz really ready to retire?

"Had there been a situation that allowed me to swim and take endorsement money, absolutely, I would have continued," he said in 2003. "The reality is that I had anticipated the end of my career, and I was accepted into dental school. Nobody who had come before me had made a living in swimming."

Brundage's 20-year rule as president of the IOC ended at the Munich Olympics. His successor, an Irishman known as Lord Killanin, immediately proclaimed that the movement must adapt. In 1974, Killanin promoted significant rule changes that wedged open the Olympic door for professionals. In 1985, the year Michael was born, FINA began to allow swimmers to accept training stipends from their national federations. After the Seoul Olympics in 1988, the IOC voted to accept professional athletes and left eligibility matters in the hands of each sport's international governing body. Soccer limited rosters to three players over the age of 23. Only boxing continues without professionals in the Summer Olympics.

The new rules made life easier for up-and-comers and welcomed back veterans who had been barred. Nearing 40, but with a 100 butterfly best that remained world-class 20 years after the fact, Spitz ended his retirement in a quixotic bid to make the 1992 Olympics. He joined some match races that Matt Biondi and Tom Jager devised as a means of cashing in on the relaxed IOC rules. Spitz didn't make the U.S. team going to Barcelona. Those who did were eligible to receive a $1,500 monthly stipend from USA Swimming. In non-Olympic years, Americans who ranked among the top four in the world got the same stipend. In 1994, Anita Nall, the reigning star of Michael's club, became the youngest American female swimmer to turn professional. Nall provided an inadvertent example of how not to go pro, as she did so without an agent, earned approximately $250,000 making speeches and working clinics over the next decade, and said that she wasted most of it.

Also in 1994, Gary Hall Jr. left the University of Texas after his freshman season and never looked back at college swimming. His contemporaries included Tom Dolan, who signed with Nike prior to the 1996 Olympics, in what was reportedly the first six-figure apparel deal for a swimmer. It paid Dolan $100,000 per year, with annual increases of $10,000.

"I got some heat for that, because the sport was based so much in the amateur tradition," Dolan said. "Swimmers work harder than anyone in athletics and deserve to be compensated, but there are some elements of it that will never change. There are still a considerable number of people in power who are small thinkers. They outnumber the ones who want to move the sport in a new direction."

The only other brand Dolan negotiated with after the 1996 NCAAs was Speedo, which in a normal year has endorsement deals with fewer than 20 Americans. No sport is easier to scout, since potential is quantified at regional and national competitions. Stu Isaac, a Speedo employee since 1983 and its lead bird dog since 1998, typically negotiates deals with gold medal–caliber swimmers after they have completed their college careers, so Michael was not the usual suspect. At the 1999 Spring Nationals, Murray Stephens advised Isaac to keep an eye on Michael, who was 13 at the time. The 2000 U.S. Trials and Olympics certified his promise, and within days of returning from Sydney, Bowman began a dialogue with Debbie and Michael about the prospect of him becoming a professional swimmer. His world record at the 2001 Spring Nationals made that more plausible. It came on the last day of March. Isaac's April itinerary already included a stop at Meadowbrook, and he asked to have an introductory dinner with Michael's parents.

Spitz had retired by 1973, when FINA conducted its inaugural world championship meet in Belgrade (Yugoslavia then, Serbia and Montenegro now). The 2001 edition was held in Japan, three weeks past Michael's 16th birthday. He celebrated his first world title with a room service feast of a corn dog, french fries, and lasagna at the Fukuoka Grand Hyatt. Twenty-four hours later, Bowman and Isaac met at that hotel and held more serious discussions. Word got out that Michael was considering turning professional, which would allow him to delay college and remain in Baltimore during the year before the Athens Olympics.

"I'd like to stay home more than anything," Michael said. "Bob is the best coach for me."

Two weeks later, at the Summer Nationals in Clovis, California, Debbie and Bowman had exploratory talks with the representative of a smaller swim apparel company. Michael increased his bargaining power with a series of eye-opening performances and the acknowledgment that he wanted to represent the United States in four individual events at the 2004 Olympics.

Bowman heard criticism that he was binding Michael to the NBAC.

Debbie had a succinct comeback to mothers who wondered why college swimming wasn't good enough for her son: He had already met the goals of most swimmers, who aspire to the Olympics, world titles, and world records. It was a radical step, however, that required serious deliberation. Michael did not have a driver's license and had yet to begin his junior year of high school. The Athens Olympics were still three years off, and there were concerns that he was signing over not just his collegiate eligibility but his innocence. Were they moving too fast? Bowman and Debbie had frank discussions, exploring worst-case scenarios about arresting Michael's development outside the pool.

"Debbie and I knew going in that there was going to be a time in his life when doing this would probably restrict his personal growth for the year," Bowman said. "The concern was that if there was no college during the 2003–04 school year, there would be a lot of free time on his hands. In the end, we knew that it was only going to be for one year and that it would allow him to focus solely on getting ready for Athens, but we went into it with our eyes wide open."

Both Bowman and Debbie knew that their influence on Michael was considerable and that the decision had to be his. Did a 16-year-old have the ability to make such an informed choice?

"It was what was coming out of my son's mouth," Debbie said. "He saw that he had already surpassed the majority of college athletes. We teach them about making decisions, and it was like Michael had done a timeline in his head—what he had done, and what he was going to do. Was it a risk? Sure, it was a risk, but life is about taking risks."

The businessman making it possible weighed his own issues.

"There's an internal debate involving anyone that young, because you're not dealing with an adult," Isaac said. "Is this kid mature enough to accept the pressure? Are the expectations we're placing on a prospect that young realistic? Are the parents doing it solely for financial reasons? Is this the right thing to do? The last thing I want to do is have a negative impact on someone's career."

Frank Morgan, who had children in the NBAC, a share in Bowman's thoroughbred business, and a practice with a Towson law firm, reviewed the Speedo contract that Bowman and Isaac negotiated. It escalated from an initial payment that was less than $100,000 annually, and there was a clause that would pay for Michael's college education if his career didn't pan out. Morgan was the agent for some musicians but told Bowman that they needed to find a specialist who could market Michael beyond his Speedo contract. It tied him to the company through 2005, but on the night Michael signed it, Morgan tossed out a casual aside. Around Michael's 18th birthday, they needed to review the matter. He was a minor, and in certain courts of law, it could be argued that the contract was invalid.

The news that Michael had signed with Speedo broke on October 3, 2001. Three days later, he worked a Speedo clinic in Portland, Oregon. Debbie accompanied him to a photo shoot in Phoenix. Before Michael raced for the first time as a pro on Thanksgiving weekend, at a U.S. Open short-course meet on Long Island, he described his new life.

"I'm working for Speedo," he said. "My attitude has to change. I have more responsibility now. When I come to practice every day, it's different. I used to be able to say, 'I'm not feeling good.' I can't have as many of those as I used to. My attitude has definitely changed. It's more positive now than it's ever been. Conference championships are big. The NCAA championships are big, but what I'm trying to do is bigger than that. I'd rather set an American record than win an NCAA title. When you go to the Olympics and set a world record when you're 15, and win a world championship when you're 16, you look at your goals and realize they're closer than you think. Everyone dreams of going to the Olympics, and I had no idea I'd get there so fast. The Olympics, the world records, the world championships—when you have all those things happen to you when you're that young, things change. This will help me focus on what I have to do."

The good news was that Michael's 3-year path to the Athens Olympics had been plotted. The bad news was the potential strain that it might place on his already intense relationship with Bowman. The initial clash they had in the summer of 1997, when Bowman remade his strokes, began a pattern. Bowman would push, and Michael would push back. Usually, he acceded to the demands, but there were times when Michael got his way, as when Bowman tried to introduce double practices in the fall of 1999.

"Michael flipped out," Bowman recalled. "I tried to set up some sessions where it was just him and me, and we could work on his stroke one-on-one, but he did not like being by himself. It was clear he wasn't ready. He was so young, it didn't matter. At the time, I thought he wasn't going anywhere."

The resistance to double practices was premeditated.

"That first workout," Michael said, "when Bob was trying to get me to do doubles, included a set of 100s. I purposely didn't break a minute. I knew what buttons of Bob's to push. The next day, he said, 'It's not working.' I got my way."

In February 2000, Michael acquiesced to two morning practices per week. He was in the process of shooting up from 5 foot 7 and 115 pounds to 6 foot 3 and 165. At the Olympic Trials, Bowman said, "With the growth spurt he's gone through, he needs nine hours of sleep a night. When he's not pleasant to deal with, neither am I." After the Sydney Olympics, the two had a public snit at Meadowbrook, and Bowman kicked his only Olympian out of practice. Most days, they seemed determined to prove the cliché that familiarity breeds contempt. When Bowman ran out of patience, he would give instructions in mock baby talk. Michael ceremonially removed his swim cap to signal that he was ignoring Bowman.

Now the jury was still out on Michael's choice to go pro, since other swimmers had made a painless transition from high school to college in a pre-Olympic year. Before the 1992 Games, Jenny Thompson made a seamless move from a club in New Hampshire to Stanford University. In the buildup to the 1996 Olympics, Tom Malchow executed a similar shift from a Minnesota club to the University of Michigan. Not all of those moves, however, worked. As Michael turned pro in the autumn of 2001, runner Alan Webb, America's great hope in the mile, began a rocky year at the University of Michigan. He juggled a full schedule of classes with cross country, indoor track, and outdoor track. Webb left Michigan in 2002 and turned pro, supporting the argument that an athlete could not serve two masters as demanding as college and the Olympics.

Besides competition and a full-time load of courses, collegians flaunted their freedom from parents with keg parties and serious relationships, what Michigan swim coach Jon Urbanchek euphemistically called sleepovers. Michael was not attending toga parties in Ann Arbor, or Baltimore, for that matter. Out of Towson High, he had been accepted into Loyola College and planned to take a course or two there in the fall of 2003, but the demands placed on him after the world championships in Barcelona scuttled that option.

The short-term benefits of being a professional were tangible. Michael furnished his bedroom with a 46-inch high-definition television. For Christmas 2002, he dropped the keys to a 2003 Mercedes in Debbie's stocking. For himself, he paid $15,000 down on a used Cadillac Escalade that sold for $36,000, and accessorized it with the bonuses USA Swimming paid for world records and titles. After the 2003 Duel in the Pool, he bought rotating wheel covers and bruised a big toe by mindlessly trying to stop one with a foot. Michael talked of owning a dog, initially a retriever, but the truth was that he didn't have the time to care for a gerbil, let alone a working breed that required exercise.

He had completely assumed the rhythm of the full-time endurance athlete, which resembled the directions on a shampoo bottle: awake, eat, train, eat, rest. Repeat. When he was at Towson High, morning practices began at 6 a.m. Now he could sleep in, albeit for only an extra 15 minutes. He did dry-land exercises, but intervals in the pool comprised the soup, salad, meat, and potatoes of his training. A workout could entail infinite permutations, involving a distance (say 100 meters), the number of times it was repeated, the stroke, and the time—the interval—between repeats. The faster he did them, the more rest he got. Michael had to develop the speed to catch Ian Crocker in the 100 butterfly and the endurance to hold off Laszlo Cseh in the 400 IM. During the shorter training phases when he built speed, Michael logged 60,000 meters per week, about 37 miles, but 600 to 800 meters of each day were at race pace. The phases when he built endurance lasted as long as 7 months and included 80,000 meters, nearly 50 miles, per week. The effort was comparable to running a marathon a day. There were periods when Bowman pushed the pedal even harder. In the winter of 2002–03, in the run-up to Barcelona, Michael averaged 85,000 meters, or 53 miles, per week. That spring, they backed off to 75,000 meters per week, still 7 miles a day.

It was what ambitious swimmers did, but with one difference: Michael never took a substantial break. He had one day off in 2002, when a snowstorm kept Meadowbrook from opening. Had it not blown in on Christmas morning, it would have been business as usual. Pragmatism created two days off in September 2003, when he went to an oral surgeon to remove problematic wisdom teeth. Counting meets, Michael worked in a pool 550 times a year, so Bowman figured he could do that 2,200 times between the 2000 Olympics in Sydney and the 2004 Games in Athens. His man was on his way to logging more than 9,000 miles between Olympics, enough to swim from the Chesapeake Bay to the Aegean Sea and back. By the time they got to Athens, Michael was going to have several more months of training in his background than the layabouts in college who took days, even weeks, off.

Bowman worked from the far end of Meadowbrook's indoor pool, away from civilians exercising on the other side of its short-course bulkhead. His backdrop included an eraser board that counted the days until the 2004 U.S. Olympic Trials, and a laminated poster he had brought back from the Sydney Olympics. The Cyrillic lettering for Athens meant nothing to most Westerners, but all of the NBAC swimmers understood the significance of the year 2004, the olive wreath, and the five interlocking rings. They were working their way to Athens. Bowman barked out orders to maintain fluids. Occasionally, one of the females might request to be excused for a bathroom break. Michael stopped for nothing, including nature, as the males relieved themselves between intervals where they stood, in the pool.

He did the work because he believed in Bowman.

"Michael shows up with an almost biblical faith in what Bob has laid out," Jamie Barone said. "He trusts that Bob is going to deliver him to where he wants to be. As far as Michael is concerned, he doesn't need to have any input. Do what you're told, and success is inevitable. Bob knows exactly what to say to elicit a reaction from Michael. In the summer of 2003, we had a 100 free set that had Bob squatting on the deck, in Michael's face, screaming, 'These next five are going to give you the edge at the Worlds; everyone else is sitting on their butt while you're swimming! This is going to give you an extra boost when you have 20 minutes to recover for the 200 IM!' Sure thing, Michael churned out five more reps faster than anyone else."

The downside of more than 6 years together and an uncommon dedication to their craft was that Michael and Bowman could now jangle each other's nerves more than ever. In the summer of 2002, Bowman took his group to the U.S. Olympic Training Center in Colorado Springs, Colorado. The change of scenery did not leaven the increased workload, which coincided with Michael's 17th birthday. As he ran his mouth, Bowman forgot that a synchronized swim team was preparing to take the next shift in the pool, and he snapped an obscene order to Michael, "Shut the fuck up!"

Michael estimated that those episodes occurred 20 to 30 times a year, once every two weeks. Bowman insisted they were down to twice a year, but both understood that the most threatening interludes came when major international meets were far off, like they were now, in December 2003. Michael began the month in the midst of a 25-day road trip that saw him sleep in five hotels and at least as many jets. Four days after he returned home from his trip to Australia, the NBAC Christmas Meet began. Bowman put him through a grinder of seven individual events, including his annual mile race, and three relays. The meet was notable for Fred's presence more than any of Michael's performances. A few days before Christmas, with Michael suffering from exhaustion, jet lag, and the dog days of winter, Bowman tossed in a grueling set: 50 100-meter sprints, kicking only, more than 3 miles of laps without benefit of the arms. Without raising his voice, Michael began to object.

Bowman: "If you don't want to do this, just get out."

Michael: "Fine, I'm not going to do this."

Bowman: "Fine, see you, Merry Christmas."

"It is a childish game we play," Michael would say, "but that time, we were very adult about it. After a while, we need space. That was one of those times. We both know that we get that way and have to give each other as much space as possible."

That episode came 8 months out from Athens. What were they going to be like in April, or June? They needed an outlet, a diversion from the absence of balance that strained their bond.

The cause of that ailment was about to deliver the cure.

RAINMAKER

AUBURN, JANUARY 2004

A few minutes past 1 p.m. on January 17, the public address announcer at Auburn University's James E. Martin Aquatics Center called attention to the contestant in lane five, heat two, of the men's 200 IM. "A man who needs no introduction," the announcer began, "but we're going to do it anyway." Michael took immediate control and won easily in 1:59.54, more than 3 seconds slower than his world record but 2 in front of training partner Kevin Clements and a field that included collegians from Auburn and the University of Southern California. The performance seemed routine. It was not. Michael was in a heavy training phase. Only four other men had ever gone faster, and two of them had won gold medals at the Olympics.

"To show how high he has set the bar," the man on the P.A. gushed, "Michael just missed producing one of the 10 fastest times ever!"

Scattered applause followed that news.

There were perhaps 200 people in attendance for Michael's first race of the Olympic year. Auburn, emptied for semester break, was too remote for all but the most dedicated family and friends, but the crowd was not an anomaly. Major competitions in large metropolitan areas were accustomed to a similar reception. Swimming barely registered as a spectator sport in the United States and was rarely seen on television outside of the Olympics.

Michael knew the economic impact of that reality. In June 2001, near the end of his sophomore year at Towson High School, he had become the youngest winner ever of Baltimore's High School Athlete of the Year Award. He had gone to the Sydney Olympics and set a world record during the school year, but there were other deserving candidates in a metropolitan area that included more than 130 high schools. That week, Gavin Floyd was the No. 4 selection in Major League Baseball's June draft and got a $4.2 million bonus just to sign with the Philadelphia Phillies. Carmelo Anthony attended a high school a mile from Michael's, went on to lead Syracuse University to the NCAA basketball championship in 2003, and signed a four-year contract with the Denver Nuggets worth $15.1 million.

In 2004, Floyd floundered in the minor leagues and Anthony dealt with a number of public relations blunders, but neither worried about money. Their lucrative contracts were guaranteed, because they played sports that provided core TV programming. Networks pay leagues hundreds of millions of dollars, which is distributed to franchises and filtered down to the athletes. A swimmer's earnings are paltry by comparison. In 2003, arguably the greatest non-Olympic year ever by a swimmer, Michael brought home a little over $280,000 in what golf and tennis would call official earnings. Most of it came in the form of bonuses from USA Swimming, which rewards world record setters and medalists at the major international meets. Still in the dark ages of professionalism, FINA offered no prize money at its world championships in Barcelona.

In addition to Americans' obsession with sports as televised entertainment, millions also tune in to reality shows. Both fascinated the man who completed the roster of what came to be known as Team Phelps. All of his endorsement deals, such as the marketing hook that made Speedo synonymous with Michael and a soon-to-be ubiquitous Visa ad, were the work of Peter Carlisle, who increased his client's visibility and made him a very wealthy teenager.

In September 2001, Frank Morgan reviewed the Speedo contract that had made Michael a professional athlete. David Pessin, one of his firm's partners, represented several NBA players, and both agreed it was imperative that Michael hire an agent with Olympic experience. Pessin had contacts at Octagon, where the client roster included John Elway, Steffi Graf, David Robinson, and Anna Kournikova, whose striking good looks had made her one of the most recognizable faces on the planet despite never having won a professional tennis tournament. In December 2001, Morgan and Pessin escorted Michael to Octagon's American headquarters in Virginia for some introductions. On the 80-mile drive back from Tysons Corner, the weary 16-year-old took a nap.

Two months later, during the 2002 Winter Olympics in Salt Lake City, Bob Bowman was watching the *Today Show,* when Matt Lauer introduced Carlisle, an agent who explained the leap that sports like snowboarding had made from ESPN's X Games to the Olympics. Two of his clients, Kelly Clark and Ross Powers, were gold medalists, and Carlisle was discussing marketing strategies and what he called Generation Y.

"There's this huge demographic out there, and marketers are intimidated by it," Carlisle explained. "Action sports and music and computer games seem to be able to reach it, but most companies are unwilling or hesitant to market to Generation Y, which could be anyone from 8 to 26. There's a kid in my office who wears shoes and shorts that are endorsed by core action-sports figures. The kid doesn't skateboard or surf. He plays lacrosse. These are the kids we're ultimately going to market to."

Watching Carlisle's appearance on the *Today Show,* Bowman put down his coffee cup and said, "That's our guy."

Carlisle, 6 foot 2 and as trim as his close-cropped hairstyle, didn't appear much older than the athletes he represented. At 34, he was the director of Olympic sports for Octagon, which had acquired his self-named agency in 2001. Maine was his home state, and he kept his office in Portland. He had played ice hockey on a state high school championship team, then tennis at the University of New Hampshire. Carlisle transferred down for athletics but up for academics to Bates College, a member of the New

England Small College Athletic Conference, what is considered the Ivy League of Division III athletics. He finished his law studies at the University of Maine, and along the way learned how to play hardball.

Carlisle met Michael in April 2002 and became his agent that summer. The Athens Olympics were still two years off when he watched Michael compete for the first time at the 2002 Summer Nationals in Fort Lauderdale. Carlisle completed a deal with Visa that created the possibility of Michael being one of the company's featured 2004 Olympians, then took a year to cultivate other potential sponsors. When Michael made history at the 2003 World Championships in Barcelona, Carlisle became one of the most popular observers at the Palau Sant Jordi. As Michael accumulated world records and titles, Carlisle's cell phone and e-mail received fresh inquiries from companies wanting to link their brand to his client. On July 25, 2003, 90 minutes before Michael became the first swimmer to improve world records in different events in the same day, Carlisle discussed his wait-and-see approach.

"It would have been foolish," Carlisle said, "to negotiate any deals before this meet. Look at him now. I got lucky."

For a year, Carlisle had relied upon periodic briefings from Bowman.

"My ability to come up with a creative deal," Carlisle said, "is totally reliant upon Bob's ability to forecast performance."

Using those projections, Carlisle brainstormed about how best to capitalize on Michael's aspirations. After morning workouts, Michael turned on *The Price Is Right* and watched Bob Barker make screaming audience members happy. Carlisle's guilty pleasure was reality TV. He studied the ratings and listened to checkout clerks take sides over *American Idol* and *Survivor*. His thoughts always returned to a staple of the genre: *Who Wants to Be a Millionaire?*

As Bowman said, while Speedo knew that Michael was going to be good, it had no idea he was going to be Mark Spitz good. One afternoon at the Hotel Fira Palace in Barcelona, while Michael took his afternoon nap during the 2003 World Championships, Carlisle asked to meet Speedo executives Craig Brommers and Stu Isaac there. The small talk ended, and Carlisle got to the business at hand.

Carlisle: "We need to renegotiate the contract, for all the right reasons."

Isaac: "What do you want?"

Carlisle: "A million bucks."

Only a handful of Speedo swimmers had six-figure deals, let alone a seven-figure one. Brommers and Isaac were taken aback, then listened to Carlisle's pitch: If Michael matches Spitz's seven gold medals at the Athens Olympics or at Beijing in 2008, Speedo pays him a $1 million bonus. The other details, his base compensation, whatever four or five or six gold medals would warrant in the way of bonuses, was secondary to coming to terms on the $1 million, which would bring attention to both their company and his athlete.

"How do we make this guy relevant outside of swimming?" Carlisle said. "I was accustomed to fighting for publicity a month before the Games, for one of our Olympians from Octagon. This was a way to get Michael not just on the sports page, but in the business section."

In November 2003, a few weeks before Michael went to Australia, Speedo announced that it had extended their agreement through 2008. The big news was the $1 million bonus, but even if Michael never got that, he had what was reported as the richest swimwear deal ever. Speedo contracts include confidentiality clauses, but Isaac did not dispute estimates that Michael's annual base compensation from the company was approaching $400,000. That figure was a reflection of his world records and world titles, and he worked hard for the money. The weekend after the deal was announced, Michael took his first solo business trip, to South Bend, Indiana, where he conducted a Speedo clinic.

The Speedo deal was the linchpin in an Octagon strategy that sought to balance conflicting goals, connecting Michael to Spitz while simultaneously maintaining some separation between the two. Spitz would become the reference point for Michael's potential, but the ambitious teen should have his own individual identity, one that wasn't overshadowed by Spitz, whose poster from the 1972 Olympics remained an iconic image to Americans over 50. Michael needed to stand alone, and it was paramount that he not be photographed with Spitz until the time was right.

That plan could not have developed better for his first sponsor. In the spring and summer of 2004, a Google search for "Michael Phelps" and "Speedo" produced similar results. Nearly every magazine or newspaper article written about Michael before Athens mentioned two other subjects: Speedo and Spitz. His first sponsor also received a considerable residual bounce. Beyond the *Sports Illustrated* swimsuit issue, the company rarely advertised in the mainstream American media, but Michael wore Speedo gear as he posed for his other major sponsors.

As the year unfolded, there was criticism that the dominant brand in competitive swimwear placed undue pressure on Michael. That contention overlooked the fact that the Speedo bonus originated with Carlisle and had been done with Michael's blessing. Considering that the prize money for the White Marlin Open, a sportfishing tournament in Ocean City, was $1.3 million, there were suggestions from the other side that it wasn't a just reward for matching the greatest feat in Olympic history. NBA phenom LeBron James had a 7-year endorsement agreement with Nike worth $90 million, but he and Michael had little in common besides being fellow members of America's high school class of 2003. James was on television 81 times a year. Michael came from a system where many were grateful to qualify for USA Swimming's $15,000 annual stipend, and the Speedo bonus was unprecedented for an Olympic athlete.

"There aren't any $3 million signing bonuses for swimmers," Michael said. "If I'm in it for the money, I'm in the wrong sport. I knew that people thought about swimming once every 4 years, and that it was going to take something outrageous to get attention."

When Michael met Carlisle, he had already raced in Asia, Australia, and Europe, and received paychecks from Speedo and stipends and bonuses from USA Swimming. Practice was hard work, but Michael was sincere when he said that he had his dream job. He loved what he did and delighted in the benefits. Michael was like a kid in a candy shop, with walk-around money that allowed him to buy lunch for his friends, any digital gadget he wanted, and that Mercedes for his mother. There was little security in his status, however, because the notoriety of swimmers and other Olympic athletes was fleeting. Michael figured that if he could accomplish things that no swimmer had done before, then he could achieve something even more difficult: expanding the sport's appeal. The more recognition his sport received, the greater Michael's wealth, but this wasn't about the money. At 13, he was already frustrated by the attention the lacrosse players received at Dumbarton Middle School. The older Michael got, the more irritated he became with swimming's second-class status. He raised the point the first time he met Carlisle, and the two would think long and hard about how they could make his sport more prominent in a crowded marketplace.

Michael was spending a long weekend at Auburn, a member of the Southeastern Conference, where football is king and the basketball season was heating up. Television was flooded with NBA games featuring players like James, but that league's ratings rarely approached those of NASCAR, which was gearing up for Daytona. College basketball and football, pro basketball, stock car racing, and Major League Baseball all envy the status of the National Football League. Swimming is also conducted in a rectangular space, so it seems well suited for television, but in 2003, Michael's sport was not seen on live network television. USA Swimming had to pay NBC $750,000 for two 90-minute windows to air Duel in the Pool highlights a week after the fact.

Several factors combine to restrict swimming's appeal, among them socioeconomics, a culture fixated on speed and violence, and the very nature of its own cult, which adhered to a training regimen that seemed more daring than inviting to outsiders.

In May 2005, *Sports Illustrated* had a cover story on lacrosse and proclaimed the old Indian game as America's hottest growing sport. One week later, it called rodeo the next big thing. A week after that, it trumpeted softball. Combined, those three sports were not televised as frequently as poker, as sedentary an activity as they come. Like American football and auto racing, rodeo had an element of danger and the threat of bodily harm. A softball game could be played in 2 hours or less. Lacrosse combined hitting and movement, but its greatest appeal is that it is easy for children to pick up a stick and play catch. Anyone can sit down at a card table and acquire the basics of Texas Hold 'Em.

Homo sapiens evolved out of the sea, so the instinct to swim appears to be wired in our DNA. Playing in the water is a shared experience, but swimming fast and well is hard to do and takes years of training. Baseball men argue that the most difficult thing to do in athletics is to put a round bat on a round ball, but middle-aged men can go to a batting cage and make contact, just like Barry Bonds. Nearly 300 times a day, a golfer gets a hole in one, and is every bit as proficient as Tiger Woods for that one stroke. The recreational cyclist can approach the speed that

Lance Armstrong maintains during some stretches of the Tour de France. Few, conversely, ever sense the exhilaration that Michael experiences in a pool.

A relatively small percentage of the population has regular access to a competition-size pool. From Beijing to Buenos Aires, basketball has spread for the same reason that soccer became the world's most popular sport in the 20th century. Dozens of children can occupy themselves with one ball. Organized baseball in American cities has dwindled not just because of the difficulty and tedium of the game. Large, green spaces can be as limited as the money for gloves, bats, and balls, and monetary issues also limit swimming. It costs millions of dollars to build Olympic-size, 50-meter pools, and most in the United States are found on college campuses. Off campus, most Olympic-size pools are not equipped with roofs, making them seasonal facilities. Swimming is a country club sport, with demographics narrower than its brethren, golf and tennis. Public facilities spawned Woods and the Williams sisters, Serena and Venus. If perception is reality, swimming in America is a white, suburban sport. Woods lacked what the marketers called street credibility. Swimming had none.

International meets take as many as 8 days, and even regional ones stretching over 4 are as much a test of a parent's endurance as the 1,500 freestyle is a swimmer's. The resistance of water makes it a comparatively slow form of racing. Swimming is devoid of physical contact, as competitors are divided by lane lines, and even relay teammates do not physically touch one another. If Michael and Ian Thorpe shared one lane and threw elbows at the start of a match race, TV ratings would soar. The very act of a swim race, distilled to one imperative—first to touch the wall wins—lacked the gray area that fueled talk radio and Internet chat rooms. Swimmers themselves are anachronisms, wishing each other well before a race and congratulating one another afterward. Even their medium made it hard for them to connect with the public. Like hot dogs and apple pie, Armstrong's drenched yellow jersey was a summer staple. A swimmer's sweat is undetectable. Modern suits leave nothing to the imagination, but the curves and sex appeal of marvelous physical specimens are lost in a pool. A swimmer in goggles is as indistinguishable as an NFL lineman, anonymous under his helmet and face mask.

Most damning was the limitation of frequency. Armstrong was a celebrity not just because he beat cancer, but because his signature event occurred annually. He and Michael had finished 1-2 in the U.S. Olympic Committee's Sportsman of the Year balloting for 2003, but a more accurate gauge of their Q rating, their marketability, was found in *ESPN* magazine's ranking of the "Defining Sports Moments and Personalities" of the year. Armstrong's fifth straight Tour de France title rated among the top 10. Number 62 was teammate Tyler Hamilton's fourth-place finish, despite a broken collarbone. Number 64 was a Division III women's college basketball player who had turned her back on the flag during the National Anthem to protest the war in Iraq. In between, at No. 63, was Michael's performance at the world championships in Barcelona. It was a landmark accomplishment, but Michael was just a swimmer, and it wasn't the Olympics.

"You don't get to see swimming on TV, and you don't get to dial into the personalities," Spitz said in 2003. "That is the reality of the Olympic sports. At the end of the day, it's difficult for swimmers to make money. Athletes are no different than *Playboy* magazine. There's always going to be a next month. Who's going to be the next darling?"

Athletes in traditional Olympic sports had a desperate dedication to an event that was both ancient and urgent. They were not like tennis star Kim Clijsters, a Fila athlete who passed on playing in the Athens Olympics because adidas sponsored the Belgian team, or the NBA veterans who were about to abandon the U.S. Olympic basketball team.

"When the Dream Team plays basketball, an Olympic medal is nothing more than a souvenir for them," Gary Hall Jr. told a radio interviewer. "But in sports like swimming, it is the pinnacle of a lifetime of work. We do not have the luxury to say, 'Ah, the Olympic Games, I can blow it off this year.'"

Sprinter Michael Johnson had done well in 1996, Marion Jones was the main beneficiary of hype for the Sydney Olympics, and Carlisle set about using Michael's accomplishments and aspirations to provide him with similar status. Few prospective sponsors other than suit manufacturers cared about swimming, but they were attracted to winners, and Michael stood to claim more medals in Athens than anyone. Argent Mortgage, a broker based in Southern California, added Michael to a group that included Indy Racing League driver Danica Patrick. A deal with AT&T Wireless followed. Combined, those two agreements were worth approximately $500,000 in 2004, according to *USA Today*. For a reported $150,000, Omega, the watchmaker, secured Michael's services for the Olympic year.

Visa didn't pay quite that much, but it supplied most Americans with their first glimpse of Michael. "The only card accepted at the Olympic Games," Visa was one of the 11 companies that paid $30 million to become a major International Olympic Committee sponsor in Athens. It spared no expense in the Park Pictures production of the spot it called "Lap." Lance Acord, who had assisted in the making of offbeat movies like *Being John Malkovich* and *Lost in Translation*, directed the commercial that depicted a swimmer passing a fishing boat in the Aegean Sea and some ancient Greek ruins. The athlete was seen making his way through towering waves, then pulling into the Hudson River and touching the base of the Statue of Liberty. It cut to a close-up of Michael, breathlessly saying "One," and then reversing course in the longest interval workout ever.

Sharp-eyed swimming experts noticed something odd. Michael breathed on every butterfly stroke. The swimmer in the commercial did not. By the time Visa filmed the spot, Michael had become too big and busy to dive into the Aegean Sea or the Hudson River. Carlisle volunteered a suitable stand-in. Sean Foley, an Octagon employee, had been an All-American swimmer at the University of Texas and stood just over 6 foot 7, a suitable approximation of Michael's wingspan. Michael was in Indianapolis when Foley performed near the Greek islands of Hydra and Poros, where Acord shooed away curious townspeople. Foley put on a skin-colored bodysuit and lathered it in Vaseline to combat a water temperature of 43 degrees in the Hudson River. Besides churning into the Statue of Liberty, he was filmed near Battery Park, where ferry passengers applauded who they thought was Michael. The only location shoot Michael attended was in Miami's Biscayne Bay, where the wake caused by departing cruise ships was supposed to simulate the choppy Atlantic Ocean. Carlisle instructed Michael to pass on that scene. Foley filled in there, too, while cameramen fretted over being sucked under a cruise ship or getting stung by a man-of-war or other sea creature.

That scene was filmed in April. It was not the first time Michael worked with a crew hired by Visa, nor the first time a sponsor supplied him and his teammates from the North Baltimore Aquatic Club with a change of scenery. During the Visa shoot in Biscayne Bay, Michael and the NBAC's other Olympic candidates were housed in Sunny Isles and trained at Florida International University. In March, the group accompanied Michael to the Bahamas, where he played with dolphins while a crew filmed him for an Argent commercial. Carlisle knew that the sponsor demands had the potential to disrupt Michael's training. When they did, they became exercises in stress management, another of the wrenches that Bowman had begun to throw into Michael's machinery on their recent trip to Australia.

"When we were in Melbourne, I began to disrupt Michael's protocol, delaying his rides, messing with his sleep patterns," Bowman said. "When Argent took us to the Bahamas, Michael had a morning practice, then did the 4-hour photo shoot with the dolphin, and immediately came back for an afternoon practice. Ideally, he could have taken it easy, but I said, 'Let's go for it.' I made it a hard practice. Michael has such low body fat, he shivers if he stays in cold water too long, and it was a cold, overcast day in a pool that was solar heated. When he's getting to his room after midnight because of a press conference and has to get up in 5 hours to race, that day in the Bahamas, like any day that makes him tougher mentally, could be a benefit.

"The thing that the coach in me worries about, does the inconsistency of maybe training one day in New York instead of in Baltimore, or moving a normal Sunday afternoon practice to Monday, is that going to affect Michael's progress? He seems to really not be affected by that."

A part of Bowman knew that he was rationalizing the sponsor demands.

"You have to make a decision: Do you want to do these promotional things? Do we not want to do any promotional things?" Bowman said. "That's not an option if you get money."

Bowman and Debbie had some long discussions about Michael's heart, soul, and mind before he turned professional. They knew that his formal education would take a backseat during the pre-Olympic year. His contemporaries from the Towson High School class of 2003 were midway through their freshman year of college, a semester of writing papers and cramming for exams behind them. All training and no intellectual stimulation had the potential to make Michael a dull boy, but fulfilling sponsor demands forced him to broaden his horizons. Michael's formal education was on hold, but he was being offered the equivalent of postgraduate courses in geography, marketing, and negotiations. He was learning that some decisions were made for business reasons, not personal ones.

The cutting-edge nature of the "Lap" ad made up for Michael's first experience with Visa. On January 13, he had jetted solo to Los Angeles. The next day, he swam in the chilly Pacific Ocean surf off Malibu, then took a red-eye flight back to Baltimore. Twenty-four hours later, he was back at Baltimore/Washington International Airport, boarding a flight to Atlanta and then a van to Alabama, where the NBAC in general and Michael in particular were brought in to spice up the college dual meet between Auburn and USC. Fatigue from three flights in four days worth approximately 7,000 miles of air travel was offset by excitement. The Visa footage was going to be used in a commercial, and Michael was going to be a part of Super Bowl XXXVIII. The game was annually the nation's highest-rated television program, and a case could be made that Super Bowl Sunday had replaced the Fourth of July as America's major secular holiday. Patriotism hadn't become passé, it had just moved from the town square to the family room. In some households, Super Bowl ads were watched more closely than the game itself, and Michael got goosebumps, anticipating that he was going to be seen by the same 90 million who had ogled Britney Spears in his favorite Pepsi spots.

Visa's advertising firm, however, went in another direction with its Super Bowl ad. The publicity still for the spot was an overhead shot of Misty May that looked down her cleavage as she spiked a volleyball. Visa's Super Bowl ad showed May and teammate Kerri Walsh playing not on sand, but on snow. It would win industry awards, but the two beach volleyball players in bikinis were initially obscured by the hysteria over the most notorious flash of a woman's breast in television history. Even a thrilling Super Bowl between the New England Patriots and Carolina Panthers was overshadowed by the halftime show, when Janet Jackson's top came undone in what her people insisted was a "wardrobe malfunction." Michael was too disappointed and Bowman too livid over the disruption the filming had caused to their training schedule to note the irony.

At the Auburn-USC meet, Michael posted four easy victories and helped the NBAC beat the collegians in the medley relay. A few hours after the 2-day meet had concluded, he unwound at The Lodge and Conference Center at Grand National. The lounge was the only location in the golf resort that had arcade games. With a soda-sipping Debbie serving as chaperone, Michael had one eye on the NFC Championship game between the Carolina Panthers and Philadelphia Eagles and the other on an arcade game, where he tried to beat a gaggle of NBAC girls that included 13-year-old Courtney Kalisz.

"I can change from being a kid to being a professional," Michael said. "That's something I've learned to do over the past few years."

Ten days later, he had to adjust to another bump on the road to Athens. A power outage on January 28 canceled exercise and instructional classes at Meadowbrook. With the glow of cell phones as their only light, Bowman put Michael's training group through its paces. He completed the afternoon's practice in the dark.

"It's good for them to swim in the dark," Bowman said. "It takes away their vision, and they have to go by feel. Plus it's different, and there aren't too many ways we can make this different. Doesn't matter. Fourteen days out from Nationals is a perfect day for this to happen."

RANGE

ORLANDO, FEBRUARY 2004

The Butterfly Effect.
Big Fish.
Miracle.

The marquee on International Drive advertising the fare at the Muvico Pointe 21 cinema complex could have been an homage to Michael Phelps.

He was in Orlando, Florida, for the Spring National Championships, a misnomer since his home in Baltimore was in for another five weeks of winter. It was the end of an era. After four decades of conducting two national championships a year, USA Swimming was eliminating the redundancy. In future years, the Summer Nationals would become the focal point of the American racing calendar. This was the final Spring Nationals, and Michael immediately made the gathering memorable for something other than a sentimental farewell.

On February 11, the first full day of competition, Michael displayed the full scope of the widest array of skills the sport had ever seen in a man. At 5:45 p.m., with rush-hour traffic backing up on Interstate 4 flanking the Central Florida YMCA Family and Aquatic Center, fans in that dank, drab hut witnessed a race that would have serious repercussions on the 2004 Olympics. As Michael won the 100 freestyle in 49.05 seconds, the veteran sprinters in attendance digested that performance and its possible impact on the American lineup for the 400 freestyle relay in Athens. Seventy-five minutes later, a cell phone spread more breaking news to Texas, that the world record in the 200 backstroke was intact, but only by .15, the length of a hand. Michael had dipped all the way down to 1:55.30. The collegian on the other end of the line in Austin was the only man who had ever gone faster.

In some ways, this double was more significant than the one that Michael had achieved at the 2003 World Championships, when he lowered the world records in the 200 IM and 100 butterfly on the same night. He was already considered the leading contender for an Olympic gold medal in those events when he made history in Barcelona. The 100 freestyle and 200 backstroke, conversely, were supposed to be afterthoughts in his repertoire, which now packed the credentials of three world-class men, maybe four. In 2003, Michael had won world or national titles in eight of the 13 individual events that would be contested at the Olympics. He now held the world record in three, was No. 2 all-time in two others, and held the American record in two more. At a national championship meet, he was the fastest American in the 100 freestyle, his *eighth* best event on paper. Ian Thorpe wasn't that versatile. Even Mark Spitz, the last American to simultaneously hold five American records, couldn't do some of the things Michael was doing.

Six weeks into the Olympic year, while swimmers around the globe were narrowing their focus, Michael continued to broaden his, defying an era of athletic specialization. Designated hitters, men who could no longer competently field a baseball, were paid millions, and American football teams had specialists for every situation. Michael, meanwhile, was a jack of all trades and master of most. He had already met the qualifying standard in 11 of the 13 events for the U.S. Trials that would come in July. If the Olympics stretched over a month, he had the potential to medal in seven individual events, but swimming at the Games would be contested over 8 days, which would tax even Michael's powers of recovery.

Amid speculation over what exactly he would swim in the Athens Olympics, not everyone fawned over his talent and titles. Bowman and

Michael had already determined what he would swim at the U.S. Trials, but they were keeping that information to themselves. That guessing game was creating resentment among other American men, since Michael's ambition could cost them medals and money.

There were also questions about Michael's reach exceeding his grasp, but those skeptics hadn't been paying attention to the arc of his career.

In the matter of professionals being welcomed into the Olympic movement, Michael came along at the right time. Similarly, he was part of the first generation to develop after the completion of a decades-long expansion of the Olympic program, which coincided with a reevaluation of man's—and woman's—perceived physical limits.

Track and field was preparing to mark the 50th anniversary of its landmark achievement: Roger Bannister breaking 4 minutes in the mile in May 1954. Voices of reason had cautioned that the effort to broach that barrier would imperil the man foolhardy enough to try, but Bannister has lived to see Hicham El Guerrouj knock another 15 seconds off that first sub-4. Women had been thought to be too delicate for strenuous exercise, but times had changed there, too. As late as 1968, Debbie Phelps was barred from interscholastic sports, and the 800 was the longest Olympic footrace for women. In 1984, the year before Michael was born, the equal rights movement helped birth the first women's marathon in the Olympics. Women routinely break 2 hours, 25 minutes, which would have won the men's gold medal at the 1956 Olympics.

For much of the 20th century, a swimmer's versatility was similarly restricted by the size of the Olympic program. In 1952, it included none of the events that Michael had set records in at the 2003 World Championships. It wasn't until 1988, the first Summer Olympics after his birth, that the International Olympic Committee settled on the men's program that would be used in Athens.

While the men's track and field program has been in place since before World War II, the men's 1,500 freestyle is the only aquatics event that has been contested at every Olympics. It wasn't until 1956, when the butterfly was separated from the breaststroke, that four distinct strokes were recognized, creating the possibility of an individual medley. The first Olympic IM came in 1964 and was part of a push that doubled individual events from six in 1960 to 12 in 1968. Each of the four strokes added a race during the expansion, which came too late for some champions. In 1924, Johnny Weissmuller won gold in the 100 and 400 freestyles. He was clearly the world's best in the 200 and most likely the 50, but those events weren't on the Olympic program, leaving him enough time to play on the U.S. water polo team in Paris. Forty years later in Tokyo, when Don Schollander swept the 100 and 400 freestyles at the 1964 Olympics, there still wasn't a 200.

Schollander's young teammates in 1968 included Mark Spitz, who benefited from the expansion of the Olympic program. Four years later, he became the first American swimmer to qualify for four individual Olympic events since 1904, when the program included one-time oddities like the dive for distance. Spitz, however, wasn't even the busiest swimmer in Munich. Shane Gould, a 15-year-old Australian girl, mocked the term "fairer sex" by medaling in five individual events. Then, as now, the issue of Olympic gigantism was a hot topic. Jerry Kirshenbaum of *Sports Illustrated* wrote this in an Olympic preview:

> "If either Gould or Spitz goes home with even five golds, it will equal Paavo Nurmi's 1924 record for the biggest hoard in a single Olympics. The fact that both went into the games with a chance to win seven medals lent fuel to a proposal being considered by the International Olympic Committee to eliminate eight events from swimming competition in the future, the rationale being that some races involved virtual duplication of skills. The idea was supported by the Soviet Union, a nation of modest aquatic achievement, and opposed by the sport's superpowers, Australia and the United States. It was true that when compared to, say, track and field, the talent in swimming did seem rather concentrated. For example, only four U.S. track athletes were entered in two individual events. But 19 American swimmers were in at least two individual events, five were in three, and Spitz was in four. And this did not include the relay races."

The three men besides Spitz who have won four individual gold medals in their Olympic careers did so by repeating a double. Germany's

Roland Matthes swept the 100 and 200 backstrokes in 1968 and 1972; Hungary's Tamas Darnyi took the IMs in 1988 and 1992, and Russian Alexander Popov owned the 50 and 100 freestyles in 1992 and 1996. Spitz was the exception to the rule, that a man could not win more than two individual events at the Olympics. John Naber took both backstrokes in 1976 and surprisingly led the 200 freestyle until teammate Bruce Furniss caught him in the final meter. A more realistic chance to surpass the two-gold limit came in 1984, when Michael Gross won the 200 freestyle and 100 butterfly, but the German was upset in the 200 butterfly by Jonathan Sieben, a 17-year-old Australian. Four years later, Matt Biondi's shot at matching Spitz's seven golds was undone early, as he followed a third in a loaded 200 freestyle field with the narrowest of losses in the 100 butterfly, to Anthony Nesty of Suriname. In 2000, Pieter van den Hoogenband beat Thorpe in the 200, then Popov in the 100, before his genius finally gave out in the 50 freestyle, five-hundredths of a second behind Americans Anthony Ervin and Gary Hall Jr., who shared the gold. Furniss, Sieben, Nesty, Ervin, and Hall were specialists, reminders of the challenges that awaited the well-rounded swimmer.

The Olympic program hadn't just gotten bigger, it was also more prolonged, as heats, semifinals, and finals were introduced for races covering 200 meters or less in 2000. In Spitz's day, only events that covered 100 meters were contested in three rounds. All events were conducted in two rounds in 1988, when Biondi became only the second American man to attempt four individual events in the modern era. He too got a program break, when the 50 freestyle returned to the Olympics. Since Biondi, only one American man had qualified for three individual events. In 1996, Tom Dolan won the first of his two gold medals in the 400 IM, was seventh in the 200 IM, and didn't reach the final of the 400 freestyle. The effort to become the best all-around swimmer in the world, however, had left him with chronic fatigue syndrome. In 1976, Shirley Babashoff became the first American to qualify for five individual events, but she dropped one in Montreal. Four years earlier, Gould won three golds, a silver, and a bronze in her five individual events. The scrutiny and stress turned her into a recluse.

Michael was unaware that no man had ever won Olympic races at three different distances. He did not study the record books to see that no male Olympic champion in an individual medley had ever won gold in one of the four strokes. In 2000, Michael ate up the passion and rhetoric that came out of Dolan at the Sydney Olympics, but he did not comprehend what the IMer had endured in 1996, knew less of Biondi, and knew little more of Spitz. Bowman wanted it that way. In the autumn of 2002, he was handed three yellowed copies of *Sports Illustrated* that encompassed coverage of Spitz at the Munich Olympics. Bowman read the pertinent articles but did not share the magazines with Michael. He wanted to keep his prodigy in the dark about the accepted notions of a swimmer's capabilities.

"I always felt," Bowman said, "that the less Michael knew, the more he thought was possible."

When the hype from the Speedo bonus and comparisons to Spitz threatened to spiral out of control, Bowman disingenuously pointed to the media as the source of it all. He conveniently neglected to acknowledge that the deal had been the doing of Peter Carlisle, in response to Bowman's own projections, which were all coming true. Bowman could have gone into handicapping if he picked winners at the thoroughbred track with the same proficiency that he had predicted Michael's ascent. He could pinpoint a week in 2002 when he realized that Michael could medal in seven or even eight events at the Athens Olympics, but that epiphany was easier to define than the gifts and influences that had created such a unique talent.

Why was Michael able to do so much? The distinctions between his genetics and his environment had blurred. What was more important, his body or the way he used it? Was he a stranger to oxygen debt because his club had stressed aerobic conditioning or because he had found a more efficient way to swim? Was he more hydrodynamic than his competitors?

"We got very lucky in that he came to our sport," Bowman said at the 2003 World Championships. "He's got a very long torso, very long arms in relation to his body, and his wingspan is taller than his height. That's very important. He has excellent flexibility in his shoulders and upper body, everywhere but his hamstrings, which at this point hasn't mattered. He has very good ankle flexibility, which is important. He also has a body that is narrow and wide, so that he planes really well on top of the water. He was made to swim, no doubt about it. You could see that when he was 11."

By then, the North Baltimore Aquatic Club had already poured 4 years of training into that body.

"With training," Bowman explained, "prepubescent children can significantly impact their heart and lung size, more substantially than they can after puberty. The larger the heart and lungs, the bigger the engine."

Those parts had been produced in the same factory that had streamlined his strokes. Murray Stephens had developed two Olympic champions in the backstroke, an American record holder in the breaststroke, and an Olympic finalist in the 400 IM. Whitney Phelps, Michael's sister, had been a major factor in the butterfly.

"I knew from the get-go, as a little kid," Michael said, "that I was not going to be someone who specialized in one event, one stroke. I was going to do multiple events. I was going to do everything. Bob reinforced that when he re-did my strokes."

In 1996, Michael established a national age-group record for boys 10 and under in the 100 butterfly that still stood in 2006. Over the next 4 years, while he was building toward his surprising run to a berth in the Sydney Olympics, he did not zero in solely on that stroke. The morning after Michael made the 2000 Olympic team, he swam a preliminary of the 200 IM at the U.S. Trials. Two months earlier, in a meet at the University of Michigan, he made the Olympic Trials qualifying standard in all five of the events he entered. When Michael celebrated his 15th birthday in June 2000, he held six American NAG records for age 13–14 boys in both IMs, both butterflys, and the 400 and 800 freestyles. As he readied himself for Athens in 2004, none of those marks had been bettered.

That range was a boon to Michael's aspirations to turn professional. He got noticed for his first world record and world championship in 2001, but Speedo's Stu Isaac was more intrigued by Michael's performance at the Summer Nationals a month later. Michael won the 100 butterfly and then the 200 IM with a time that would have gotten a medal at the world championships. He opened that meet by shaving 11 seconds off his personal best in the 200 backstroke. Michael placed second in that event and also made the 200 freestyle final. The 200 butterfly wasn't even on his program in Clovis, California, where he first acknowledged the scope of his Olympic aspirations.

"I don't want to be just a one-event athlete in Athens," Michael said. "I'd like to make the team and have a chance to medal in both the 100 and 200 fly and 200 and 400 (individual medleys), at least."

It was around that time that Michael began to ask, "Why does everyone keep asking me about Mark Spitz?" The comparison gained weight in the summer of 2002, which began with 3 weeks of altitude work at the U.S. Olympic Training Center. Bowman was pointing Michael to Fort Lauderdale and the Summer Nationals, which served as the U.S. qualifier for the 2003 World Championships. The meet in Florida clearly indicated that Michael had the potential to make a serious run at Spitz's record, at least in the individual events.

Michael opened with the 200 IM, posting an American record and coming within a half-second of the world mark. He placed third in the 200 freestyle, recorded his second-fastest time ever in the 200 butterfly, and delivered a calculated response to a serious challenge in a landmark 400 IM. Erik Vendt, a feisty native of Massachusetts who had taken silver behind Dolan in the 2000 Olympics, was coming off a narrow victory over Michael at the Janet Evans Invitational. In Fort Lauderdale, Vendt appeared headed for another win going into the final wall, until Michael unleashed his underwater dolphin kick, a technique he had learned watching his Thorpe video. Instead of fluttering alternately, the feet and legs move in unison, creating a whipping action that mimics the movement of a dolphin.

"Because I was a butterflyer, the dolphin kick came naturally," Michael said. "It was one of the things we added to the IM, and it became the equalizer. People could catch me on the breaststroke, but I could use the dolphin on the turns, just as they were getting tired. Vendt flipped first, but I was able to stay with him and regain the lead. It's the reason I set that world record."

Jumping Vendt off the final turn, Michael touched in 4:11.09, taking two-thirds of a second off of Dolan's world record. Less than two tenths back, Vendt also bettered the old world mark. It was a marvelous, mature effort from Michael, who did not fit the customary mold of an IM champion. It had been a blue-collar discipline, attracting swimmers who were unable to make an impact internationally in one of the individual strokes—but now it had been hijacked by the best 200 butterflyer in the world.

He wasn't done.

On the final day of the 2002 Summer Nationals, Michael was an underdog in the 100 butterfly, but he chopped a second off his personal best, upset Ian Crocker, and matched the second-fastest time ever, 51.88. The meet made Michael the first man since Spitz to simultaneously hold four American world records, and he had just turned 17. It was the first meet of Michael's that Carlisle attended, and the one that made Bowman believe that he could do very big things at the Athens Olympics, which were 2 distant years off.

"I had thought about that a little until Fort Lauderdale, which made me really grasp Michael's capabilities," Bowman said. "The 400 IM had been the focus of our training, so the 100 fly was a total shock to me. I thought that Michael could do a lot of stuff, but it was then that I thought about Spitz's record and told myself, 'Wow, he can really do this.' That was in the back of my mind, but I still didn't want to think about seven medals. The way to think about seven medals isn't to talk about it, it's to train. When we left that meet, we knew at the least, that Michael was going to be our Ian Thorpe."

In order to have any chance at matching Spitz, Michael had to become a player in all three relays, which Bowman promptly discovered could be a point of contention. At the 2002 Pan Pacific Championships in Yokohama, Japan, against strong opinion that the 17-year-old was being spread too thin, American head coach Dick Jochums overruled the dissent and placed Michael on the 800 freestyle relay. Minutes after his yearlong neglect of his signature event resulted in a runner-up finish to Tom Malchow in the 200 butterfly, Michael swam an inspired third leg on the relay, which gave the Americans their first lead over the Australians since the 1997 Pan Pacific Championships. Thorpe came back on the anchor leg, but Michael had made a point. He set meet records in both individual medleys in Yokohama, established himself as a comer in the 200 freestyle, and helped the United States lower the world record in the medley relay with history's fastest butterfly split.

"Our goal," Bowman said upon their return from Yokohama, "is to get Michael fast enough in the next year that, going into Athens, he can kind of transcend everyone's concept of what is fast. I want him to be in that ballpark, because then he doesn't have to be 100 percent perfect to win gold medals. You don't want to be in a situation where everything has to be right."

That margin of error and Michael's confidence grew in 2003, at the Duel in the Pool in Indianapolis, the world championships in Barcelona, and the Summer Nationals in College Park. That August, Michael convinced Bowman to let him go for an unprecedented six individual events at the 2004 U.S. Olympic Trials. He could hold something in reserve and still win both individual medleys and the 200 butterfly in Long Beach. He wanted to challenge two world record holders from the University of Texas, Crocker in the 100 butterfly and Aaron Peirsol in the 200 backstroke. Michael was also anxious to test himself in the 200 freestyle, where Thorpe and van den Hoogenband were even more daunting. If his form suffered or something went wrong, he could always drop an event or two before or after the Trials, but now was not the time to be cautious. It was a time to be secretive. Michael and Bowman told no one, not even his training partners, of what they called Plan A.

Michael enjoyed the camaraderie on American teams, but he had a sense of what he was stepping into.

"Some of the guys," he said, "were on a shuttle bus at the world championships in Barcelona, and I mentioned that I was going to swim the 100 freestyle in College Park, at the Summer Nationals. Scott Tucker (a relay silver medalist in 2000) said, 'You'll never break 50 seconds.' I didn't say anything back."

That race in College Park, where Michael went 49.19, was the one that allowed him to cannonball his way into the pool of candidates for the Athens 400 freestyle relay. Six months later, he was in Orlando, taking charge of another national championship meet and forcing Olympic coach Eddie Reese to pay him more attention. The sprint relay had been the only one that Michael didn't participate in at the world championships. He wasn't fast enough to medal in the 100 freestyle at an international meet, and didn't want to waste his energy on it at the Trials, but he wanted to leave no doubt that he deserved a spot on the relay in Athens. To that end, every 100 freestyle was a precious opportunity to impress Reese, who came to Orlando to scout and run a relay minicamp. The focus would be starting on the fly, timing the takeoff to coincide with the coming touch on the wall by a teammate. Michael was a relative novice to the skill, which was old hat to the college guys.

The shorter the race, the less time Michael had to find his rhythm, and the 100 freestyle in Orlando unfolded miserably for him. His reaction time off the blocks was a sluggish 1.21 seconds, and he was dead last in the eight-man field at the turn. In the second half, however, he pounded past some of the best sprinters in the world and finished in 49.05. It was a milestone, the last time he would set a national age-group record for 17–18 boys. Michael finished more than a half-second in front of Ryk Neethling. Roland Schoeman, another South African, was fourth. Neil Walker was fifth. Hall, resting his 29-year-old bones in anticipation of a long Olympic year, swam in the consolation final. Jason Lezak, the only American besides Tucker who had gone faster in 2003 than the time Michael just turned in, was in attendance but sat out the event. Hall, Lezak, and Walker made up three-fourths of the American sprint relay at the 2000 Olympics and had reason to be concerned about Michael encroaching on their turf. They were in line for the same bonuses that USA Swimming and the U.S. Olympic Committee would pay in Athens, but legacies were just as important as money.

The nation's premier college swimmer in 1997, Walker was a reliable relay hand. He was a Texas graduate who swam for Reese at Longhorn Aquatics. A late bloomer, Lezak had won his first national title at age 22 but continued to develop for Irvine Novaquatics, his hometown team in Southern California. All raced in the shadow of Hall, an iconoclast who injected some personality into what could be a very dry sport. Hall had flowing blond hair and wore star-spangled boxing trunks during introductions. His biography noted that he was the first endorser of the Grateful Dead line of sunglasses. A drug test that produced a positive for marijuana had cost him his Speedo contract, but he had overcome diabetes and become a role model in that cause. His bloodlines were intriguing. When Hall collected two gold medals and two silvers at the 1996 Olympics, his maternal grandfather, 1946 NCAA 200 butterfly champion, Charles Keating Jr., was in federal prison on securities fraud. His father, Gary Hall Sr., had been the second-best American swimmer in the Spitz era.

As they all digested a 100 freestyle that made him the seventh-fastest American ever, Michael faced a quick turnaround for the 200 backstroke. It was the domain of Peirsol, the world record holder, two-time world champion, and Michael's roommate at the Sydney Olympics. Had Peirsol not been such a sure thing in the backstrokes, Michael would have been exploring them even more than he was. Peirsol was a sophomore at Texas, which was in the midst of an NCAA championship season. He and Crocker did not go to the Spring Nationals, and it was up to Lenny Krayzelburg to relay the news of Michael's 200 backstroke to Austin.

"Do you want the play by play?" Krayzelburg asked, when Peirsol answered his cell.

Krayzelburg had a compelling story of his own. His family had fled religious persecution in Odessa, Russia, and settled in Los Angeles when he was a boy. He was an Ashkenazi Jew and bore a striking resemblance to a father and son with similar ancestry, actors Kirk and Michael Douglas. Krayzelburg had been the only American male swimmer to win three gold medals at the 2000 Olympics. He had been unbeatable in the backstroke events until shoulder injuries and Peirsol caught him. Now Krayzelburg wasn't even No. 2 anymore in the 200 backstroke, but he laughed at the development. He had been the first big-name swimmer to hire Carlisle as his agent, and treated Michael like a younger brother. Similarly, Malchow had gone from dismissing Michael when he was an up-and-comer in the 200 butterfly to supporting him once the younger man had proved himself beyond that event. Not everyone, however, was infatuated.

"The only guys who aren't mad at me," Michael would say, "are the breaststrokers."

What made Michael's double in Orlando astounding was that he wasn't fully rested for the Spring Nationals. As Michael cooled down, Bowman was asked what he could have done if he had been fresh.

"We stopped thinking that way a long time ago," Bowman said. "Of course, this doesn't clarify a thing. It makes it more confusing."

It was another of the stress tests that Bowman created to see how Michael would handle a crowded schedule at the Athens Olympics, specifically day 6 of swimming's 8-day program. It would include the finals of the 200 backstroke and 200 IM, and semifinals of the 100 butterfly. Plan A revolved around that day. The world rankings now showed that

Michael was closer to Peirsol in the 200 backstroke than he was to Crocker in the 100 butterfly, but if he passed on that, then he would forgo the medley relay. The permutations made Bowman's head spin.

"Something," he said, "has to give."

NBAC teammates Kevin Clements and 14-year-old Katie Hoff won their first national titles the next night, but Bowman was visibly angry. Michael had begun the Spring Nationals with two personal bests, which were always a major motivation, but now he was unable to lower his American record in the 200 freestyle. A day later, on Friday the 13th and with 6 months to go until the Athens Olympics, Michael won the 100 butterfly in the same time he had taken the 2003 Duel in the Pool. As a steady rain soaked Valentine's Day, Michael concluded the meet with a 5-second win over Clements in the 200 IM. He was less than a second off his world record but got little help from a lethargic crowd.

"Success gets tougher," Bowman said. "At Michael's level, all of the ingredients that go into a great swim are not always present. I don't care what the announcer said to the crowd, there was nothing there. To break a world record takes an emotional component that the athlete can't generate by himself. I'm not blaming the people here. We're all guilty."

As oblivious as the crowd seemed to Michael's fifth title of the meet, and the 20th of his career, some spectators were too close for comfort. One morning in Orlando, Michael moved to Bowman's side and pointed out a man who had been stalking him throughout the meet.

Security was loose at the 2004 Spring Nationals, and that concern was not going away.

INSECURITY

ANNAPOLIS, MARCH 2004

Michael Phelps was going to be prepared for the Athens Olympics.

The host city of the Games of the XXVIII Olympiad was another matter.

Michael's diligent, methodical preparation proceeded amid a series of alarming updates from Greece, where the Athens Organizing Committee (ATHOC), dawdled through urgent construction deadlines. It seemed to be the only nation on earth that wasn't alarmed by the conditions found at many of its Olympic venues. On February 16, while Michael worked on relay starts, a rare chink in his armor, with Eddie Reese in Orlando, ATHOC officials conducted a briefing in Athens. The resurfacing of the marathon route was behind schedule. The situation was troubling at the main Olympic park (OAKA) in the northern suburb of Maroussi. In jeopardy was the $158 million retractable steel and glass roof over the Olympic Stadium. Most of the trees and landscaping touches that were supposed to turn OAKA into an oasis would be scrapped. It looked more like a desert, and come August, the Athens Olympics loomed very dry and hot under the Mediterranean sun.

That force of nature was a concern at the Olympic Aquatic Center, where another architectural touch was on the ATHOC chopping block. The International Olympic Committee oversees the Olympics, but competition in each sport is conducted by its own international governing federation. FINA officials knew that a pleasant breeze could cool swim finals, which would be held at night. In the morning, however, as preliminaries unfolded past high noon, baking concrete and synthetic surfaces could burn bare skin. Blinded by glare, backstrokers could miss the 5-meter flags that alerted them to a coming wall. The needs of NBC and other broadcasters were no small matter. From the time Athens had been awarded the Olympics, FINA had pushed for an indoor facility as the most obvious solution to the elements. As work stalled or never began, Athens lowered its expectations and FINA assumed a stance of resignation. There would be no indoor pool, but there would be a canopy, which would cover the facility, cool swimmers, and keep broadcasters in the shade. Now even that protection was in doubt, and a member of the FINA press commission used sarcasm to describe ATHOC's state of readiness.

"If they manage to get water in the pool," Elena Vaitsekhovskaia said, "we'll be happy."

The temperature of the water Michael would be racing in and the comfort of observers at the aquatics center were minor compared with the life-and-death matter that made the delays in Athens more frightening than frustrating. Terrorism, the 21st-century horror, was the primary reason that venues needed to be completed. The longer it took for them to be built, the greater the possibility of a security breach, of someone or something doing harm to the Athens Olympics.

ATHOC's lackadaisical preparation and the realpolitik of the era juxtaposed neatly at Michael's next meet, in Annapolis, the capital of Maryland. The low-key Maryland Local Swim Committee (LSC) Championships were held at the pool in Lejeune Hall, on the grounds of the U.S. Naval Academy. For most of Michael's life, tourists could drive their cars into the Academy, but civilian automobile traffic was no longer allowed on the grounds. Security was as tight in Annapolis as it had been loose in Orlando at the Spring Nationals. To gain entrance to the Academy, athletes and their parents at the Maryland LSC Championships had to display photo identification at Gate C to soldiers outfitted with sidearms. The meet began on March 19, the first anniversary of the U.S. invasion of Iraq. News bulletins recounted death and destruction around the world, which threatened the status of the first Summer Olympics since September 11, 2001.

It was a surreal stretch of Michael's road to Athens, as he attempted to go about his business amid speculation that the 2004 Olympics would be canceled. The doomsday chorus included Mark Spitz, who had a unique perspective on terrorism. Long before Osama bin Laden became the most notorious man in the United States, one of the initial reference points to Islamic extremism had come at the 1972 Olympics, hours after Spitz's crowning achievement.

WELCOME HOME

The motto of the 2004 Olympics was a nod to both the host city of Athens and the nation of Greece. In a stroke of inspiration, the shot put for men and women would be conducted a half-day's drive from Athens, in remote Olympia, the site of the ancient Games. The marathons would conclude at Panathinaiko Stadium, where the modern Olympics had been revived in 1896. That elongated oval sat beneath the Acropolis and its main structure, the Parthenon. The marathon itself was rooted in the legend of Pheidippides, who ran a long distance to bring news of victory over a Persian invasion around 490 BC, before dropping dead of exhaustion. Scholars found the tale to be apocryphal, the stuff of myth, like the gods themselves, but there was no minimizing the historical significance of Greece. The birthplace of Western Civilization had long been a chaotic crossroads, and 2004 wasn't the first time that outsiders doubted the ability of Athens and Greece to meet the logistical challenges of the modern Olympics.

Paris and London were mentioned as potential sites when Baron Pierre de Coubertin, a nobleman from France, had suggested an Olympic revival, but Athenians were passionate and persuasive about their city being the first modern host in 1896. They needed something positive to stem a period of economic upheaval, mass emigration, and political uncertainty. The Games returned to Athens for what would be remembered as the "Intercalated," or intermediary, Games of 1906. Its contributions included the parade of nations at the opening ceremony, but an IOC commission ruled in 1949 that it should not be included in the Olympic record. Athens was shunned again by the IOC when the centennial Games of 1996 were awarded to Atlanta instead of returning to their birthplace. Despite concerns that Athens and Greece lacked the economy and infrastructure to successfully stage the Games, the IOC made amends with the awarding of the 2004 Olympics.

With just under 11 million people, Greece would be the smallest host nation of the Summer Olympics since the 1952 Games were held in Helsinki, Finland. Greece had half the people of Australia, a sluggish economy, and little of the organizational expertise required to stage the Summer Olympics. Athens immediately fell behind schedule. In 2000, when an IOC commission determined that progress was unsatisfactory, a soccer term was used to characterize its warning to ATHOC: Athens was being given a yellow card. Another 3 months of dithering, it would get a red card, and the 2004 Olympics would be moved elsewhere.

The 9/11 terrorist attacks heightened security at the 2002 Winter Olympics in Salt Lake City, as isolated and as easy to police as a city on the American mainland gets. Soccer's 2002 World Cup featured unprecedented cooperation, and cohosts Japan and South Korea were hailed for their organizational skill. Now the international sporting community in general, and the United States in particular, fretted that Athens was the wrong place at the wrong time. Americans had warmed to a small independent film, *My Big Fat Greek Wedding,* but cooled to the notion of going to Athens. Compared with orders for Sydney in 2000, tour operators reported that Summer Olympics requests were down 20 percent. Australia was an enchanting, popular destination, but the Summer Games that Americans most remembered came in 1996, when a bombing by an abortion rights opponent named Eric Rudolph had shattered the joy and taken life at Atlanta's Centennial Park. Now bin Laden had joined Rudolph on the FBI's Most Wanted List, but there was more than the specter of al-Qaeda to consider.

Greece was ringed by unrest. Beyond its eastern border with Turkey lies the Middle East, where Islamic extremists like bin Laden had proclaimed holy war against all things American, several years before 9/11. Beyond the obvious threats, could Greece even protect its Balkan borders? To the north were violent flashpoints like Kosovo and Bosnia. Alexander the Great had slept there, the Ottoman Empire had ruled there, and there was a real fear that nefarious forces would harm Athens, Greece, and the Olympics.

The Games were to open in August, on Friday the 13th. That superstition meant nothing in Athens, where suspicion walked a two-way street. One opinion poll found that 95 percent of Greeks were opposed to America's foreign policy, and a portion of that resentment could be traced to a man from Michael's hometown. In 1971, a military junta had taken control of Greece. White House approval came in the form of an official state visit from an American of Greek ancestry, Vice President Spiro T. Agnew, whose political base was Towson, Maryland, where Michael would attend high school. In response to the junta, radical groups espousing anarchy sprang up. The most powerful, called 17 November, was dedicated to fighting the establishment and shutting down U.S. military bases in Greece. For nearly three decades, the radical group had assassinated U.S. officials and influential Greeks, with little reprisal.

In 1999, President Bill Clinton formally apologized for the White House's 1971 endorsement of the military junta, which had long been overthrown, but American security officials continued to criticize Greece's laissez-faire approach to terrorists. In January 2002, CBS news program *60 Minutes* aired an alarming segment on 17 November. Later that year, the Greek government finally began to crack down on the radical groups. After a decade of Socialist rule, Costas Karamanlis of the conservative New Democracy party was elected prime minister of Greece on March 7, 2004. One of the first dignitaries he met was IOC President Jacques Rogge, who told Karamanlis to get ATHOC's house in order by April 1 or allow some of his inspectors to poke around Olympic construction sites.

Two days after the Greek elections, Michael, Amanda Beard, Lenny Krayzelburg, and Jenny Thompson were in Manhattan for the North American unveiling of Speedo's new line of high-performance suits. It was held at a dance club, the kind of nightspot that didn't open until after Michael went to bed. His itinerary had included an appearance on the NBC morning program the *Today Show*. Two days later, on March 11, 190 people were killed in a series of bombings in Madrid, Spain, the second deadliest terrorist attack the world had seen since 9/11. On March 15, the *Today Show* passed along an unconfirmed report that the U.S. ambassador to Greece had informed officials there that if security was deemed inadequate, the Americans would not send a team to the Olympics.

The option of returning to Sydney was no longer viable, but it was never too late for the IOC to cancel the Games. World wars had meant no Summer Olympics in 1916, 1940, and 1944. Politics could disrupt the Games. The People's Republic of China had not been welcome at the Olympics until 1980, and South African athletes were banned from 1964 to 1988 because of their nation's apartheid policies. Even though its athletes weren't even welcome, a trip by a South African rugby team led to an African boycott that devalued distance running at the 1976 Olympics. In 1980, in protest of the Soviet Union's invasion of Afghanistan, President Jimmy Carter ordered a U.S. boycott of the Moscow Olympics. In 1984, the Soviets retaliated and did not go to Los Angeles. Now the Athens Games were in jeopardy. When Spitz said that cancellation was a very real possibility, he spoke from experience, since he had been at ground zero of the worst moment in Olympic history.

At some point during his run through the Munich Olympics, Spitz shared his amazement over his burgeoning celebrity.

"I suppose I could always postpone dental school for a year," Spitz told *Sports Illustrated*. "If everything goes the way I planned this week, I may need a bodyguard."

The remark was prophetically tragic.

Spitz's Olympic debut had come in 1968 in Mexico City, which was rocked by student riots and the violent death of more than 250 people 10 days before the Games opened. Munich was supposed to be different and provide a break from Germany's past. West Germany was nearly 2 decades from reunification with the East, and trying to shed history.

At the 1936 Olympics in Berlin, the Third Reich and Adolf Hitler's notion of Aryan supremacy had been upstaged by Jesse Owens, a black American. Olympic visitors were subjected to goose-stepping soldiers and the "heil Hitler" salute. The "serene Olympics" of 1972 were to be not about armed soldiers, but open arms.

Spitz won his seventh gold medal on the evening of September 4. After a celebratory dinner, he returned to his room in the Olympic Village and retired for the night. Security was loose in the Village, and jocks who had broken curfew were accustomed to hopping a fence and sneaking back to their rooms. In the predawn hours of September 5, at 4:30 a.m., armed men in disguise attempted to enter a suite of rooms that was occupied by members of the Israeli delegation. Moshe Weinberg, a wrestling coach, jumped from his bed, blocked the door, and screamed to his countrymen to flee. The intruders gunned down Weinberg and another coach, tossed his body outside the door, and took nine other Israelis hostage.

Spitz was waiting to be interviewed by ABC when he was drawn to a television monitor in the studio. It showed a Black September terrorist negotiating with a German policeman. Spitz is a Jew, a people who had been decimated in the Nazi Holocaust, which was less than 30 years in the past. Representatives of the IOC, the U.S. State Department, and the local law authorities met to discuss Spitz, and agreed that he should be moved to a safer location. That evening, he boarded a flight to London, where he sat for the *Stern* magazine photo shoot that had been scheduled for a Munich studio. Spitz was one less headache for the local authorities, who made assurances that they had the hostage situation under control and rejected offers of assistance from Mossad, the Israeli intelligence unit.

The military airport at Furstenfeldbruck, 28 miles from the city's center, was used to lure the Black September terrorists out into the open. The drama that unfolded for American television viewers made its conclusion all the more tragic. ABC announcer Jim McKay read a report that the nine hostages, bound and blindfolded, had been rescued, then told America that the optimistic bulletin had been premature. The tens of millions who were watching ABC remember the words that McKay used to update the fate of the nine Israelis in the firefight at Furstenfeldbruck.

"They're all gone," McKay said, sadly and softly.

A hastily arranged memorial service for the first two Israeli victims at the Olympic Stadium became one for all 11. Amid calls for the cancellation of the remainder of the Munich Olympics, IOC President Avery Brundage declared that the Games must go on. The 1972 Olympics moved from the tragic to the absurd, when security officials neglected to notice an impostor playing a prank who entered the Olympic Stadium just before marathon champion Frank Shorter. Spitz followed that denouement from the safety of his home in Sacramento.

The Olympic Village evolved into an armed compound. Black September would be linked to the Palestine Liberation Organization. Three decades after the Munich Olympics, the situation in the Middle East was as muddled as ever.

"If 9/11 hadn't happened," Spitz told an Australian reporter in 2002, "I don't think the 30th anniversary of the Munich massacre would even register."

On September 11, 2001, Michael's group at the North Baltimore Aquatic Club was not yet in a phase of double sessions. He was beginning his junior year at Towson High, and as he walked from English to history class, Michael got his first glimpse of the morning's horror on television. As schools closed early, he hitched a ride home with a friend, not bothering to inform his mother, who frantically conducted a phone search to determine his whereabouts. That afternoon, he reported to practice at Meadowbrook. As much of the nation huddled in shock, the NBAC went to work. One girl who traveled Interstate 95, which was rumored to be shutting down, was excused, but everyone else in Michael's training group showed for practice. It began with a defiant pep talk.

"We don't stop for snow, we don't stop for rain, we don't stop for a flood, and we sure aren't going to stop for terrorists," Bowman told his swimmers. "They can kill innocent Americans, but they can't kill our dreams. Why let them change our way of life? They want us to sit home and be scared. That is not us."

Spitz's seven gold medals had been overshadowed by terrorists. Could they disrupt Michael's bid for greatness? The weekend after the 9/11 attacks, Michael and Bowman were to be honored as Swimmer of the Year and Coach of the Year at a convention in Dearborn, Michigan. The awards banquet was canceled. Major League Baseball put its season on hold. The Ryder Cup, one of golf's biggest events, was postponed for a year. Had the 9/11 bombings occurred earlier in the summer of 2001, the world championships in Fukuoka, Japan, and the Summer Nationals in Clovis, California, might not have been held. Bowman says a scenario that would have wiped out those pivotal competitions would not have affected Michael's decision to turn professional, a major step in his effort to match Spitz's Olympic feat.

As much as they wanted Michael to live a normal life, the members of Team Phelps knew that adjustments had to be made. Some already had been. Like many youth activities, swimming faces the issue of pedophiles. At two meets during Michael's youth, NBAC coaches asked Fred Phelps, a Maryland State policeman, to eject adult males who were suspected of spying on boys in a locker room. As Michael's fame grew, fans went to great lengths to get near him. His first taste of obsession came in Yokohama, Japan, at the 2002 Pan Pacific Championships. After a woman repeatedly tried to get onto Michael's floor, the hotel's security escorted her off the property. He took to using an alias, Robert Davisson, which combined Bowman's first name and Debbie's maiden name. Bowman stopped announcing their movements, and Michael knew to keep his guard up.

When he told Bowman about the fan that made him uncomfortable in Orlando, Michael was applying the teachings of Larry Buendorf. Since 1993, Buendorf has been the chief security officer for the USOC. A native of Minnesota, he had played basketball and been a hurdler on the track team in college. In 1971, Buendorf entered the Secret Service and spent two decades protecting American presidents. He helped foil a 1975 assassination attempt on President Gerald R. Ford. Buendorf was now in his late 60s and had a shock of white hair, but he stood a ramrod-straight 6 foot 1 and had a commanding presence. The older and more famous that Michael grew, the more attention he paid Buendorf's periodic briefings to the American swim team. Buendorf explained that his office was like any other in the USOC, where the objective was to help Americans medal. That job included monitoring the movements of what he called the athletes on his "high-profile list."

"When I was in the Secret Service, the whole basis of our daily operations was preparing the appropriate reaction to what-ifs," Buendorf said. "With the USOC, educating the athletes is part of the process. I talk to them about awareness. If you're uncomfortable with a situation, bring it to my attention. We want to put everyone in a controlled environment and allow the athletes to focus on what they went to a competition for. The people in USA Swimming listen to what you say. They stick together. They are a team in the truest sense of the word. They support each other and travel together. It's a controlled group, and that makes it easier for me."

At the 2001 World Championships in Fukuoka, Japan, Michael and Ian Thorpe shared the last shuttle bus leaving the pool. Two years later, USA Swimming used dedicated transportation at the world championships in Barcelona. Buendorf's presence and the readiness of the local authorities were assurances on Michael's first trip to Europe since 9/11.

"I was worried about Barcelona and the world championships," Bowman said, "but as soon as we got to the Fira Palace, our team hotel, I saw four guys with submachine guns working the front door. That's also where we started dealing with dedicated buses, and wherever Michael was, Larry was."

On their final night in Barcelona, Michael made time in a seemingly secure basement corridor of the Palau Sant Jordi for a brief one-on-one interview. Before he could answer a question, two young men rounded a corner and thrust a Barcelona FC jersey in his hands. Michael asked for a pen, to sign the soccer jersey, until one of the men gestured no, that it was a gift for him to wear. It was a warm gesture, but evidence that celebrities are never 100 percent secure.

The USOC could take steps to protect its athletes, but it could not stem the hysteria that was mounting over the 2004 Olympics. American tourists weren't going to Athens, but the nation's journalists were. They were receiving inoculations and gas masks, attending antiterrorism training, and being instructed in the use of a tourniquet, should a co-worker get a leg blown off in a bombing. They forwarded their anxiety to an American public already accustomed to monitoring the threat-of-attack level.

An Associated Press poll showed that 53 percent of Americans "believed a terrorist attack of some sort was either very likely or somewhat likely in Athens. Many Americans also think their country's athletes would be targeted in any attack." Athletes shared that apprehension. Serena Williams would withdraw from the Olympic tennis team. Most of the veteran basketball players dropped off the team headed to Athens. Their excuses ranged from fatigue to wedding plans, but Mike Bibby stated the obvious, that players feared for their well-being. Asked about the pool controversy in Athens, American swimmer Lindsay Benko said, "I'm more concerned about my family. The water's going to be the same temperature for all the athletes, (but) it is a little nerve-wracking to go over there and be a target."

Krayzelburg, the reigning Olympic champion in both backstrokes, was even more explicit.

"Think about it," Krayzelburg said. "For terrorists to make a statement, there isn't a bigger place than the Olympic Games."

Michael always staked out a remote corner at a meet, and he dropped his bags in an area of the deck where he could be as far as possible from the pool and fans but still be in Lejeune Hall. As he stretched, he was less than 200 yards from the Naval Academy checkpoint at Gate C. The report of a possible American pullout of the Athens Olympics had been discounted, but 90 minutes before Michael's first race at the Maryland LSC Championships, Bowman addressed the prospect that the Athens Olympics were not a sure thing. Bowman works in a profession that does not attract fatalists, and as interested as he was in world politics, he never let Michael think of a doomsday Olympic scenario.

"When I heard that report, I thought that a lot of very different circumstances than the ones that exist now have to come up for something as severe as a boycott or cancellation to happen," Bowman said. "Besides, that's the kind of thing you consider after it's too late. Worrying about it is not gonna help. It's really out of our hands."

Michael never concerned himself with world politics or the possibility that the 2004 Olympics might not occur. It was another distraction to block out, another example of his remarkable ability to wrap his mind around what he could control.

"I didn't even think about it," he later said. "That was all out of our hands. My job was to focus on what I had to do and make sure that I was as ready as I could be."

Michael had no say in the global situation, but he could control his fitness. After the Spring Nationals, Bowman had increased Michael's mileage and its pace, and also piled on the dry-land work. Michael went to Annapolis drained from the 3 hardest weeks of training he had endured since the world championships.

"He has had some days where he has pushed himself to the absolute wall," Bowman said. "Anything he does here is gravy."

Michael's first race in the short-course (25-yard pool) format was the 200-yard freestyle. After an easy win, he was stopped by some autograph-seekers who were unaware that his work was just getting started. Another piece of paper was thrust under his nose. It was Bowman, angered by one of Michael's unenthusiastic splits. Michael shook his head and smiled as he made his way to the practice pool. He won the 400 IM by 14 seconds, but he didn't better Tom Dolan's American mark, let alone Ryan Lochte's national age-group record. Bowman's displeasure became louder and more vehement. Michael made a move to his corner, but Bowman stopped him and resumed his diatribe over some turns that were even sloppier than normal.

The next day, ATHOC announced that there would be no roof over the Olympic pool in Athens. "The experts," an official statement read, "concluded that due to the delays there are no guarantees for the timely construction and delivery of the roof—a fact that could jeopardize the swimming event."

The Times of London, the same newspaper that had infiltrated OAKA and documented its shoddy security, passed along the apoplectic reaction of the head of British swimming.

"It's symptomatic of the chaos in Athens," David Sparkes said. "After all the time they've had to prepare, they've failed to allow enough time to build a roof. Only 2 weeks ago, they said they would go ahead with a temporary tarpaulin-type structure that would provide shade. It's very disappointing. There has been an appalling lack of leadership."

What did Michael make of it all?

"A pool is a pool," he said. "Roof or no roof, I'm going to be there, and hopefully ready to swim. I've swum outdoors before. It's a meet where people are going to swim fast."

Michael had just posted a time in the 500 freestyle that stacked up nicely alongside his 200 backstroke from the Spring Nationals. He finished the 3-day meet in Annapolis with eight wins in as many individual events. Since losing to Ian Crocker in the 100 butterfly at the 2003 World Championships, Michael had won 37 straight races.

In April, the IOC would take out a $170 million insurance policy against the cancellation of the games because of natural disaster, war, or terrorism. Spitz was among those who did not like the odds.

"We know there is a high degree of probability that something could happen in Athens," he told BBC Radio. "Would that be political suicide to send a team there if you were the Bush administration? I would say that about 6 months ago, it was highly unlikely, but each day as it goes on with current world affairs, it becomes more probable than not that ongoing conversations will take place as to how important it is to put athletes in harm's way."

By the time Spitz made that assessment, Michael knew that trouble could be found in something as seemingly harmless as dinner.

KARMA

INDIANAPOLIS, APRIL 2004

At 8:30 a.m. on April Fools' Day, the pecking order for Southwest Airlines' 10 a.m. nonstop from Baltimore/Washington International Airport to Indianapolis had already been determined. A slight, gray-haired lady sat in the lotus position, behind a circle of young men doing the same. She appeared to be someone's grandmother, but the boys paid her no mind as they passed the time playing dominos. A 14-year-old girl in their traveling party leafed through a copy of *Cosmopolitan*. Jamie Barone, the oldest in the circle, pretended to pick his nose. He was not the first passenger at Gate B16, sitting beneath the "A" that would determine who boarded the jet first. An 18-year-old, his face shaded by a baseball cap, occupied that spot, unaware that he was applying principles that were 2,500 years old. In *The Art of War,* Sun Tzu decreed that the first to arrive at the battlefield wins. Bowman had read Sun Tzu, who had rubbed off on Michael. First to the pool wall, first to an airline gate. He wasn't going to let a little old lady, let alone a training partner, beat him onto his flight.

Michael was returning to a venue that carried great sentimental attachment, the Indiana University Natatorium, the site of his triumphs at the 2000 Olympic Trials and the 2003 Duel in the Pool. The Doc Counsilman Classic was insignificant by comparison, but Bowman had pointed to the USA Swimming Grand Prix meet as a major checkpoint in Michael's preparation for Athens. Even the most routine aspirations to that competition needed good health, good timing, and good luck. A teen who attempted to match or surpass the Games' greatest feat required that wide-ranging fortune, times seven or eight.

Michael's first-day itinerary in Indianapolis took him from airport to pool to a promotional appearance at Conseco Fieldhouse, which would be the site of FINA's 2004 world short-course (25-meter pool) championships. That meet was scheduled for October, 2 months after the Olympics. Michael would be racing in Athens in 135 days, and his destiny was unfolding so rapidly that some developments were difficult to process. As their morning flight departed BWI, Michael had been among the handful of people from the North Baltimore Aquatic Club who knew that Bowman had accepted an offer to coach the University of Michigan men's team. It was a foregone conclusion that after the 2004 Olympics, Michael would leave the only club he had ever known and follow Bowman to Ann Arbor.

Michael had trained diligently, deferred the fun his friends had enjoyed, and adopted a single-mindedness that extended to beating a senior citizen to a Southwest Airlines gate. His physical well-being was closely monitored, at home by specialists from one of the world's renowned hospitals, and on the road by physiologists from USA Swimming and security experts from the USOC. Bowman had mapped a course through the swimming world, and Debbie Phelps had guided Michael through the real one. Team Phelps could cross every t and dot every i, but it could not avoid the unpredictability that is at the core of athletics' appeal. Not all contingencies could be anticipated, and Michael was involved in a tenuous enterprise. In the previous 24 hours, it had been determined that his path to the 2008 Olympics in Beijing would go through Michigan. In the next 24, he would discover that all of his dreams and hopes, along with all of the deliberation and planning that had gone into them, were a bite of chicken at a mall food court away from coming undone.

A young Michael and sisters, Hilary (*left*) and Whitney, on photo day at the North Baltimore Aquatic Club (NBAC).

A rite of passage for boy swimmers: the first pre-meet shave.

On deck with Tom Malchow, Michael searches for the right track on his portable CD player before their 200 butterfly semifinal at the 2000 Olympics in Sydney, Australia.

A 15-year-old Michael (*fifth from the top*) knew he needed work on his starts after this near-jackknife entry in the Sydney Olympics final left him in an early hole.

Michael passes time with NBAC teammates Claire Hutchinson (*left*) and Ellen Brooks (*second from left*) before the meat and potatoes of his training regimen, another interval workout.

Michael (*right*) explains some of the NBAC's history to Jamie Barone after a 2003 practice at Meadowbrook.

Back in Baltimore after an unprecedented performance at the 2003 World Championships, Michael and Bob Bowman were sitting on top of their sport.

"I don't want to get into the specifics of Michael's performance mentality," Bowman said. "I don't want to mess with it."

Michael stands 6-foot-4, but his wingspan of nearly 6-7 is on display once he finds the proper rhythm in the butterfly.

Ian Crocker, Neil Walker, Michael, and Jason Lezak (*in pool*) show the dismay and dissatisfaction of a bronze medal in the 400 freestyle relay, the worst finish ever for the Americans at the Olympics.

Karl Merton Ferron, The Baltimore Sun

Michael and Ian Thorpe didn't mask their feelings after the Australian's win in the semifinals of the 200 freestyle in Athens. The next night, Thorpe took the gold medal, Michael the bronze.

Karl Merton Ferron, The Baltimore Sun

Peter Vanderkaay, Michael, Ryan Lochte, and Klete Keller (*in pool*) celebrate their upset of the Australians in the 800 freestyle relay.

Karl Merton Ferron, The Baltimore Sun

Stuck in third place in the closing meters, Michael catches Ian Crocker with a late surge to take gold in the 100 butterfly, securing his fourth individual gold medal at the Athens Olympics. The victory allows Michael to represent the U.S. in the final of the medley relay.

Michael adds an unconventional twist to his sixth gold medal at the Athens Olympics, as he gives his spot in the final of the medley relay to teammate Ian Crocker. The two hug after Crocker's record butterfly leg helped the Americans cap swimming at the Athens Olympics with a world record.

Karl Merton Ferron, The Baltimore Sun

Chicago Cubs fans ended each season with the rallying cry, "Wait 'til next year." Failed Olympians have to wait 4 years for another opportunity, which compounds their joy, heartache, and need for everything to go right. The most poignant images of the finest middle-distance runners America has ever produced are of them sprawled on an Olympic track: Jim Ryun in Munich and Mary Decker in Los Angeles, their greatness undone by a clipped heel. Reebok dropped $25 million on its "Dan vs. Dave" advertising campaign in 1992, when Dan O'Brien was the best decathlete in the world and American teammate Dave Johnson was another medal contender. O'Brien never got to Barcelona, as he couldn't clear his opening height in the pole vault at the U.S. Trials. O'Brien made amends and won gold in 1996, but track and field athletes were always one hamstring pull or missed height away from oblivion. Save for curling, nearly every Winter Olympian was a similar disaster waiting to happen. Figure skaters had pratfalls, lugers skidded out of control, and downhill skiers sometimes lost their lives.

Hazards appear to be fewer for swimmers, who are cushioned by their medium and separated from the competition by lane markers. Disqualifications are rare, but one of the most tempestuous in the sport's history was being debated as Michael headed to Indianapolis. On March 27, at the opening session of the Australian Trials, Ian Thorpe fell off his block while awaiting the start of his 400 freestyle preliminary and was disqualified. He was as big an Olympic lock as Michael was in the 200 IM, and Australian officials pulled some strings to ensure that Thorpe swam his premier event in Athens. America's best understood that there would be no similar gifts from USA Swimming in an individual event. If Michael took ill or screwed up at the Trials in Long Beach, he wasn't going to swim that event in Athens. End of discussion.

There was no shortage of ways that Olympic plans could end. External issues, like boycotts, were beyond an athlete's control. Training mistakes, injuries, and simply choking under the weight of the moment could conspire against gold medal favorites.

Years before there was speculation that the United States might not send a team to Athens, Bowman and Debbie knew that Michael was not involved in a sure thing, and attempted to minimize the risks he faced outside the pool. That required vigilance on their part and sacrifice on his. Like most teenage males, Michael felt invincible, but he was also among the group of world-class athletes who had the disposable income to test their limits. Basketball player Jay Williams had just wrecked a motorcycle and his career. Football player Kellen Winslow Jr. would do the same and endanger his future. Professional franchises protected their investments by prohibiting activities like skydiving and snowboarding. Peter Carlisle, who had carved out his niche in daredevil sports, did not have to enforce limits on his client, because Bowman and Debbie had conspired to do that for years.

"Debbie was pretty valuable there," Bowman said. "She was always willing to help frame for Michael what made sense and what didn't. I had to pick and choose my battles. It sounds counterintuitive, but I couldn't put the hammer down on things that didn't pertain to swimming, so she did. She regularly read him the riot act. She knew where he was, what he was doing, and with whom he was doing it. On the home front, she was the bad cop. On anything that had to do with swimming, I was the bad cop."

By 1997, Michael had dropped all other organized sports to concentrate on swimming, but even recreational fun could lead to an emergency room visit. The more Michael became immersed in his career, the more Debbie drove that point home. In January 2003, a blizzard hit Baltimore and closed its schools for a week. Michael wrapped himself in a parka and prepared to go sledding with friends when Debbie piped up, in jest but in a way that made her son consider the ramifications of his actions.

"Where are you going?"

"Who are you going with?"

"Are they going to Barcelona next summer, to race in the world championships?"

A swimming career was not conducive to a normal social life.

"I had to pass up a lot of things with my friends," a 15-year-old Michael said the night he qualified for the 2000 Olympics. "At the time, I was upset, but right now I'm happy that I passed up things like late-night movies and parties."

Michael made those comments at his first press conference, where Jill Lieber of *USA Today* caught him off guard: "Do you have a girlfriend, and have you kissed her?" He nodded yes, and mumbled something about a girl at Dulaney High, Towson's rival school. Having two older sisters made him comfortable around the opposite sex, and by the time he was in the sixth grade, he was assured enough to go to the movies with girls who were in the eighth grade. Gerry Brewster, his American Government teacher and chief advocate at Towson High, chaperoned a dance there during Michael's freshman year. During a slow number, Michael bent over at the waist and draped his arms over his date's shoulders. Brewster pulled Michael aside and told him that it was all right to stand tall and pull the girl in closer. By 2004, that innocence was long gone.

"Every decision Michael makes," Bowman said, "has a litmus test: It will hurt swimming or help it. As long as you are doing what you need to do, and you're happy, anything you want to do is fine. But it would be better not to have a commitment that might take your emotional energy this year."

Living under his mother's roof, Michael didn't face the temptation that comes in coed college housing, but he was a public figure with a seven-figure income. Beyond the normal caution regarding an 18-year-old falling into a serious relationship in an Olympic year, there were days when Bowman spoke in the frankest terms possible, that famous athletes who were careless opened themselves to paternity suits. He sounded like Rocky's manager: Stay away from dames; kills the legs. No topic more infuriated Michael.

"Bob knows how I get when he brings it up," Michael said. "After you hear the same thing over and over again, you understand it. 'I know, I know, I know, I know, I know.' We've had multiple conversations, and he's gotten it into my head."

The payoff, in acclaim and experiences, let alone the money, made it easier for Michael to accept the restrictions that he lived under.

"I hadn't even started my sophomore year of high school when I went to Sydney," he said. "I had nothing to complain about, because I didn't think I had missed anything. Swimming had taken me so many places that I would never have gotten to otherwise, and allowed me to do so many things. It was neat, going around the world. There were times when I wanted to tell everybody to lighten up, but then I'd remember what was at stake and what I stood to gain."

The Olympic year had begun at a farmhouse north of Baltimore. Michael was one of the first guests to leave that New Year's Eve party, because January 1, 2004, was just another day in his training regimen. Between the Olympics in Sydney and Athens, he would log more than 9,000 miles of training and live a paradox. His mother could build a cocoon around Michael outside the pool. In it, Bowman took him to the precipice that confronts all endurance athletes, the point where the demands of training lead to diminishing returns.

Piled on the aerobic base he had built as a child, all of the mileage Michael did after Sydney left his resting pulse in the 40s. Thousands of hours in the pool had allowed him to maintain his ability to hyperextend his elbows, knees, and ankles, flexibility that allowed him to incorporate a ritual that intimidated swimmers around the world. On the blocks, before the starter called for them to set, Michael rapidly but fluidly raised his arms above his spine until the hands touched and made an audible whap. He repeated that motion, which evoked a massive bird in flight.

All of that laxity in his joints, however, may have made him injury-prone on land. Michael had the hand-eye coordination and leverage to pound a baseball over a fence, but watching him circle the bases was not a pretty sight. After the 2003 World Championships, running had been discarded from his cross-training. Too many of his 3-mile jogs had finished with skinned knees and elbows after a slip on gravel. He might attempt to break his fall with a hand, and a swimmer in a cast was a civilian. The threat of a broken bone was secondary to the fact that Michael's knees ached after a run. That pain led him to "sort of cheat on turns, do things with my body that I should do with my knee," a disruption to the symphony of moving parts that all champion swimmers had mastered.

Bowman was Michael's conductor, but a battery of doctors and physical therapists kept that harmony in tune. They did not have to go far for medical advice, as there may not be a better club than North Baltimore for an ailing swimmer. Joanna Zeiger was a member of the NBAC when she placed fourth in the triathlon at the 2000 Olympics. She came to Baltimore not just to train, but to study epidemiology at the Johns Hopkins School of Public Health. Hopkins is one of the world's premier medical institutions, and some of its leading physicians are members of Meadowbrook or have children who train with the NBAC. A 2001 photo shows Michael playfully tossing 9-year-old Andy Cosgarea into the outdoor pool at Meadowbrook. Cosgarea's father was the director of sports medicine at Hopkins. Peter Rowe, another NBAC parent, was a professor of pediatrics at Hopkins. He became Michael's personal physician in 2000, initially to expedite USOC paperwork for the Sydney Olympics.

Rowe marveled at Michael, the way he was more resistant to fatigue and less susceptible to the common cold. The only medication he took was an occasional sleeping pill, administered by USA Swimming team doctors, to hasten rest on intercontinental flights and at international competitions. There were red flags, however, in Michael's build and family background. He had the elongated limbs, flat feet, and asymmetrical chest that were indicators of Marfan's Syndrome, a potentially fatal hereditary disorder that affects the body's connective tissue.

Well-to-do college basketball teams screen their players for Marfan's. Bowman knew that both Tom Dolan and Tom Malchow had undergone that precaution, and had Rowe test Michael for Marfan's in June 2000. The test results were negative, but Michael's distinct build led to other concerns. *The Da Vinci Code,* the *New York Times* bestseller that mixed a fictional plotline with biblical figures, had readers measuring themselves. It shed light on the so-called "divine proportion" that recurred in nature. Divide your height by the distance from the top of your navel to the bottom of the feet. The quotient should be approximately 1.618. For Michael, that quotient was more than 1.7. At 6 foot 4, Michael bought pants with a 32-inch length. Hicham El Guerrouj, the great Moroccan miler, was 5 foot 9 but wore 34-inch length trousers. El Guerrouj was all legs, and Michael was all torso. That allowed him to plane atop the water, but it also meant a larger back, which needed monitoring.

Other than a broken collarbone he had sustained while roughhousing with a friend at age 5, Michael had a clean physical record, but did his long torso and heredity make him predisposed to back problems? Spinal conditions had helped disrupt his sister Whitney's career in 1996. In 1999, NBAC teammate Anita Nall was making regular visits to Scott Heinlein, a physical therapist. When Michael began to experience some mild shoulder pain around that same time, he also began to see Heinlein.

"In 2000, I was seeing Michael twice a week for shoulder pain," said Heinlein, who remained his physical therapist in 2004. "Now he might go 6 months between visits. When Michael does come in, he'll say something like, 'Bob said my hips are not moving because my knee doesn't feel right.' It's obvious that he knows how he's supposed to feel in the water. We look for any cheats he's developed and ascertain if there are any related deficits in strength. The way the coach looks at it, if you can keep everything efficient, you can keep the kid training."

Bowman did that, mindful of what had happened to Whitney.

"One morning," Bowman said, "we worked with a pool buoy between the ankles instead of the knees, the typical way we maintain body position from the core. The next 2 days, Michael had nothing in practice. No one else was bothered, but his back hurt. He handles the major stresses, but the little things throw him off. His body is so sensitive. Just watching how he does things, he's taught me a lot about strokes. When people first see him swim butterfly, their reaction is, 'He doesn't swim properly, his head position is wrong.' The fact is, he redefined butterfly."

Mark Spitz critiqued Michael's method of breathing on every stroke, but the variance in their times was considerable. Michael swam the 100 butterfly nearly 3 seconds faster than Spitz and had gone nearly 7 seconds faster in the 200 butterfly. Technology was partly responsible for the drop, as wider and deeper pools minimized waves, but technique was also a major factor. Michael, for instance, had taken Thorpe's version of the dolphin kick and contributed his own advance.

"I haven't had this proven yet," Bowman said, "but Michael actually has an extra (third) kicking action when he's really doing the butterfly. He only does it when he's going really fast."

Swimming was similar to golf, in that, past a certain tension, the stroke deteriorated. In order to reach and maintain the speed that produced a revolutionary dolphin kick, Michael had to be at peak fitness. When did mileage cross from just right to too much? Bowman knew the cautionary tales. Tim Shaw won three events at the 1973 World Championships but was so burned out by the time of the 1976 Olympics, his only medal was a silver in the 400 freestyle. In April 1994, Dolan, then a University of

Michigan freshman, became the first man since Spitz to hold four national titles. The Curl-Burke Club in northern Virginia had supplied Dolan with a strong aerobic base, but Michigan coach Jon Urbanchek wanted him even fitter. Urbanchek took Dolan to the U.S. Olympic Training Center in 1995 and loaded on the work. An asthmatic who did not know when to quit, Dolan passed out in a pool later that year.

"What if this kid dies?" Urbanchek thought. "I killed him at altitude."

Diagnosed with chronic fatigue syndrome, Dolan won the 400 IM at the 1996 Olympics primarily on the residue of training he had done in the 3 previous years.

That gold medal came in Atlanta, where the U.S. coaching staff included Urbanchek and Murray Stephens. Each admired the other's work, and after the Games, when Urbanchek visited his daughter in Baltimore, he also checked out the NBAC operation.

"Murray was working a jackhammer when I got there," Urbanchek said. "He told me, 'I want you to watch this kid.' He was odd-looking, had an unconventional butterfly, a different looking stroke. Murray introduced me to him, and said, 'This boy is going to go to the University of Michigan.' It was Michael."

He was soon wearing a Michigan cap. Michael was attracted to the college, where Urbanchek recruited dedicated athletes and made them into the world's best. He was an assistant coach on every U.S. Olympic team from 1992 to 2004, and might have been a head coach if not for his thick accent and aversion to bureaucracy. A short, wiry man with political leanings that he said place him somewhere between "John Wayne and the John Birch Society," Urbanchek was out of step on a liberal college campus but at home in a hard sport. He had immigrated from behind the Iron Curtain to Ann Arbor in 1957. Only one man in America went faster than Urbanchek in the 1,500 in 1960, but Hungary didn't want him back and he wasn't yet a U.S. citizen. Urbanchek could assume a gruff exterior, but his swimmers saw his other side and responded to the way he nurtured their needs while coaxing them out of their comfort zone. The Wolverines didn't always have the sprint depth that is required to win an NCAA title, but Michigan men delivered at the most important swim meet of all. Mike Barrowman in 1992, Dolan in 1996, Dolan again, and Malchow in 2000, all won individual titles at the Olympics.

In January, Urbanchek had officially announced that the current college season would be his last as head coach, and he began to talk up his successor. Bowman agreed to meet Athletic Director Bill Martin, who happened to be the president of the USOC, but remained noncommittal until a Michigan administrator tracked him down in the Bahamas, where Michael was filming a commercial. Stephens had groomed Bowman to run North Baltimore, but the heir apparent had tired of waiting for that transition. There was nothing to fix in Ann Arbor, where Urbanchek had created a culture as stringent as the one in Baltimore. Bowman could go from a private club that sold Christmas trees to raise funds, to a college athletic department that had one of the biggest budgets in the nation.

For his own personal development, Michael needed to leave home after the Athens Olympics, but that call wasn't Bowman's.

"Michael and I talked on the flight from the Bahamas to Baltimore, the morning after Michigan offered me the job," Bowman said. "He said that he would go wherever I went. Even if he had said no, that he was going to stay in Baltimore, it was too good of an opportunity for me to pass. I told the people at Michigan, 'Don't hire me, thinking you're going to get Michael.' Even with what he told me, I took the job on the assumption that he would not follow me to Ann Arbor. It was the only approach to take."

Bowman accepted the Michigan job on March 31. The next morning, Bowman, Michael, and his North Baltimore teammates traveled to the Doc Counsilman Classic. When their flight landed in Indianapolis, Bowman powered up his BlackBerry and saw 15 new messages. A Web site had broken the story. Bowman gathered his swimmers in a hallway at the Indianapolis Hyatt and informed them that after the Athens Olympics, he would be changing jobs. It made for an awkward news conference promoting the world short-course championships at Conseco Fieldhouse, the home of the Indiana Pacers. Larry Bird, the Pacers' general manager and one of the stars on the Dream Team at the 1992 Olympics, gave Michael a jersey bearing the number 7.

"It's Jermaine O'Neal's number," Bird said, "but we all know what it stands for."

Talk turned to the Counsilman Classic, the real reason they were in town. The meet would cover 3 days, and Bowman wanted to close it with a bang. In short order at the final session, Michael would race the 200 backstroke and 100 freestyle, then an exhibition in the 200 freestyle.

"I guess I'm a guinea pig," Michael said at the April 1 press conference. "The more stress I'm under now, the better."

As always, Michael was hungry. He went to one of his favorite haunts in Indianapolis and devoured a dinner of bourbon chicken.

"When I woke up the next morning," Michael said, "something wasn't right."

The Counsilman Classic opened on April 2. Ninety-five days before the start of the U.S. Olympic Trials, Michael got through the morning preliminaries but didn't respond that evening when Jenny Thompson playfully poked him in the ribs before his first final, the 200 freestyle. Coming off the turn at 100 meters, Michael began to vomit, but choked it back and soldiered on. He finished a half-second behind Ryk Neethling, in 1:48.78, nearly 3 seconds off his American record. (Neethling trained in Arizona but was from Bloemfontein, South Africa, the same town that had produced Zola Budd, who got infamously tangled with Mary Decker in track's 3,000 at the 1984 Olympics). Three weeks away from posting some fast times at South Africa's Olympic Trials, Neethling graciously noted that he and Michael were at different stages of their training. Michael knew there was another explanation for his first loss since Crocker had beaten him at the 2003 World Championships, a streak of 37 straight finals. After an earnest discussion with Bowman, Michael pulled out of the 400 IM. He could not recall ever withdrawing from a race before.

Bowman said that Michael wasn't feeling well and assured everyone that he would be back, if not for day two of the Counsilman Classic, then definitely for day three. Bowman put on a blasé front and attributed Michael's shaky performance to possible food poisoning from the previous night's dinner of bourbon chicken. Privately, the coach who bragged about the winter when he successfully predicted the day Michael would get sick wasn't so cocksure. Bowman's mind raced with worst-case scenarios, that he had overtrained Michael and that the impending move to Michigan had blurred their priorities.

"See what you've done!" Bowman raged to himself. "You've screwed the whole thing! We had a good thing going, and you've screwed up the karma!"

Back at their hotel, Bowman railed about Michael's fluid levels. Instead of an IV, Debbie suggested a lukewarm coke and mothered her son. Room service delivered chicken soup and a grilled cheese sandwich. Michael watched a Keanu Reeves film about a Little League baseball team. Debbie tucked him in, and he didn't stir until 8:30 a.m. Saturday, too late to prepare for the morning's preliminaries. He watched one cycle of ESPN *SportsCenter,* turned off the TV, and slept past noon. The day would have seemed like a vacation, if not for the anxiety. Michael went to the IU Natatorium that night, swam a leisurely 2,400 meters, and cheered on his teammates.

"It's good for me to try to get in the water and race under those conditions," Michael said of the circumstances behind the loss. "If something happens in the Olympic Trials or at another big meet, you know how to react. If it was the Trials, I would have gone ahead and competed in my other events. I'd rather this happen now, rather than in a few months."

"It shows how ultimately fragile the thing is," Bowman acknowledged. "We make Michael out to be a machine, but he's human."

The Counsilman Classic closed on Palm Sunday, April 4, on a reassuring note. The 200 backstroke went off at 7:19 p.m., and Michael won with a time that only Aaron Peirsol and Lenny Krayzelburg had ever bettered among American men. He moved to the practice pool, where one of his earlobes was pricked for a tiny blood sample to monitor his lactate level; the higher the reading, the greater the oxygen debt. Years of training had enhanced Michael's lung capacity, what the sports scientists might call a "specific adaptation to an imposed demand." When Michael had scared the world record in the 200 backstroke in Orlando, his lactate had read 8.0 millimoles per liter of blood. Other world-class swimmers routinely doubled that in competition, and Michael's readings fascinated the director of physiology for USA Swimming.

"The harder you work, the more lactate you produce," Genadijus

Sokolovas said. "Michael is the only one who can set a world record with very small lactate in the blood."

Michael downed a can of Carnation Instant Breakfast, and was back on the blocks at 7:41 p.m. for the 100 freestyle. Trailing Neethling by nearly a second at the turn, Michael came back and won in 49.45, a fine time given the 20-minute turnaround. He supplied another drop of blood for the lactate monitors as the sparse crowd exited. Fewer than 50 spectators remained when the announcer noted an exhibition in the 200 freestyle. At 7:54 p.m., on 22 minutes' rest, Michael dove in and went 1:48.30, faster than he had gone in Friday's loss.

"Whoo!" Bowman whooped. "Big Dog!"

The three races had taken 37 minutes. Michael's lactate had read 12 at the start of the last exercise, and 14 when he finished. He had never pushed his body this hard during a competition, and all of the fears that had multiplied during an unsettling weekend were groundless. Michael was exhilarated, and Bowman was relieved.

"What Michael did tonight is as tough as it gets," Bowman said. "What he did in 37 minutes is something you can't gain in practice. This doesn't rule anything out."

Michael warmed down until 8:29 p.m., when his lactate finally returned to the preferred reading, 2.

"Yes!" Michael said.

One month later, Michael went to a bowling center for a charity event hosted by Ray Lewis, the Baltimore Ravens' All-Pro linebacker. Michael mingled with NBA all-star Tracy McGrady but did not roll a single ball. That had been taboo since Bowman told him about the swimmer who threw out a shoulder bowling and was never the same. It was Mother's Day weekend, and Michael accompanied Debbie on a visit to his grandmother. Leoma Davisson, 84, weakened by pancreatic cancer and recovering from pneumonia, showed the source of Debbie's instincts. Nursing homes were full of sick people. She did not want her grandson catching something, and shooed him from her room. Michael was in the backseat of his Cadillac Escalade, watching *Scarface* on the SUV's DVD player, when Debbie returned.

"She's afraid you're going to get sick," Debbie said. "We're too close into this now."

STAYING CLEAN

SANTA CLARA, MAY 2004

In describing his inability to maintain weight as a teen, humorist Garrison Keillor said he had the metabolism of a wolverine. Now that it had been determined that Michael would head to the University of Michigan and swim for Club Wolverine after the Athens Olympics, the comparison applied more than ever to a boy who could, would, and needed to eat nearly anything.

His friends in middle school and high school had laughed as he went through three cafeteria lunches. In June 2001, Jamie Barone introduced Michael to Pete's Grille, a greasy spoon 4 miles south of Meadowbrook where they went to refuel after morning practices. Barone would order a breakfast platter and a side, and enjoy the floor show that centered on the counter in front of Michael. He started with a sandwich of fried egg and cheese, with lettuce, tomato, and mayonnaise. Then he had another. In rapid order, he polished off three slices of french toast with butter and syrup, a western omelet, and a bowl of grits. Michael would then order a milkshake for the short drive home, tumble into bed, and nap before the afternoon's workout.

The recommended daily intake for an active 200-pound man is 2,500 to 3,000 calories. Michael's brunch usually exceeded 4,000 calories, but he still had trouble keeping his weight at 195. Other than being troubled by the occasional order of bourbon chicken, Michael had the constitution of a farm animal. While his sister Whitney had been affected by bulimia, an eating disorder, he was constantly consuming food and drink. He was still growing, and his body needed to be replenished after being drained 11 times a week by Bob Bowman. Michael had an astounding ability to recover from an exercise, which only made it harder to instill postrace protocols that would aid and hasten that process. Bowman had observed the deliberation and diligence with which Ian Thorpe took fluid and nutrition immediately after a race, and knew that Michael had to take the matter more seriously.

"There's a window after the exercise when you can replace glycogen," Bowman said of the substance found in the liver and muscles that the body converts into energy in the form of glucose. "That 20-minute window catches up to Michael during the blood (lactate) testing we do, and the swim down. That means that the second he gets out of the pool, we have to add carbohydrates to his system. He needs PowerBars, and he needs to be drinking Gatorade. His mindset is, he just got out of the pool, he's breathing hard, and now the physiologists want to prick his ear to sample his lactate—all while I'm trying to shove food and drink in him. He really doesn't want to be bothered."

After a race at the 2003 Santa Clara International Invitational, they clashed about the matter.

Bowman: "You have to have this Gatorade and PowerBar."

Michael: "I already know why, you don't have to tell me that."

Bowman: "Fine, Thorpe's got a team of six doctors working on it. Since you've got all of this science mastered by yourself, I'll just go upstairs, take a seat in the stands, and leave you alone."

Bowman's nagging seemed pointless a day later, when Michael broke the oldest men's world record on the books, a mark in the 200 IM that had stood since 1994. En route to the San Jose airport that night, Bowman rewarded Michael with a stop at a Carl's, which he had never seen on the East Coast. On the red-eye flight home, Michael turned 18. He pounded his young body in practice and produced in meets, but he had an extremely low percentage of body fat and needed more than Gatorade, PowerBars, and gorging at Pete's Grille, not the most efficient method to take nutrition to begin with.

Athletes expecting to do big things needed more than three square meals a day, and regular food and drink needed to be supplemented. In the early 1990s, the North Baltimore Aquatic Club had experimented with the use of creatine, which added bulk, but Murray Stephens stopped the practice when he couldn't determine a link to improved performance. In December 1999, around the time he started doing double sessions of practice to prepare for his long-shot bid at the Sydney Olympics, Michael began to use Endurox, a nutritional supplement that could be purchased at a GNC store at the mall or online. After a workout, he poured some of the powder into a water bottle, shook it vigorously, and guzzled the mixture.

Endurox promised to "reduce muscle and oxidative stress." Bowman had Dr. Peter Rowe, Michael's physician, study the label, which said that, among other ingredients, Endurox contained electrolytes, carbohydrates, and whey protein. Bowman had found the supplement beneficial and reputable, as Michael had passed dozens of drug tests with Endurox in his system. As they returned to the West Coast for the 2004 Santa Clara International Invitational, however, it had been dropped from his regimen. Before the Doc Counsilman Classic in Indianapolis, Michael had switched to a product that was regulated by the Food and Drug Administration, in response to a warning that he was playing supplement roulette.

In 2001, the International Olympic Committee financed a study of the dietary supplement industry. Nearly 15 percent of the products tested contained substances not listed on the label that would have led to a positive doping test. That rate was 18.8 percent for supplements that had been manufactured in the United States. The level of contaminants may have been too low to affect performance, but it was enough to taint the supplement and the athlete who took it.

One cautionary tale, in particular, hit close to home. Michael was attempting to become the first member of the NBAC to win an Olympic gold medal since Beth Botsford in 1996. Now Botsford was all grown up and engaged to Kicker Vencill, a sprinter she had met in Tucson, Arizona. Vencill's long-shot dream of a berth in the Athens Olympics was squashed in January 2003, when an out-of-competition test detected a high limit in his system of 19-Norandrosterone, a by-product of the steroid nandrolone. Vencill was banned from competition for 2 years, but continued to proclaim his innocence, that he had not knowingly taken a banned substance. At his own expense, Vencill had his supplements tested at a private lab, which determined that a multivitamin he had taken was tainted. He became the face of the caveat emptor that was being issued by the U.S. Anti-Doping Agency (USADA).

USADA's 2004 guide included the following message: "Antidoping rules make the presence of a prohibited substance in an athlete's urine a doping offense regardless of how the substance got there. Any athlete who takes a vitamin, mineral, herb, amino acid, or other dietary supplement does so at his or her OWN RISK of committing a doping violation." The point was reiterated in the back of the guide: "Ignorance is never an excuse. It is the personal responsibility of each athlete to ensure that he or she does not allow any prohibited substance to enter his or her system or use or allow the use of any prohibited method."

Cases of sports drinks were stacked on the back porch at Michael's home in the Baltimore suburb of Rodgers Forge. They were sent there unsolicited by companies hoping to get Michael to endorse a product that contained a high amount of caffeine or electrolytes. Inside the kitchen, one magnet was stuck on the refrigerator. It was from USADA, listing its Web address and 1-800 number. Athletes could get answers to simple yet vital questions. Does my doctor's prescription include a substance that was banned by the IOC? Is the cold remedy I bought over the counter safe? Just as important, is the dietary supplement I am taking clean of banned substances, or could it get me bounced out of the Olympics?

In the wake of the Vencill case, some veterans wouldn't take as much as a vitamin C tablet, and a few coaches decried the supplement hysteria as unwarranted. In 2000, Stanford coach Richard Quick had taken 33-year-old Dara Torres back to the Olympics after an 8-year absence, thanks in part to the liberal use of supplements. The issue divided the swim industry. While some senior officers of the American Swim Coaches Association (ASCA) joined the warning chorus, the home page on ASCA's Web site included an advertisement for a supplement.

Michael's generation was accustomed to receiving mixed messages of how a pill or powder, needle here, or nip and tuck there could improve a person's drab existence. Cosmetic surgeons could enhance your sex appeal, and a dose of Viagra provided relief from erectile dysfunction. "Whatever it takes" had long been part of the athletic parlance. NFL fans were indifferent to the evidence that the synthetic means that bulked up offensive linemen to 350 pounds also shortened their life spans. Anabolic steroids had boosted Arnold Schwarzenegger's body-building career, helping him become Hollywood's top box-office attraction and then the governor of California. Before he entered politics, President George W. Bush had owned the Texas Rangers, and no spectator sport had turned more of a blind eye to doping than Major League Baseball.

Michael's father was in law enforcement, and his mother's home economics curriculum included a segment on nutrition. He chose drug cheats as his topic for a presentation in his ninth-grade American Government class. While he wasn't as zealous as the distance runners and other endurance athletes who had sworn off carbonated beverages, Michael knew what belonged in his body and what did not, and he was galled by a double standard for American athletes. The U.S. Olympic Committee had been one of the first bodies to sign on to the World Anti-Doping Code, which had been enacted on January 1, 2004. A positive test for a banned substance meant a 2-year suspension. A second offense brought a lifetime ban. Tests were conducted in competition and out of it, on a random basis. Depending on the rules of their international federation, Olympic athletes could miss a random test or two and still compete, but in essence, swimmers, runners, gymnasts, and cyclists announced their retirement when they stopped notifying the authorities of their whereabouts. They were not unionized, and their privacy was secondary to a level playing field. It was a marked contrast to baseball sluggers like Barry Bonds, Mark McGwire, Rafael Palmeiro, and Sammy Sosa, who had compiled Hall of Fame numbers in an era when their sport did not ban substances that would have gotten an Olympian suspended.

"I was done playing baseball by the time Mark McGwire and Sammy Sosa had their big home-run chase," Michael said of the summer of 1998. "That was the main headline on *SportsCenter* every day. Kids look up to baseball players and want to be like them, but what do you do when somebody you look up to 'roids up, cheats? What's a kid supposed to do then? When I hear about what goes on in some other sports, it makes me mad. It's sad, that all sports aren't created equal."

In the first 5 months of 2001, from a World Cup meet in Stockholm, Sweden, to an out-of-competition test at Meadowbrook, a 15-year-old Michael had provided seven samples of blood or urine to doping control officials. The samples collected in the United States were sent to a lab at the University of California at Los Angeles, which was accredited as a testing facility by both USADA and the World Anti-Doping Agency (WADA). Over 19 days in the summer of 2003, encompassing the world championships in Barcelona and the Summer Nationals in College Park, Michael was drug tested 10 times, but the aftermath of the first meet pointed to the paradox of doping control.

After Barcelona, FINA announced that it would retest more than 300 urine samples for THG, a designer steroid that had only recently been detected. None of those retests turned up a positive sample, but the doping cops were always a step behind the chemists, and a career's worth of clean, negative test results, like Michael's, proved nothing. Innocent athletes like Vencill got trapped, while cheating athletes had gotten away with Olympic gold. Quick, the Stanford coach, lamented that every great performance had a cloud over it. The cynics presumed that any athlete who enjoyed a groundbreaking achievement had to be dirty, and Mark Spitz assumed that cheating was so rampant, he had told a 2002 interviewer that he would be tempted to use banned substances. The more records and titles an athlete won, the more he was subjected to testing. Michael pointed to his dozens of negative samples and said, "The results don't lie," but that didn't quiet the whispers that he couldn't possibly be doing what he was without some method that was unethical, secretive, and against the WADA code.

"We all do it," Bowman said. "Somebody overseas does something, and your first reaction is, 'He's juiced.' Michael and I have talked about the unfairness of that reality."

Nothing tainted an Olympian as badly as being labeled a drug cheat, but now good intentions and a clear conscience weren't enough. Caution and vigilance were also required to avoid tumbling into the pool of Olympic athletes who had been tainted by steroids, human growth hormone, and a laundry list of other synthetic concoctions that had given a perverse twist to the ideal of higher, faster, farther. Bowman's nightmare was that Michael would do something great and then test positive for a banned substance.

"It's very frightening to think that there are gray areas there, and that there are very minute degrees of reading that could have a huge impact on what we do," Bowman said. "It requires some faith. It comes down to the fact that this is sport, we enjoy it, and we've taken every possible precaution to protect Michael. You could take this to the nth degree. It could become a 24-hour obsession with everything he puts in his mouth. I don't know if we could live and train and handle everything that he's doing, if all I thought about was supplements. The food he eats is wholesome, but as much as we try to make sure that it's 100 percent pure, who's to say? That drives me crazy, but at the end of the day, we can't lose every ounce of innocence that goes into this, because that's what makes it fun."

The urgency that accompanied an event held once every 4 years compounded the pressure to win, medal, or just qualify, side effects be damned. The opening ceremony of the Olympics included one athlete taking an oath for all, that they will play cleanly and fair, but Faustian bargains were as old as the Games themselves. En route to winning the gold medal in the marathon at the 1904 Olympics, Thomas Hicks fortified himself with an elixir of brandy and strychnine. Cycling's dirty history, which included the death of a Danish athlete at the 1960 Olympics, dogged Lance Armstrong. His sport had looked as bad as ever on February 14, 2004, when Marco Pantani—Armstrong's predecessor atop the Tour de France until he had to serve a doping suspension in 1999— died under mysterious circumstances. Amphetamines and other stimulants were the early drug of choice for men on the road, like baseball players, long-distance truckers, and cyclists. In the 1950s, Soviet weight lifters were using anabolic steroids, which elevate testosterone levels and help build mass. Boxers and wrestlers needing to make weight used diuretics.

The IOC banned specific substances for the first time at the 1968 Games. The 1976 Olympics were the first where steroid users were caught and disqualified, but Montreal is not remembered as a watershed year for the antidoping movement. Historically dominant in the Olympic pool, the American women did not win an individual gold medal. Ten of the 11 went to East Germany, whose star was Kornelia Ender, the only swimmer before Michael to have world record times in different events in the same day. Officials from the state-run Sports Medical Service had given Ender and scores of young women harmfully large doses of testosterone and skirted the era's primitive controls by falsifying documents, providing bogus urine samples, or tapering their drug use just like they did their training. That East German system was still in place through the 1988 Olympics, where swimmer Kristin Otto became the second athlete after Spitz to win six gold medals in a single Games. The East German system was done in not by the IOC, but by politics, as the fall of the Berlin Wall in 1989 unified Germany and sent the dirty doctors packing.

Some took their medical bags and syringes to China. While East German women won 10 of the 15 gold medals in swimming at the 1988 Olympics, the 1992 Games saw only the Americans top China's four golds. A year later, five Chinese women bettered the world record for the 3,000-meter run in a preliminary heat at a track and field meet. In 1994, Chinese women won 12 of the 16 events at FINA's world championships. One of the youngest competitors in Rome was 14-year-old Whitney Phelps, who came home and told her little brother how manly the Chinese women were. A month later, two of China's gold medalists tested positive for steroids.

That country was not invited to the 1995 Pan Pacific Championships, but cheaters continued to slip through the cracks. Michael's NBAC teammates included Canada's Marianne Limpert, who would have won the 200 IM at the 1996 Olympics if not for Michelle Smith, an Irishwoman who would later be banned. Two weeks after Massi Rosolino won the 200 IM at the 2000 Olympics, an Italian newspaper reported that he had been among 61 of the nation's Olympians to register abnormally high levels of human growth hormone (HGH). A reputable doping test for HGH was several years off, and Rosolino finished third behind Michael at the 2003 World Championships.

Now the rumor mill centered on genetic doping and track and field, which had always been at the forefront of athletics' brave new world. Endurance athletes like distance runners were the first to boost their ability to produce oxygen through the use of EPO, Erythropoietin. At the 1976 Olympics, Finland's Lasse Viren employed a more primitive form of blood doping, banking his own blood, then returning it to his system via transfusion. While not prohibited, the ethically dubious aid helped Viren become the first man to repeat in the 5,000 and 10,000 runs. At the 1988 Olympics, Canada's Ben Johnson trounced Carl Lewis and set a world record in the 100 dash but did not hold his gold medal for long. Johnson immediately tested positive for high levels of stanozolol, an anabolic steroid.

Dick Pound, the Canadian who heads WADA, argued that Johnson wasn't the only cheater at the 1988 Olympics and crusaded to have USA Track and Field come clean about what he claimed had been an extended, systematic cover-up of its own dirty athletes. The saddest circumstantial evidence came from Florence Griffith-Joyner. Her body had been transformed between 1984 and 1988, when she set world records and won gold medals in the 100 and 200 sprints. She retired a year later, just as random drug testing was about to be instituted and amid accusations that she had taken growth hormone. Griffith-Joyner was 38 when she died in 1998. Her autopsy cited complications from a congenital brain abnormality.

Pound's claims gained credibility with the case of C. J. Hunter. One of the world's best shot-putters, Hunter finished second at the 2000 Olympic Trials but later withdrew from the American team, ostensibly with a knee injury. That was a ruse to deflect attention from a series of positive doping tests that showed his testosterone raised to outrageous levels. The deceit came to light during the Sydney Olympics, and the Hunter scandal lingered because of two of the people who stood by him at a press conference. The first was a curious man named Victor Conte, who had played the bass in a popular rock band in the early 1970s. He had found a second career as a supplement guru, producing potions at his Bay Area Laboratory Cooperative (Balco) that boosted the performance of famous athletes, among them home-run champion Barry Bonds and All-Pro linebacker Bill Romanowski. In Sydney, Conte went into a laborious explanation of how legitimate dietary supplements could become tainted in the factory. Somewhere in the production process, he insisted, Hunter's supplement had passed through a vat that had once contained steroids. (Kicker Vencill would tell a similar tainted-supplement story, albeit with miniscule traces of banned substances in his system.)

Before Conte made Hunter's case, another person even closer to the burly shot-putter gave a brief statement of support, then excused herself to get back to her work at the 2000 Olympics. Hunter was married to Marion Jones, who did not meet the profile of a drug cheat. Jones had set national age-group sprint records while growing up in Southern California, and then played point guard for the University of North Carolina's 1995 NCAA basketball champions. Jones returned her focus to track and field, became the second-fastest woman ever, after Griffith-Joyner, and attempted to become the first track and field athlete to win five gold medals in a single Olympics. She won three in Sydney, but would be haunted by her associations to Conte and Hunter, whom she would soon divorce. In December 2003, Hunter told the *San Jose Mercury News* that officials from track and field's international governing body suggested he feign his injury as a way to deflect attention during the Sydney Olympics away from his positive doping tests and from Jones, the sport's most marketable athlete at the time.

Craig Masback, the chief executive officer of USA Track and Field, admitted, "We have not done everything we could in the past" when his organization proposed a zero tolerance policy for doping cheats in 2003. The gesture was more publicity stunt than realistic possibility, but people in high places were about to take an interest in the issue.

The day after Michael returned from Auburn University and his first meet of the Olympic year, President Bush gave the annual State of the Union address. The country was at war in Iraq and there seemed to be more pressing matters, but the president used his platform to mention the impact that doping in general, and steroid use in particular, were having on the integrity of American sports. The election-year remarks stirred a brief debate, but as the Athens Olympics neared, doping became a very hot topic.

In the first week of May, a group of men emerged from a closed-door meeting in Washington, D.C. They included USOC President Bill Martin, who happened to be Bowman's new boss, since he was also the athletic director at the University of Michigan. Martin and officials from USADA went to Capitol Hill to lobby Senator John McCain, a cochairman of the Senate Committee on Commerce, Science, and Transportation. They wanted McCain's committee to help USADA keep dirty American athletes from competing in Athens. USADA would use calendars, e-mails, and other documents it received from an ongoing federal investigation of Balco—what it called "nonanalytical" evidence—to bar athletes linked to banned substances.

Jones was among those under suspicion.

"To keep an athlete out of the Olympic Games because of something that's not been tested for, that's totally unfair," she said. "We live in the United States, where you're innocent until proven guilty. If I make the Olympic team and am held out of the Olympic Games, you can bet that there will be lawsuits. I'm not going to let people take away my livelihood because of a hunch."

Four years after she had been an Olympic darling, Jones was being grilled at the USOC's Media Summit on May 16. Michael was the only other athlete who merited an individual press conference in that packed Manhattan ballroom. Jones wished him well but said that her "Drive for Five" gold medals in 2000 had been viewed more harshly than his effort to match Spitz.

"I hope you guys are as difficult on him as you were on me," she said. "Just because he's a guy . . . my five gold medals revelation was viewed as cocky. I don't think there's any reason to beat around the bush. He's going there (to Athens) to make history. I wish him the best."

Four days later, Michael traveled to the 2004 Santa Clara International. In a Silicon Valley pool, about a 40-minute drive south of the industrial park where Conte had built his Balco lab, Michael attempted a schedule that unethical athletes and coaches would have been tempted to alleviate with banned substances. Bowman had inserted an exhibition into the Doc Counsilman Classic, but he needed no contrivances like that now that the college season was done. Ian Crocker and Aaron Peirsol were in town. So were Gary Hall Jr., Jason Lezak, Tom Malchow, Erik Vendt, and a cool spring breeze. On May 21, as Michael raced outdoors for the first time since June 2003, the air temperature was 62 degrees.

"We would all be bitching if it was hot," Bowman said. "The best place to be is in the water, but it sucks when you get out."

Michael opened with a substantial win over Vendt in the 400 IM, despite an awkward slip on his block that plopped him into the pool on all fours. From that point on, he toweled his block dry before a race.

"I'm glad that happened now, instead of in 6 weeks," he said. "I want the Trials and I want the Olympics to be now. The Olympics are getting closer every day, but I wish it was here now."

The next night, Michael took the 100 butterfly from Crocker, who was fresh from acing a chemistry exam and sporting a beard. After Michael lost to Peirsol by more than a second in the 200 backstroke, the furor over the fact that he hadn't formally announced his program for the U.S. Olympic Trials resumed. Speculation centered on July 12, which was crammed with the finals of the 200 backstroke and 200 IM, and the semifinals of the 100 butterfly. None of the American men knew exactly what he was going to swim down the California coast in Long Beach.

Santa Clara closed with Michael's most demanding day, which began with a reminder of the vigilant attention that had to be paid to detail, items that had to be triple-checked. As the penultimate heat of the 100 backstroke preliminaries progressed, the announcer noted Michael's absence. The men in the sixth and final heat were ready at their blocks when the starter sensed a commotion behind him. Bowman had neglected to pick up a revised heat sheet, and Michael had missed his race. Could he fill the vacancy in lane seven? The referee granted the request. That leeway did not come in international meets, and had a run-of-the-mill swimmer asked for the same break, he would not have been given the same consideration. For years, Michael had admired Michael Jordan, and now he had the kind of pull that had birthed the phrase "Jordan Rules."

Michael had three finals coming up that evening, but he spent 30 minutes doing a photo shoot for PowerBar, one of his new sponsors. Wasn't that an unnecessary distraction, at a time when Michael needed his rest?

"So what?" Bowman said. "What are we going to do in Athens, when it's midnight, and he's still not out of doping control?"

Minus a pair of racing trunks that had either been misplaced or stolen, Michael returned for the evening's finals. He won the 100 freestyle in 49.26, an excellent time considering the chilly conditions. He won the 200 IM by 4 seconds. In the 100 backstroke, he was last at the turn against a loaded field, but stormed back and caught everyone except Peirsol. The three races were admirably handled, all in the span of 66 minutes.

"That was definitely more painful than Indianapolis, because of the competition," Michael said. "This is the best of the best, the same faces I'm going to see at the Olympics."

He got another reminder of the stakes.

"Good luck in the Trials," the public address announcer said, "and then there's a meet in Europe this summer."

SCRUTINY

BALTIMORE, JUNE 2004

On the last day of July 2003, Michael had returned to Baltimore after being on the road for nearly a month, first for the world championships in Barcelona and then a scouting trip to Athens. Michael usually headed straight to his room for some peace and quiet after exhausting road trips, but on that day, he dropped his bags inside the front door, climbed into his SUV, and drove to a custom auto glass shop. Before he had gone overseas, Michael asked Gerry Brewster, the former Towson High teacher who was among his fans in Barcelona, to research the Maryland vehicle code regarding tinted windows. Michael wanted his as dark as the law allowed.

"He likes to be in the car," Debbie said of her son. "He feels, 'They can't see me, and I can see you.' Michael wants to be noticed, but only in certain parts of his life."

"On the TV show *Cribs,*" Michael said, "the big-name stars always had tinted windows. That's the one place I'm able to get away, be a normal person somewhat, somehow. The baseball cap had the same purpose."

Michael was well known in swimming's small circle when he went to

Barcelona, but left the city in Spain as the leader in the race for Athens hype. Between the 2003 World Championships and the 2004 Olympics, he would undergo scrutiny that few drug-free athletes, if any, have ever experienced before the Games. Just as he had arrived after the Olympic swim program had expanded and professionals were allowed in, his celebrity was boosted by another perfect storm of circumstances courtesy of the United States. Marion Jones and the track and field team were being dragged into the muck of the Balco scandal. The men had failed to qualify for Athens in baseball and soccer. The women's gymnastics team lacked a charismatic star. The men's basketball team was newsworthy because of who wasn't going to Athens.

Both the American and international media had their antenna up for a story that did not involve drugs or terrorism. Michael's times and titles had attracted endorsement contracts. The sponsors who had given him the freedom to train wanted to see his image and name, not just in their advertisements, but in the print and electronic media. Bob Bowman plotted his career and Peter Carlisle mapped out a media strategy, but now Team Phelps had executed its job so well, Michael had to get behind the wheel of his SUV to find anonymity.

Mark Spitz recalled doing one press conference before the 1972 Olympics, 8 years before the founding of ESPN. Cable television and then the Internet fragmented the traditional media and multiplied the number of reporters, bloggers, columnists, essayists, newspapermen, and television types, let alone fans with their own Web sites. Ian Thorpe had been a hometown hero at the 2000 Olympics, but the American and European press could not easily make its way to Australia. Baltimore was an hour's drive north of Washington, D.C., the capital of the free world, and 3 hours south of New York City, a media center. Athens was preparing for 10,500 athletes, but they would be outnumbered by a press horde of 12,000, and there were days when Michael felt as if each one had thrust a microphone in his face or asked him to pose for just one more photo.

Michael was repeatedly asked to take stock of himself as he prepared for the Argent Mortgage Invitational, which would serve as both his final tune-up for the U.S. Olympic Trials and a farewell to Baltimore. The media prefer their athletic heroes as Renaissance Men, but Michael was intently focused on swimming, not taken to introspection, and was in the midst of the transition from adolescence to adulthood. That step had been underlined at his high school graduation, where fellow members of the Towson High School class of 2003 tried to sabotage NBC's record of the rite of passage by making farting noises.

Michael readied for the Invitational as his contemporaries completed their freshman year of college. Spitz had started college in 1968, when campuses were rocked by protests against the Vietnam War. The kids in Generation Y had vague memories of the toppling of the Soviet Union and the first Gulf War, but could take credit for refining spring break to a science. Born in 1985, Michael had never worn cloth diapers or played Pacman, and always had cable television. He was a child of the digital age, albeit a clumsy one, who went through an estimated 10 compact disc players, which he was always dropping on the pool deck. In September 2003, when Hurricane Isabel left parts of Baltimore without electricity for several days, he said, "I can't imagine not being able to play video games for a week." On a road trip in 2004, Michael developed a rash on his back, took a photo of the troubled area with his cell phone, and e-mailed it to Dr. Peter Rowe, whose diagnosis and treatment were made long-distance. His deal with AT&T Wireless supplied BlackBerrys to several members of Team Phelps, and he immediately took to the gadget.

His favorite motivational saying was "Actions speak louder than words," and with his boyhood lisp, Michael had never been much for idle conversation with adults. In the spring of 2001, British butterflyer James Hickman and his coach came to Meadowbrook to train. Several nights, to her son's dismay, they lingered at Debbie's dinner table.

"Michael learned to sit at the dining room table for hours after you eat a meal," she said. "You drink tea and eat crumpets, and chat and chat and chat. One night he said in a stage whisper, 'Mom, I can't do this every night.' It was enjoyable for me, torture for Michael. He just wanted to go play his video games."

Because of his ADHD, Michael had little interest in the written word but possessed the intelligence and habits to qualify for honors classes as a ninth-grader. When he returned from the 2000 Olympics, his sophomore course load included English, French, chemistry, and geometry. Less than a month into his junior year, he became a professional athlete, and over his final 2 years at Towson High, he took only the basic courses required to earn a Maryland High School diploma. On his third attempt, after he finally took the time to read the manual, Michael acquired the learner's permit necessary to attend driver's education. As his classmates hired tutors and feverishly prepared for the Scholastic Assessment Test that affects the college options for most, Michael crammed for the 2003 World Championships.

He had traveled the world, but hadn't always had the chance to see the sights. In Barcelona, USA Swimming's curfew policy lumped Michael in with the kids who had never gone to college. The night the meet concluded, he had to be in by 11 p.m., so his celebratory dinner with family and friends was held at the team hotel.

At the 2004 Santa Clara International, Dominic Szabo, a recent addition to the training group, relaxed with a fictional account of the Battle of Thermopylae. Jamie Barone breezed through *The Da Vinci Code* and told Michael to read something other than the sports section in *USA Today*. Szabo had graduated from American University, Barone from Baltimore's Loyola College. Michael was listed as a volunteer assistant coach at Loyola but had yet to set foot in a college classroom. He was unaware that his 19th birthday, June 30, 2004, coincided with the deadline for the American-led occupying forces to turn over sovereignty in Iraq to the Iraqi people. The collegians had eggs in other baskets, but he was totally absorbed in his work and at a loss as to why anyone would want to know what he thought about world affairs.

"I'm here to swim," he would complain to Bowman. "Why are they asking me those questions?"

"This is bigger than that," his coach explained. "You're a public figure. They want to know what you think about things. The least you can do is think about them."

He had his own Web site and logo, courtesy of Octagon, but the media had a substantial say in his image, and dealing with minicams and tape recorders was integrated into his training. The process that had begun with the study of a videotape of a polished 15-year-old Thorpe had advanced to pointers from professional media consultants. On at least four occasions, Paul Green, an employee of Brenner Zwykel, Speedo's public relations firm, arrived at Meadowbrook to "ambush"

Michael. After practice, the two would record an interview on video. Michael would return after lunch, and Green would review his performance, in the same way that Bowman would critique his turns.

"We came up with answers to the questions he would be asked, and practiced the answers," Bowman said. "Michael's problem was that he would lean on one word or phrase that would become a crutch. For months, it was 'awesome,' then it became 'incredible.' 'This is going to be an incredible meet. The times are incredible. It's going to be incredible to be here.' He needed to do better than that."

Michael had turned professional at age 16. Before one of his first speaking engagements, at a senior center, one of the residents raised his hand, reminded Michael that he was indoors, and ordered him to remove his Michigan cap. He wore Nike shoes, the competition's brand, to an early Speedo shoot. After he was schooled in the ways of product placement, some of his attempts brought laughter from Bowman and Carlisle, who kept telling themselves, he's only a teenager.

"How do you remain a kid?" Michael was asked at a packed press conference.

"I'm a normal 18-year-old," he said. "I like video games, hanging out with my friends, going to the movies. I text message a lot. AT&T Wireless makes it so easy to text message."

Michael had been burned at his very first press conference, the night he had qualified for the 2000 Olympics. Besides learning the value of "no comment" when asked about his love life, that session held a lesson in interpretation, how an offhand comment could become gospel on the Internet. That same night in Indianapolis, Michael mentioned that he had eaten clam chowder before his big race. Five years later, writers who had never met him were citing clam chowder as his secret weapon.

Michael knew that every step he took, every fist he pumped, and every grimace at the end of a race was being analyzed, and that reporters would put their own spin on his actions or comments. He noticed that some interviewers tried to blindside him; "Butter me up, get me off topic, then spring another Spitz question." Carlisle told Michael that if he didn't have an opinion about something, then he shouldn't make one up. Swimmers are healthy and half-naked, and a self-conscious one is a bit of an oxymoron, but he became guarded with the press. Michael was a willing interview subject, but the process became repetitive, work to be approached like another set of intervals. Tarrah Smith Pollaro, a publicist for USA Swimming, mentioned that to Michael one day.

"You always give the same answers," she said.

"They always ask the same questions," he responded.

The more the press prodded, the less he had to say. Out of respect to the NBAC, he wouldn't even confirm the obvious, that he would be following Bowman to the University of Michigan. Michael sighed as writers repeated the same old questions, and couldn't understand their complaint that he revealed little. On a Web site for PowerBar, six of its high-profile athletes were asked to list "one fact no one knows about you." Lance Armstrong's entry read: I can relax. Brandi Chastain mentioned her hobby, knitting. The listing for Michael: I think everyone knows everything about me.

"Most of it was fun, but it got on my nerves sometimes," Michael said. "People usually asked, 'Is there anything we don't know about you, that you care to share?' I would say, 'You guys know everything about me.' My life, my past, nothing was private."

Asked if he took exception to anything that had been written about him, Michael said, "The truth can't hurt me," but he was sensitive to criticism and found motivation in the media. In 2003, a skeptic in the Finnish press said that Michael couldn't break Jani Sievinen's 9-year-old world record in the 200 IM, which spurred him to do so four times in 42 days. The novelty was long gone from the day in 1999, when he gave his first interview to the *Towson Times,* a weekly newspaper. In the spring of 2000, the only publication that knew of his Olympic aspirations was the *Talisman,* the Towson High newspaper. Those articles were clipped and saved, but now he didn't have the time to read everything that was written about him.

"If there's a quote about me, Bob passes it along," Michael said. "Other than that, I read nothing that's written about me. If I did, I'd get nothing done."

Speedo's Stu Isaac had been on the mark when he described Michael as an "ordinary boy who did extraordinary things." Like most American teenage boys, he spent his idle time in front of a video display or the television. His favorite show was *Cribs,* where an athlete or musician from the hip-hop generation shows off his luxury home and fleet of cars. He was keenly interested in the Baltimore Ravens and televised sports, but rarely watched the evening news. Tom Brokaw, the avuncular anchorman at NBC, showed a clear admiration for Michael and what he was trying to do. When they were introduced, Michael had never heard of the famous newsman, but he came to know Brokaw and other personalities from NBC.

The International Olympic Committee's biggest single source of income is from the American television network that pays for the exclusive rights to broadcast the Games in the United States. As the number of viewers worldwide grew, from 2.5 billion for Los Angeles in 1984 to 4 billion for Atlanta in 1996, so did the rights fee. Sydney and its 14-hour time difference from the crucial Eastern time zone lowered NBC's ratings in 2000, but the network paid $793 million, approximately 60 percent of the IOC's broadcasting revenue, for the right to be the sole provider of 2004 Olympic programming in the United States.

Like Michael's sponsors and NBC, the Olympic press was lukewarm about swimming, but it loved a winner, especially one who had overcome some kind of hardship and dreamed big. Four American newspapers sent reporters to the 2003 World Championships in Barcelona, including the *Baltimore Sun*, which then created a Michael Phelps beat, an Olympic reporter whose sole responsibility would be following him around the world and chronicling what it called "The Road to Athens." In January 2004, the *Washington Post*'s Mike Ruane was assigned to cover Michael on a full-time basis. Everything was fair game in the rush to dissect the boy who was the presumptive star of the Athens Olympics, and about the only thing the media failed to produce was a nickname that stuck. Because of the city's homicide rate, "The Baltimore Bullet" was deemed politically incorrect.

In November 2003, the *Baltimore Sun* explored his family dynamics. Wayne Coffey of the *New York Daily News* was the first to notice in print that Michael had a tattoo of the Olympic rings on his right hip, which was usually hidden by swim trunks. *The Times* of London called regularly, for Michael's take on topics of Olympic interest. In February, *ESPN* the magazine had a clever counter to the *Sports Illustrated* swimsuit issue, a cover story titled "The Hottest Thing in a Swimsuit." Eric Adelson's article recounted the basic elements of Michael's story: Spitz and the greatest feat in the history of the world's biggest sports event, the prospect of a pot of gold at the end of the Olympic rainbow, and an otherwise typical American teen estranged from his father.

His parents and sisters were sought for interviews. So many reporters and photographers talked to Lou Sharkey, the proprietor of Pete's Grille, Barone joked that he should get a kickback for introducing Michael to the diner. In August 2003, Bowman heard someone whisper, "That's Michael Phelps's coach," in an electronics store. It was then that he fully comprehended that everyone in the training group, not just Michael, was being watched. Bowman told his swimmers that they had an opportunity to present swimming to the largest audience the sport had ever seen. Bowman made at least five of their 11 practices a week observer-free, but the other NBAC swimmers didn't seem to mind the attention. Kevin Clements, who had done some modeling, was featured in a spot on ABC's *Good Morning America*. Bowman's practice attire went from a T-shirt and gym shorts to a golf shirt and pressed khakis, and he made an effort to sanitize the mildest obscenities from his banter. As reticent as Michael could be, Bowman was that expansive. Reporters needed to be educated, and besides, from April on, every interview was a chance for Bowman to drop the University of Michigan into stories that might be read by prospective recruits.

After 7 years together, Michael and Bowman had developed a good schtick.

"Today, I'm running a little on empty," Michael said. "I had some extra special encouragement this morning."

"My foot connecting with a part of his anatomy," Bowman said.

Bowman's symbolic kick in the ass was promptly parried by Michael, who was asked what was in the CD changer in his SUV.

"Overnight Celebrity," Michael said. "I just burned it for Bob."

Bowman listened to classical music, not hip-hop artists like Twista.

Those exchanges came at the end of the first week in May, when Bowman and Carlisle began to shut down availability to Michael. It was his most demanding week to date, but he liked the way it started, as he reached the semifinals of ESPN's online competition to determine America's best athlete. There were worse fates than being eliminated by Atlanta Falcons quarterback Michael Vick.

May 5 marked 100 days until the start of the Athens Olympics. To mark the occasion, three small bombs were detonated outside a police station in the Kallithea section of Athens. Michael's day began with a live remote for one of Baltimore's morning television shows. Mike Sokolove of the *New York Times Magazine* and Matt Lauer of NBC's the *Today Show* followed him for much of the day. Two days later, the European press was accommodated with interviews at Meadowbrook, and returned the next morning to get visuals at practice. The BBC, a German television network, two from France, and a reporter from the *Financial Times* documented the morning workout on May 8. The Baltimore media got its last chance to question Michael en masse that evening, before a black-tie gala fundraiser for the NBAC. Eight days later, hundreds of reporters attended Michael's May 16 press conference at the USOC Media Summit in Manhattan.

May 8 typified the squeeze that Carlisle and Marissa Gagnon, the Octagon assistant who served as his press agent, had to manage on Michael's calendar. Media attended the morning practice and an evening press conference, which came in between a Speedo appearance at a department store and the NBAC fundraiser. In midday, Michael was invited to be the grand marshal of the Preakness Parade. The synergy was seamless, as the race was an NBC property and Argent Mortgage, one of his sponsors, backed the Triple Crown, but there just wasn't enough time. Carlisle had spent his career drumming up interest in his athletes, but now he had to decline most invitations. Among other charities, Michael had adopted the Harford Boys and Girls Clubs and Baltimore County's Riverside Elementary, one of the schools his mother Debbie oversaw, but even those institutions were seeing less of him.

Media outlets that wanted to jump on the Michael Phelps bandwagon discovered that it had left town. *Newsweek*'s request to pose Michael in the Arizona desert was turned down. Maryland Public Television came around too late. By then, Bowman had already learned to say no. He erupted when a writer for *Baltimore Magazine* asked for a follow-up interview to get to know more about Michael's current girlfriend. Bowman also had a run-in with a photographer from *Time* who overstayed his welcome. A session that was supposed to last an hour stretched to 2. Having been hosed down with water for the shoot, Michael got a chill and had to warm himself in the Meadowbrook hot tub, which further delayed practice. The photographer said he needed Michael to swim in lane one, and Bowman ordered him to stay in four. The photographer protested and was then given 15 minutes to pack up his gear and leave the premises.

Bowman was sensitive to the complaint that some in the American swim community made, that Michael was overexposed.

"The ones who complain about Michael giving too many interviews are the same ones who complain that swimming never gets any attention," Bowman said. "I hope he gets his due from the swimming community for that. If he was still juggling swimming and school and homework, no one would bat an eyelash about his swimming being compromised, or say 'You've got to protect him.' A lot of factors will add up to determining Michael's success at the Trials and in Athens, and most of them don't have anything to do with swimming. One, will he be able to eliminate distractions? Two, how will he handle unforeseen circumstances? Three, can he recover emotionally from facing the best in the world in each event? Finally, there is his physical preparation. Of those four, that's the most rock solid. The volume of interviews he's done has not compromised his fitness. So people say, 'Nobody cares about swimming.' Fine, okay. We can't win."

Bowman made his point on the first day of June, from Colorado Springs, Colorado. After Santa Clara, Michael's training group was in the midst of a 17-night stay at the U.S. Olympic Training Center. Ostensibly, they were repeating the protocol that had been laid out in the summer of 2002, when Michael had followed up some rigorous preparation at altitude with a breakout meet at the Summer Nationals. That was Bowman's story as they prepared for the Argent Mortgage Invitational, but it wasn't the whole one.

Now that the media crush had eased, Michael had too much free time on his hands.

"I wanted to get Michael out of town," Bowman said. "We could do the work at home, but I didn't want any distractions. It's not as if Michael was partying out of control, but he was trying to have relationships with girls, hang with the guys from Loyola College, be a normal 18-year-old. I could see it happening before my eyes, him losing his focus, and I wasn't taking any chances. We were talking about 2 months in your life, of maintaining the discipline that was necessary to accomplish what he was trying to do."

Michael did not protest.

"Looking back, it wasn't a good time to certify my independence," Michael said. "The main reason we went to Colorado Springs is that Bob didn't want me to throw away what we had worked so hard for. In 2003, I was in the best shape of my life. In 2004, I traveled more, and I was pulling myself away from Bob's instruction. He tried to get me in an environment where it was swim, eat, sleep."

His only nonswimming demands at the U.S. Olympic Training Center were a photo session for AT&T Wireless and an interview with Tim Layden of *Sports Illustrated*. Like Omega and Visa, the magazine is an official Olympic sponsor.

June 5, their final Saturday in Colorado Springs, was not a good day. Bowman lost one of his heroes, as former President Ronald Reagan died, and Michael was disappointed by the result of the Belmont Stakes, where Smarty Jones, the winner of the Kentucky Derby and Preakness, was the runner-up. Bowman had told him that winning seven gold medals would be harder than taking the Triple Crown, which remained untouchable since 1978.

On June 10, they returned to Baltimore. A day later, the Argent Mortgage Invitational began. Usually known as the North Baltimore Aquatic Club Long Course Championships, the meet had its first corporate sponsor. The more pertinent news was that it would be the last time Michael would compete in his home pool while representing the only club he had ever known. After this meet, he would gear up for the U.S. Trials and then the 2004 Olympics. After Athens, he would move to Ann Arbor, Michigan. Time was fleeting, and his days in Baltimore were coming to an end. His hometown was obsessed with the blight of the 17-year locust, and the official Argent Mortgage Invitational T-shirt included a sketch of the insect and this message: "Every 17 years or so, a fast little bugger will come around and blow away the competition." Michael had been in diapers in 1987, the last time the locusts sang what Bob Dylan called their "high, whining trill." Murray Stephens, the club's founder, remembered an NBAC meet when Michael stood near the official's tent, howling and in tears, because no one was paying attention to him. That was no longer an issue.

Two television minicams and two newspaper photographers captured a cordial exchange between Michael and his father, Fred, and his wife, Jackie. Fred had been away too long and did not miss a day of the Argent Mortgage Invitational. On day three, one of the Baltimore TV stations led its 11 p.m. newscast with a bulletin that Michael had lost. The report did not provide the context, which was that Clements had beaten him in the 200 breaststroke—about as newsworthy as Michael Jordan striking out in a minor league baseball game. The meet concluded on June 14, a Monday. A dozen parents used digital movie cameras to record Michael in the preliminaries of the 200 butterfly. When he was done, mothers returned to their paperbacks.

Michael autographed an Athens visor for one of the NBAC's age-groupers, and patiently sat with a young girl from a visiting team who was concerned that she was no longer able to lower her personal best in one of her favorite events. Michael recalled his stagnation in the 200 butterfly, of how he erroneously thought he knew everything, and told the girl to listen to her coach. Behind him, a group of boys used a tennis ball and the outside wall of the indoor pool to play a variation of dodgeball.

"I was the guy standing against the wall," Michael said, "getting hit by three balls at a time."

That night, his last race in an NBAC cap in Baltimore unfolded under threatening skies, and Bowman told the starter to interrupt the announcer and get the 200 butterfly final going. It was hard to distinguish the flash of cameras from lightning as Michael dove in at 7:39 p.m. He finished in 1 minute, 56.04 seconds. Only two Americans had ever gone faster. Michael had just pounded his body at altitude and was swimming purely on the emotion of the evening. He changed into jeans and a PowerBar T-shirt, and gave a nod to his background as he concluded one last press conference in Baltimore.

"The NBAC will always have a special place in my heart," he said. "I grew up in an environment where things like going to the Olympics and winning gold medals are not foreign concepts, they're expected."

Michael was a floor above the indoor pool that he had poured much of his life into. The deck included a greaseboard, where Bowman or Scott Armstrong, his assistant, would write the particulars of practice, often in a predawn haze being cleared by caffeine. Over the last year, the board had included a countdown, which was updated with ceremonial flourish. On September 10, 2003, the message had read 300 DAYS, an eternity for a teenager. On March 29, 2004, it had dropped to 100 DAYS, symbolizing increasing urgency. Now the board read 23 DAYS. That's how long Michael had until the start of the U.S. Olympic Trials.

Michael's Visa commercial would make its debut in 48 hours. Most of the photos that he had posed for—including the ones *Sports Illustrated* had taken of him playing with dolphins at the National Aquarium in Baltimore and the *Time* shots that had so angered Bowman—were stored in the computers of magazine designers. If Michael produced as expected at the U.S. Trials in Long Beach, he would appear on more covers than a supermodel. If he didn't, those magazines had backup options.

Michael was ready to leave Meadowbrook, when he was approached with one more photo request. He posed in the middle, his arms around strangers, as 44 members of the Lake Erie Silver Dolphins gathered for a keepsake photo of the meet.

Then he was gone.

TRIALS

LONG BEACH, JULY 2004

Michael turned 19 on June 30 with a quiet celebration. When his father called to wish him a happy birthday, he was invited to join Michael, his sisters, and his mother, who were taking him to an Oriental restaurant for one of his favorite foods, sushi. All would be going to Athens, but Debbie, Fred, Hilary, and Whitney understood that quiet time with Michael would soon be scarce. July would be spent in California, at the U.S. Olympic Trials in Long Beach, and then at a training camp for the American team at Stanford University. He figured to spend nearly the entire month of August in Athens. If all went well at the Olympics, Michael was going to hop on a bus and spend September on a nation-wide tour that Peter Carlisle and the people from Octagon were ready-ing. October would see Michael moving to Ann Arbor, Michigan, and beginning the next phase of his life.

The baby of the family was moving on, for good, and the evening marked a symbolic passage. Debbie, Hilary, and Whitney gave Michael a large shadowbox that held the No. 7 jersey he had received from the Indiana Pacers. Michael had dropped repeated hints that he wanted an

English bulldog, like the one Carlisle had. Given his travels, a pet that required exercising was not the most pragmatic gift, so Fred gave him a sand-cast model of the breed.

At nearly the same hour, the USA Swimming Web site posted the official entries for the Trials, which were 1 week off. Michael was going forward with Plan A, the one he and Bowman had plotted after the 2003 World Championships. He would compete in an unprecedented six events, the four in which he had set world records in Barcelona, plus the 200 freestyle and 200 backstroke. Michael had wanted to keep his plans quiet, in the event that they changed. Bowman had always felt that the final entry list, what swim people called a psych sheet, would be the best way to disseminate what they had agreed upon the previous August. They wanted to drop his Trials schedule into the conversation. They wanted to keep a low profile, which was no longer realistic.

A travel agent handled Trials arrangements for Michael, 11 teammates, three coaches, and the support staff from the North Baltimore Aquatic Club. A limousine service called the NBAC switchboard to confirm details about transporting the party from Los Angeles International Airport to the Long Beach Hyatt. Bowman and Cathy Lears, the traveling secretary for the trip, were pleased with the prompt attention, until the NBAC's travel agent mentioned that its office had never heard of the limo service. Authorities in Long Beach were asked to look into the matter. According to Bowman, a search of the taxi driver's house was made, and it was awash in Michael Phelps memorabilia. Bowman made other arrangements for ground transportation, and kept Michael and his teammates in the dark about the matter. As the NBAC party entered the baggage claim area at LAX, a plain-clothes police officer from Long Beach approached the group, followed by the plotting taxi driver and two of his friends. The officer flashed his badge and waived over an airport security detail, which detained the driver's group until Michael and his teammates were safely on their way to Long Beach.

"That's why," Bowman said, "Sean Foley was with Michael all the time in Long Beach."

Foley, the former University of Texas swimmer, current Octagon employee, and Michael's double beneath the Statue of Liberty in the Visa commercial, was also now his bodyguard. Bowman concocted a plausible cover story to explain why Foley had one of the NBAC's precious deck passes. Michael's possessions had become collector's items, and Foley was shadowing him at the pool to make sure that his kickboards and water bottles didn't become souvenirs. It was a way to limit distractions as Michael attacked the busiest program in Trials history. Besides, if anyone wanted a keepsake, they didn't have to look far.

The cover of the official program and a pair of large mesh murals that adorned the two main entrances to the outdoor stadium featured an artist's montage. At the top were two female swimmers, wearing triumphant smiles and olive wreaths, in front of a Greek temple. At the bottom were two modes of transportation linked to Long Beach, the Queen Mary and a Grand Prix race car. Those images surrounded the biggest figure, a male butterflyer. The meet's official logo was a more stylized version of the same subject. Those renderings were generic, but inside the official program there were nine photos of the world's hottest Olympic athlete.

At the 2000 Trials, a 15-year-old Michael had not merited one of the 130 biographies for males in USA Swimming's media guide. Now the Aqua Zone, the corporate village where fans could purchase T-shirts, hats, and other keepsakes, looked more like the Michael Phelps Zone. He was featured on giveaway posters at the booths that had been rented by Argent Mortgage and the Indianapolis organizers of the 2004 world short-course championships. Visitors to the AT&T Wireless booth heard an attendant make like a carnival barker with the come-on to get "a free picture with Michael Phelps—pretty soon he'll be too famous and you won't be able to get one." The man stood alongside a cardboard cutout that included the invitation to "strike a winning pose with Michael Phelps of the U.S. Olympic team."

That promotion was presumptuous, as Michael had yet to earn a berth in Athens. A top-two finish at the Trials was required to get to the Olympics. Relay spots also awaited the top six in the 100 and 200 freestyles, but everyone else was going home. You could hold a world record and have a closet full of gold medals from major international meets, but you had to perform in Long Beach in order to get to Athens.

The meet had nearly 700 entrants, and fewer than 50 would go to the Olympics. A majority came to the Trials simply for the experience, but

Whitney Phelps empathized with the dozens whose dreams would not be realized. The pressure at the Professional Golfers Association tour qualifying school that made grown men nauseous was multiplied fourfold at the Trials. The stakes in the American system had been tragically emphasized in February, after the U.S. race-walking Trials. Al Heppner, a product of a Baltimore suburb, had overcome depression to become one of the nation's best. After he failed to qualify for the U.S. Olympic team, Heppner drove to a bridge outside San Diego and leapt to his death. At a normal USA Swimming meet, finalists were recognized on the awards podium. After too many third-place medals had been tossed in the nearest trash can, that ceremony had been streamlined at the Trials.

Michael enjoyed a margin of error that other swimmers didn't, but there were other perils to consider. If he slipped off a block, false-started, or suddenly came down with performance anxiety, his plans for Athens would have to be downsized. NBC would ready another potential Olympic star, magazine designers would put someone else on their covers, and his sponsors would lament betting on the wrong horse. His courage was compelling, as Michael was attempting to go where no swimmer had gone. Shirley Babashoff had won five events at the 1976 Trials. Mark Spitz had been the only man ever to win four events at the meet. Matt Biondi, in 1988, had been the second to qualify for the Olympics in four individual events. Charlie Hickcox in 1968 and Tom Dolan in 1996 had been the only other men with as many as three wins at the Trials. Spitz's era included two rounds in events that covered 200 meters, while Michael's faced three. Spitz didn't need it, but in 1972, nations were allowed three entries per event. Now berths were fewer and events lasted longer, a push and pull that led Natalie Coughlin, considered Michael's female counterpart a year earlier, to enter just two individual events at the Trials.

What Michael was attempting was confusing. An Australian newspaper misinterpreted the fact that Michael had met the qualifying standard in all but two of the 13 events, and reported that he would compete in 11 of them. Spitz alluded to that prospect during a Trials eve press conference, where he was brought to supply perspective.

"I've never met Michael," Spitz said, "and I am as curious as the next person as to how he's going to manage this."

At a press conference all his own, Michael was asked repeatedly to make a prediction. He broke from his media training and said the first preposterous thing that came to his mind.

"I could get 15 gold medals if I wanted."

Easygoing and polite, Ian Crocker and Aaron Peirsol were asked about being villains, since they could get in the way of the biggest story of the Athens Olympics. Four years earlier, the three had gotten to know each other in Sydney. Crocker and Peirsol shrugged off the questions. None were wearier of talking, and more eager to race, than Michael.

Waiting for room service that evening, Michael text messaged Hilary and invited Debbie and his sisters, who were out having dinner, to join him. They were accustomed to keeping out of his way at meets, and the offer was a pleasant surprise. By the time they arrived with ice cream, he had finished his dinner and was shaving the hair from his arms, chest, and legs, to reduce friction, a ritual that swimmers observe prior to major meets. Jamie Barone stopped by and gave him a brush cut that one European writer likened to Frankenstein's hairdo, but Michael always had been more about substance than style.

WEDNESDAY, JULY 7

Wired for the East Coast, Bowman was grateful to sleep until 5 a.m. on opening day of the 8-day Trials. He needed to be in better condition to keep up with Michael, so he had begun jogging. Bowman's run was done when Michael awoke at 6:15. Making his way to breakfast, Michael noticed two Long Beach policemen patrolling the Hyatt lobby. As CNN reported that hotel workers in Athens were demanding better pay with a 24-hour walkout, he ducked out a back entrance of the hotel and strolled no more than a half-mile around Rainbow Lagoon Park to the swim stadium. In the Olympic year, only the Spring Nationals in Orlando offered better logistics, but the air there had been thick and the venue claustrophobic. USA Swimming was accustomed to holding its prime event in Indianapolis, but now it had adopted a 10,000-seat minimum for the Trials. The city of Long Beach's temporary stadium was on a convention center parking lot, where Michael had once written one of his world records in chalk. The air was light, cooled by the Pacific Ocean, and its pool was fast.

Michael waited for an NBC cameraman to step back, then climbed onto the block in lane four for the fourth and final preliminary of the 400 IM, his first race at the Trials. The event is contested in 1 day, and Michael wanted to expend minimal effort in the morning swim. He won his heat in 4 minutes, 16.11 seconds, and only two other men went under 4:20. As he walked a gauntlet to the practice pool to cool down, dozens of men and women with tape recorders, notepads, and minicams traded elbows in the Mixed Zone, the international appellation for the area where athletes take questions. At major meets, Michael made time for the press after every final. His program was usually too full to accommodate morning stops in the Mixed Zone, but the media demanded to hear his thoughts about his first race at the 2004 Trials.

"I felt relaxed," Michael said. "That's the way I wanted it to go this morning. I'm very pleased."

He moved on as reporters scribbled down that revelation. The scene evoked a Bernardo Bertolucci film about the fall of China's royal family. In *The Last Emperor,* the title character is introduced as a small child. Sycophants scrutinize his bowel movement, searching for a divine message.

Six hours later, Michael shed red basketball shorts, a full-length NBAC parka, and an iPod that throbbed *Till I Collapse,* his favorite track from *The Eminem Show,* the seminal rap CD that he used for preparation only at the most important meets. Michael meant business in the final of the 400 IM. He built a lead of a second on the butterfly leg, added to it on the backstroke, remained on world-record pace during the breaststroke, and never faltered in the freestyle. He touched the wall and turned to see Erik Vendt catch Ryan Lochte for the second spot. Michael squinted, saw the "WR" alongside his time on a scoreboard at the opposite end of the stadium, and repeatedly pumped his left fist. A time of 4:08.41 was his fourth world record in the event, but of more import, Michael was the very first athlete to make the American swim team going to Athens.

His medal ceremony segued into the parade of finalists for the women's 400 IM, who were greeted by an incongruous musical selection, a cover of The Guess Who's *American Woman*. Katie Hoff had gotten skittish in the morning preliminary and barely made it into the final, but once there, the 15-year-old won with the second-fastest time ever by an American. The NBAC not only had the most versatile swimmer ever, it also had the nation's best all-around female. It was an eventful night for the club. Back in Baltimore, the Jones Falls flooded its banks and damaged the Meadowbrook Aquatic and Fitness Center.

THURSDAY, JULY 8

Michael breezed through the first two rounds of the 200 freestyle, with the second-fastest time in the morning preliminaries, then leading the way in the evening semifinals. There was speculation that he might not swim the event in Athens, since Australia's Ian Thorpe and Pieter van den Hoogenband of the Netherlands loomed large.

FRIDAY, JULY 9

Day three of the Trials included the final of the 200 freestyle, the first two rounds of the 200 butterfly, and a lesson in resource management. Michael was eating and sleeping in the hotel nearest the stadium. At the practice pool, the NBAC canopy was erected next to a staircase that led to Jim Earley, his Baltimore-based masseuse. Every protocol had been designed to minimize effort and maximize potential, but conserving energy in races went against Michael's nature. Fred Phelps, an old cornerback, had taught his son to take no prisoners. That point had been reinforced by the loss to Crocker at the 2003 World Championships, but while wanting to win every race was admirable, now it wasn't sensible. It was imperative that Michael learn a different approach to preliminaries and semifinals.

Pete Malone, a coach from Kansas City who was giving Michael tips on his starts, made this point with some name-dropping. On opening day at the Trials, Lance Armstrong had taken the overall leader's yellow jersey in the Tour de France for the first time. Armstrong didn't have to dominate every stage, and a swimmer didn't have to win every round. Michael needed to advance with less effort, and now he was doing just that in the preliminaries of the 200 butterfly. He won his heat, but defending Olympic champion Tom Malchow, despite a torn shoulder muscle, posted the fastest time of the morning. It was a small step in the maturation of Michael Phelps. As the stadium's sound system played Richard Strauss's *Thus Spake Zarathustra,* Michael ducked under the stands, where a chiropractor worked on a seemingly minor kink in his back.

The evening's finals were moved up 10 minutes, to accommodate NBC's first live prime-time telecast of the swim Trials since it had become America's Olympic network in 1988. At 5 p.m. in Long Beach, 8 p.m. on the East Coast, NBC went live for the parade of the 200 freestyle finalists. Introduced for the first time as a two-time Olympian, Michael had the worst reaction time off the blocks and entered the water with his hands too far apart. He settled into third after 50 meters, second at the 100 wall, and had the lead at the final turn. The time of 1:46.27 was a meet record but not a personal best. The runner-up was Klete Keller, who raced for Club Wolverine, the organization Michael would soon join. The University of Michigan's Peter Vanderkaay and Dan Ketchum were third and fifth, earning Olympic berths in the 800 relay. That race was a certainty for Michael, but the 200 freestyle was not. Did he really relish the prospect of being on the podium in Athens and looking up at Thorpe in what was already being hyped as the Race of the Century?

On 44 minutes' rest, Michael won his semifinal of the 200 butterfly in 1:56.66. The effort was relaxed but still a full second ahead of the time Malchow posted in the second semifinal. Back at the Hyatt, the restaurant staff found him a secluded table, where he relaxed over dinner with his sisters, Debbie, Bowman, and Cathy Lears.

SATURDAY, JULY 10

Fans paying their own way for two weeks at the 2004 Olympics were budgeting over $15,000. Fred Phelps was saving for Athens and had no plans to go to Long Beach, until something told him he needed to get to the Trials. He made an unexpected cross-country flight and arrived at the swim stadium for the evening session, when his instincts proved true.

Michael did not have the time or inclination to read the newspapers or go online during a major meet, and was unaware that Spitz was going to be the presenter during the medal ceremony for the 200 butterfly. Carlisle's marketing strategy for Michael wanted to link his client to Spitz, without being overshadowed by him, the reason the hottest swimmer in the world had avoided one of its most famous Olympic heroes. On opening day of the meet, Bill Plaschke of the *Los Angeles Times* had weighed in on the perceived snub. "While Phelps and his handlers," Plaschke wrote, "have carefully planned an attack on the record and its $1 million bounty, they have done so without paying even chapped lip service to the most famous swimmer in the world."

NBC knew to milk the drama of the moment and left its coverage of the track and field Trials for a cut-in of the final. Michael won in 1:54.31, the second-fastest time in history after his world championship semifinal, but wasn't pleased, since in all likelihood it was his last chance at a personal best at the Trials. Michael had wanted another world record, which would have added to what has to be the most intriguing medal ceremony the meet has ever produced. NBC again left the track Trials and returned to Long Beach, where the man who had lowered the world record in the 200 butterfly nine times between 1967 and the Munich Olympics awaited Michael at the medal podium. Like power forwards establishing position under the boards, photographers shoved one another aside and widened their stances in front of the medal stand. Spitz, gray at the temples but a fit 54, shook Michael's right hand and began to talk. The teen bent forward and listened.

"I know what you're going through," Spitz told Michael. "I'll be in Athens, cheering you on. You can really do this. Don't let your focus waver."

Swim meets and the Olympics are choreographed, which made what occurred next all the more engaging. Spitz draped the gold medal over Michael's head and onto his shoulders, then showed that he had lost none of his flair for the dramatic. He leapt onto the podium, grabbed Michael's right wrist with his left, and thrust their arms to the sky, like a boxing referee signifying the winner of a knockout. Spitz nodded his approval and used his right finger to point to swimming's new heavy-weight champion, who got goose flesh as a crowd of 9,878 roared its approval.

"I had no idea what I was going to do," Spitz said on his way out of the stadium. "I was winging it."

SUNDAY, JULY 11

It was a compelling image, but the Phelps-Spitz photo did not make the first page of the *Los Angeles Times* sports section. Shaquille O'Neal, who had returned the NBA title to the Lakers, had enough of Kobe Bryant and wanted out of L.A. There was scandal at the track Trials in Sacramento, where a federal judge turned down a U.S. Anti-Doping Agency request to review sealed testimony from the Balco investigation and where a fifth-place in the 100-meter dash meant that Marion Jones would not defend her Olympic title as the World's Fastest Woman. Those events bumped the photo inside the Sunday sports section, but Michael did not have the time to peruse it over breakfast.

After eight races in the first 4 days of the Trials, Michael would face that many in four sessions that would encompass just 33 hours. Minus relays, the Trials schedule replicated the one at the Olympics, and how well he handled these 2 days would determine Michael's final program for Athens. Sunday brought the preliminaries of the 200 backstroke and 200 IM in the morning, and the semifinals of each at night. In the morning, Michael won his heat of the 200 backstroke and was in the practice pool by the time the vanquished climbed out of the stadium pool. Coming back on 52 minutes' rest, Michael took his heat of the 200 IM in a time that was easily the fastest of the morning.

Michael established a pair of Trials records in the semifinals that evening. The first, in the 200 backstroke, had a short cyberlife and never made it as far as a computer printout, as Peirsol went 2 seconds faster in the second semifinal. Seventy minutes later, Michael went 1:57.64 in the 200 IM. He was still the only man ever under 1:58, but a fine double was lost in the noise that emanated from the 100 freestyle final. Under normal circumstances, that event dictated the lineup for the 400 freestyle relay, but Michael wasn't a normal swimmer, and he was among the candidates for the relay in Athens.

Michael and a record crowd of 10,016 saw a plane pull a banner that read "Swim Fast, Have Fun." It had been paid for by America's most decorated sprinter, Gary Hall Jr. Jason Lezak won the 100 free and became the second-fastest man ever with a 48.17. Crocker finished second in 49.06, a tenth of a second in front of Hall, who had eight Olympic medals and disdain for Lezak and his comparatively miniscule international credentials. The only thing the two seemed to agree upon was that Michael didn't belong on the American 400 freestyle relay at the Olympics.

MONDAY, JULY 12

After the first round of the 50 freestyle, Hall weighed in.

"Somebody swam the 100 free and earned a spot on that relay," he said. "You're talking about a lifetime of work. I'm supportive of Michael and his goals. I want to see the relay win gold. It's only fair for the individuals who earned a place on the relay to swim in the Olympics. Four of us are swimming for one spot if Michael's there."

In fact, any member of an Olympic squad can be used in a relay. Some of Jenny Thompson's eight relay gold medals had been earned in relay events in which she didn't enter the corresponding event at the Trials. Coughlin figured on the 800 relay in Athens even though she didn't swim the 200 freestyle in Long Beach. Men's head coach Eddie Reese, however, was dealing with proud veterans willing to speak their mind, not compliant teenage girls. Once invincible, the Americans hadn't won a major international 400 freestyle relay since 1998, and Reese figured that Michael could make a difference. His 49.05 at the Spring Nationals remained faster than Crocker's new personal best. Michael had beaten Lezak head-to-head in Santa Clara. Reese explained that the men who finished third through sixth at the Trials had to step up in the Olympic preliminary and produce a split of 48.2 or 48.3, the rough equivalent of a sub-49 time in an individual 100 freestyle, to gain a place in the Athens final. If fewer than two met that standard, Michael would join Lezak and Crocker there.

"I'm going to put eight names in a hat," Reese started, trying to defuse the controversy. "I know what Michael has done and when he's done it. If everyone goes 48.2 or 48.3, he might not be on it. The chances of that happening . . . I want Michael Phelps in as many events as possible, and in as many as he can do well."

Michael was too preoccupied to consider the surrounding sound and fury. He won his preliminary of the 100 butterfly in an expedient 53.27, while Crocker lowered the meet record to 51.69 in his. Michael then rested for the most taxing night of his career, one that had the potential to be replayed on August 19 in Athens. He faced the finals of the 200 backstroke and 200 IM, and semifinals of the 100 butterfly. Nights like this were why he had doubled in both the 13–14 and adult age group sections of a relay for the NBAC. Nights like this were the reason he had averaged 43 miles of training a week since the Sydney Olympics. Nights like this dictated that he give blood samples to monitor his lactate while guzzling a sports drink to replenish his glycogen. Nights like this were behind his routine, why today's lunch would be a turkey and avocado sub, the same as yesterday's and tomorrow's.

At 5:11 p.m., Michael was the first of the eight finalists in the 200 backstroke to enter the tented area that served as the ready room. He stifled a nervous yawn as Amanda Beard lowered the world record in the 200 breaststroke. Michael was on Peirsol's turf, figuratively and literally. Half the crowd seemed to be from Irvine, Peirsol's nearby hometown, and it grew louder as both men were under world record pace through the 50 and 100 walls. Peirsol gained ground in the third 50, and more as Michael struggled with the final turn. Lowering his world record for the first time in two years, Peirsol responded with the most boisterous celebration the Trials had seen to that point. He leapt on the lane divider that separated him from Michael and pounded the water like a kid playing at the neighborhood pool. He was slow to see Michael's hand extended in congratulations.

The runner-up made a quick exit. In his 14th race at the Trials, Michael had finally been beaten, but he had just qualified for the Olympics in a fourth individual event. There was no time to dwell on that achievement or to consider whether the 200 backstroke would remain on his Athens program. Michael went feet first into the practice pool, surfaced, and was handed a sports drink from Foley, while Genadijus Soko-lovas of USA Swimming took a knee and drew blood from an earlobe to monitor his lactate.

Returning on 25 minutes' rest, Michael was under his world-record pace through the first two turns of the 200 IM final. He came home in 1:56.71, his third-fastest time ever. Michael had just become the first American male swimmer in a century to qualify for five individual Olympic events, but seemed more interested in the men behind him. Ryan Lochte finished second. Tommy Hannan, a friend from Baltimore who had been a relay gold medalist at the 2000 Olympics, was fourth. Kevin Clements, Michael's training partner, was fifth, more than 3 seconds slower than he had gone at the 2003 Summer Nationals. Clements pulled on some gym shorts and didn't bother to cool down. At the Canadian Trials, meanwhile, Marianne Limpert was failing to meet the qualifying standards her homeland had instituted, which meant that Michael would be the only member of his training group going to the 2004 Olympics.

He was in the practice pool, preparing for his 100 butterfly semifinal, when the public address announcer explained his absence during the medal ceremony for Peirsol. The 200 backstroke had been his wild card. Peirsol was a second faster today, but Michael could make up some of that differential on improved turns alone. On this night at least, the 200 backstroke had detracted little from his 200 IM. If he rebounded strongly again in this 100 fly, then what would be the harm in keeping the 200 backstroke on his Athens program? Barely an hour after facing Peirsol, 36 minutes after winning the 200 IM and just wanting to break 52 seconds, Michael set aside the program concerns and won his semifinal in 51.89. Crocker followed with another Trials record, 51.25.

How did Michael feel after the most daunting night a man had ever faced at the Trials?

"I thought," he said, "I would be in more pain now."

TUESDAY, JULY 13

In Long Beach, Fred had made it a point to meet Spitz, whom he took an immediate liking to. Now Fred was working on his second cup of coffee as Michael and Foley sat down at an adjoining table in the Hyatt, ordered breakfast, and father and son caught up. It was Michael's second free morning at the Trials, which included some reevaluation in the press. Bill Plaschke, the *Los Angeles Times* columnist who had criticized Carlisle's Spitz strategy, now had this to say about the flap in the 400 freestyle relay: "If whiny, jealous teammates and competitors don't appreciate the risk he is taking and pain he is absorbing in trying to equal Mark Spitz's seven gold medals, they should now. . . . Michael Jordan could skip shoot-arounds. Barry Bonds can skip batting practice. Michael Phelps can skip a time trial."

That evening, Michael raced for the 17th and final time in 7 days, as a clear underdog to Crocker. Once a week since the 2003 World Championships, the man from Longhorn Aquatics had studied the video of their final in Barcelona. Crocker again wanted to force the issue and negate Michael's stronger second 50, and he executed his plan perfectly, leading by three-quarters of a second at the turn. Crocker lowered his world record to 50.76 and raised his index finger and pinkie in the "Hook 'em Horns" sign that signified the University of Texas. Michael went 51.15, not as fast as he had gone in Barcelona, but it was a historic moment nonetheless.

In the last three U.S. Trials, Dolan had been the only man to qualify for the Olympics in three individual events. Michael had done so in six. He had won four events, something only Spitz had done, and it had taken world records from Crocker and Peirsol to beat him in the other two. He had produced under pressure for 7 straight days, and it was time to exhale. For the very last time, Michael took off the blue and gold cap of the North Baltimore Aquatic Club, the colors he had worn since age 7. Later, as he walked a victory lap around the deck with Crocker, he tossed his baseball cap into the stands, then his 100 butterfly medal. Throwing caution to the wind, he shortened his normal cool-down and opened a can of Coke for the first time in Long Beach. Having worn goggles for more than a week under the California sun, Michael had raccoon eyes as he shook hands with the press room moderator.

"I can say I've done something no one else has ever done," Michael said. "I can say I was the first Michael Phelps, not the second Mark Spitz."

Michael walked off that podium and was stopped by an old man who sported a media credential from an Italian agency. He threw an arm around Michael and handed a disposable camera to a stranger, to document his brush with a historic figure. There may be no cheering in American press boxes, but Europeans had their own customs.

Decisions had to be made, and promptly. Michael could be coy with his program before the Trials, but now the third-place finishers in the 200 freestyle and 200 backstroke anxiously waited to see if he would drop an event, which would create an opening for them in Athens. Over dinner at the Hyatt, Bowman and Michael weighed his options. Something had to give, since he had to make room in his Athens program for as many as three relays. Bowman would never forgive himself if the 200 backstroke detracted from Michael's 200 IM, and suggested he drop the chase of Peirsol. Michael agreed that it was the prudent thing to do, which made Bryce Hunt the happiest third-place finisher in Long Beach. Bowman then raised the option of dropping the 200 freestyle, which would tax Michael's body and mind with little hope of a gold medal.

"No way," was Michael's emphatic answer.

WEDNESDAY, JULY 14

At 8:40 a.m., Michael was working on his starts with Pete Malone at the practice pool, abandoned except for Peirsol and five other swimmers. On his way out of the stadium, Michael walked by a processing trailer and bumped into Crocker, who was weighed down by the apparel and luggage he had been issued by the USOC. On the walk back to the Hyatt, without Foley or Bowman running interference, Michael explained his decision to drop the 200 backstroke.

"It didn't take too much talking to figure out that we needed to drop the 200 backstroke," Michael said. "It's one less individual event, and it's the one race where I build the most lactate. I was willing to drop that, but I was not going to be talked into dropping the 200 freestyle. I want to see how close I can get to Thorpe. This will be the only time I get to go head-to-head with him in the 200 freestyle."

Four hours later, during a press briefing sponsored by the Omega watch company, one of his sponsors, Michael took a seat alongside supermodel Cindy Crawford and glanced at the script in front of him. He could do better than the words that had been written for him, and winged it, just like Spitz.

"It's an honor to be here," Michael said. "Omega sponsors so many high-end athletes, and it's a privilege to be among them."

What's it like, being alongside a supermodel?

"Once this news is out," he said, "I'll get some calls from my friends."

That evening, nearly every member of the U.S. Olympic swim team donned a football jersey with the number 04 on the back and took a bow at the Long Beach swim stadium. So did Bowman, who was named as an assistant coach. Michael did not, as he was in Los Angeles, wearing his tuxedo to a taping of the 2004 ESPY awards.

A day later, he was among the guests on the *Tonight Show* with Jay Leno, where Mark Wahlberg promoted a new cable program titled *Entourage*. A few dozen autograph seekers waited outside the NBC studio in Burbank, and Michael rolled down the window in his stretch limousine. Bowman and Carlisle promptly noticed a familiar face, the taxi driver who had been waiting for Michael upon his arrival in Los Angeles. Carlisle ordered their driver to leave immediately. The taxi driver hopped in the passenger seat of a waiting car as Michael's limo pulled away. As the taxi driver's car ran several traffic signals in pursuit, Carlisle alerted their hotel's security desk, which had men stationed at the entrance to the basement garage when the limo arrived. Michael finally understood the alarm over a man who twice in 10 days had gotten too close for comfort. There was less than a month to the 2004 Olympics, and his mind raced.

"What is happening?" Michael said. "Where have I put myself?"

Michael had always liked being one of the guys, but he also wanted to raise his sport's profile. He could do one or the other, but he could no longer do both.

ONCE IS NOT ENOUGH

ATHENS, AUGUST 2004

One Olympiad, you're an anonymous 15-year-old with big ears and the wrong identification badge.

The next, you're posing with supermodels, Internet chat rooms are describing you as "dreamy," and journalists are inquiring about your politics.

It had become trendy for Olympians to pose nude. Michael didn't go that far, but he showed plenty in a *Vanity Fair* salute to Athens hopefuls. Bruce Weber, famous for his provocative photos of the human form, posed softball pitcher Jenny Finch in a black slip and sprinter Shawn Crawford in his briefs. The first athlete in Weber's 29-page Olympic spread for *Vanity Fair* was Michael, his Speedo pulled down to reveal the Olympic rings tattooed on his right hip. The *New York Observer* reported that Michael was slated for the cover until actress Reese Witherspoon's people objected, but he was not lacking for a newsstand presence as the countdown to the Athens Olympics shrunk from months to weeks to days. *Sports Illustrated* showed him crouched on a block, wearing goggles and a Speedo swim cap. It was the first time its cover featured a solo swimmer outside the pool since 1975. On the cover of *Time,* Michael displayed a stern visage and his increasingly familiar torso. The article inside erroneously referred to his father as Frank Phelps. Michael and Marion Jones were the only athletes featured on the cover of David Wallechinsky's *Complete Book of the Summer Olympics.* The Athens edition of the reference tome altered its customary alphabetical organization and made swimming the first sport. Michael was on the cover of *Parade* magazine, where Olympic historian Bud Greenspan weighed in.

"Will Phelps be able to equal or better Spitz's record total, perhaps the greatest single achievement in Olympic history?" Greenspan asked. "For me, this will be one of the most exciting dramas at this year's Olympics."

The answer to that question would be determined in part by how well Michael handled his taper, the act of reducing training and increasing rest before a major competition. Basketball and football teams applied the same principle, minimizing their physical preparation as a game drew near. Science, intuition, and guesswork went into the seesaw of keeping a swimmer both fresh and sharp, and Olympic head coach Eddie Reese compared the taper to going to a new barber: You don't know how it's going to look until it's over. The majority of the Americans were compelled to do a full taper before the Trials, since they had to be at peak form just to get to the Olympics. Michael, however, did not have to be at his best at the Trials. He had created such a large margin of error that he trained right through Long Beach, where he raced over 2 miles and put in nearly 40 warming up and cooling down. Michael's taper had always included more mileage at a faster pace than the competition, but adjustments were constantly made to the process. It seemed counterintuitive, but as a swimmer neared physical maturity, it took longer for his body to recover. Larsen Jensen was the only male on the U.S. Olympic swim team younger than Michael, whose ongoing development had to be accommodated.

"When Michael was little, I wouldn't hesitate to push him over the edge," Bowman said. "Can I just plug in the training we did in 2003, before Barcelona? No, we have to make some adjustments. Michael is a different person than he was a year ago. He has hair on his chest. He's a man. I used to be able to pound him. Now he's fit, he's in a good place. I need to err on the side of protecting him. A sledgehammer used to work. Not anymore."

After the Trials, the Americans headed up the California coast for 2 weeks of seclusion at Stanford University, where Michael backed off his training, but not as drastically as his veteran teammates. He took it easy for 5 days after the Trials, then logged 10 hard days of practice at Stanford, which included three-quarters of his normal volume of mileage. In Palo Alto, Michael met some former Olympians and was humbled to shake hands with Muhammad Ali, a gold medalist in 1960. Parkinson's disease had withered the boxing legend, but Michael had seen some of Ali's fights on ESPN Classics and remembered the trembling man lighting the Olympic Flame at the 1996 Games in Atlanta.

Michael needed every motivational edge he could muster as he prepared to become the first swimmer to attempt eight events at the Olympics. He was favored or had a realistic chance at a gold medal in all but the 200 freestyle, where Ian Thorpe and Pieter van den Hoogenband were the fastest men ever. There was only one man to catch in the 100 butterfly, and Michael had beaten Ian Crocker before. As he went about his work at Stanford one day, Bowman added some visualization to those memories.

"What is Ian going to do," Bowman asked, "once you win the 100 butterfly?"

Michael processed the ploy. As the runner-up at the Trials, he would handle the butterfly leg in the preliminary of the medley relay on August 20 in Athens. Later that same day, he would face Crocker in the final of the 100 butterfly, and the faster man there would get the spot in the final of the relay, the climactic swim race in Athens. Bowman repeated the question: What was Crocker going to do after Michael beat him in the butterfly and took that spot in the medley relay final?

"Wow," Michael said. "Ian might not get any gold medals."

That scenario stayed in Michael's mind as he headed to San Francisco International Airport on the first day of August, a Sunday. Crossing the Atlantic Ocean overnight, the U.S. contingent of 21 men, 22 women, eight coaches, three managers, and assorted administrators from USA Swimming and the U.S. Olympic Committee sped through customs in Athens. They then escaped the anticipation and anxiety in the Olympic Village by heading to Mallorca, Spain, a Mediterranean island off Barcelona. In his downtime, Michael played poker with his teammates and read *Hacking Las Vegas: The Inside Story of the MIT Blackjack Team's Conquest of the Casinos*. On August 5, he did a freestyle workout that stopped conversation on the deck at the Poliesportu Son Hugo complex. Two days later, with one week remaining before the start of Olympic swimming, Michael and Katie Hoff, another product of the North Baltimore Aquatic Club, were the only members of the American Olympic team to do double practices, but every swimmer was different. As Michael worked on his starts in the morning, Gary Hall Jr. sunned himself on a chaise lounge.

That workout was open to fans and the media, who were curious about the most hyped member of the U.S. Olympic team. With the Soviet sports machine long disbanded, much of China's prowess concentrated in obscure sports, and President George W. Bush's Iraq policy a global point of contention, the Americans had the potential to be painted as bullies in Athens. The USOC had instructed its 2004 team to adopt a low-key approach, and made its point about ugly Americans with a video package of 2000 lowlights. In Sydney, swimmer Amy Van Dyken had spat in an opponent's lane, and a track relay team that included Maurice Greene and Baltimorean Bernard Williams tainted its gold medal celebration with over-the-top preening. Michael wasn't going to do anything stupid, but he saw no reason to mask his patriotism.

"I feel extremely safe, extremely confident," Michael said of the conditions in Athens. "The USA is doing a great job of supporting us and protecting us, especially the swim team. We wear the red, white, and blue proudly. We wear the Stars and Stripes."

Another halting question was all of three words: "Bush or Kerry?" Who was he going to vote for in the 2004 presidential election?

"The objective at hand is swimming," he said. "That's what I'm worried about right now."

"You should have said Bush," Bowman told Michael as they returned to their luxury hotel, where he enjoyed a broad, sweeping view of the Mediterranean.

Things were not as placid on the European mainland. Earlier that day, Basque separatists set off bombs in two coastal towns in the north of Spain. Steven Spielberg temporarily halted location filming in Poland on *Munich,* a feature film about the hunt for the terrorists who killed 11 Israelis at the 1972 Olympics. A Muslim cleric proclaimed that an attack on Athens during the Games would be an attack on all of Islam, and the angst in the Olympic city was palpable. Its day had begun with the news that a Greek judo player had plunged several stories off an apartment balcony, an apparent suicide attempt after a lover's spat. Athens was welcoming more members of the media than athletes, and reporters from the United States were instructed to make three copies of their passport: Carry one on your person, leave another with your supervisor, and leave one with your loved ones back home. Few tourists were arriving in comparison to Sydney. The Australian city had imported an additional 10,000 sex workers for the 2000 Olympics, but now the 700 licensed prostitutes in Athens complained about a lack of business.

The city itself seemed hungover from a surprising run by its national soccer team to the European Cup championship. OAKA, the main Olympic park in the northern suburb of Maroussi, still resembled a construction site, as heavy machinery continued to kick up dust. In addition to swimming, OAKA would also be the site of competition in basketball, cycling, gymnastics, track and field, and water polo. It included two massive office buildings for the media: Television was housed in the International Press Center, and print journalists in the Main Press Center (MPC). A metro station for the Athens subway system was built on the north side of OAKA. A fence ringed its perimeter, which wasn't as secure as the one Michael had encountered 4 years earlier in Sydney. Residential and commercial districts surrounded OAKA. A hundred yards from the MPC was a Carre Four department store, the European answer to Wal-Mart. At a checkout line, rifle-toting soldiers paid for lawn chairs. They were not about to stand under a grueling sun for 3 weeks, and some of the workers manning the x-ray scanners at OAKA would figuratively fall asleep on the job. A backpack inadvertently placed on top of the machine instead of the conveyer belt would go unnoticed, and the record $1.5 billion that Athens spent on Olympic security never seemed enough for skittish visitors from post-9/11 North America.

On the morning of August 9, when Michael took a running start and dove into the Olympic pool for his first serious work there, he may have appeared ill-informed or naïve about the condition of his surroundings.

He was neither. Along with the majority of athletes, he was staying in the Olympic Village, a 15-minute drive north of OAKA. Larry Buendorf, the chief security officer for the USOC, had assigned two members of his staff to Michael Phelps detail. One of Buendorf's men was always with Michael when he ate a meal at the Olympic Village and traveled to or from OAKA.

The USOC made Michael feel safer, but it could do nothing about the onerous heat and humidity at the open-air Olympic pool. As he did his laps, an observer briefly placed his metal-rimmed reading glasses on a white Formica counter, and burned his forehead when he put them back on. It was the proverbial 100 degrees in the shade, and there were just over 100 hours until the opening ceremony.

For all of its organizational shortcomings, Athens had a fascinating backdrop of vibrant archaeological sites. Carl Lewis carried the Olympic torch as it made its way beneath the Acropolis on August 12, when soccer preliminaries began. Iraqis who had once been brutalized by Saddam Hussein's son Uday, a sports czar who had been killed in a 2003 shootout, beat Portugal 2–1. Thorpe loomed on billboards for adidas, a major Olympic sponsor. Instead of Michael, its newest American star, Visa went with generic images of comely women. They had not been included in the 1896 revival of the Games in Athens, but now the city welcomed thousands of female athletes. They weren't just swimming and running; they were wrestling, lifting weights, and serving as de facto go-go dancers at beach volleyball. The Olympics had undergone enormous change, accepted professionals, gone commercial, and accumulated paradox and critics galore. What had begun as a tribute to Zeus, with a single 200-meter footrace in 2600 BC, was bursting at the seams with some 10,500 athletes from more than 200 nations.

Could a single individual transcend the biggest sports event on earth?

FRIDAY, AUGUST 13

Friday the 13th started ominously. Kostas Kenteris, who had become Greece's first track gold medalist since 1896 with a 200-meter win at the

Sydney Olympics, and fellow sprinter Katerina Thanou were injured in a mysterious motorcycle accident. Their appearance at an inquiry into their failure to show for random drug tests was postponed. Kenteris had been a leading candidate to light the flame at the evening's Opening Ceremony of the Games of the XXVIII Olympiad. The Olympic Village was the staging area for the Americans who would march at the opening, and Michael noticed tennis star Andy Roddick and basketball players Carmelo Anthony and Lebron James as they boarded transportation to OAKA. At the opening, a runner symbolically staggered and fell, but rose and crossed the finish line. Yes, Athens had stumbled along the way, but it was going to win its Olympic race. Greek history and myth were depicted in a pageant that included the flooding of the Olympic Stadium. Soccer veteran Mia Hamm carried the American flag. President Bush was in attendance, but Michael was not, which offended a few who were unfamiliar with the schedule he faced.

As the opening began, Michael reclined back at the Olympic Village. He was rooming with Lenny Krayzelburg, who had been voted cocaptain of the American men's swim team, along with Tom Malchow. Krayzelburg had gone from being the star of the American team to a calming influence on his heir apparent. Michael watched television coverage of the opening, then dug into his own entertainment options, which included a PlayStation2 console and 40 DVDs. He watched one of his favorite films, *Miracle,* a retelling of the U.S. ice hockey team and its improbable gold medal in 1980. At 10 p.m., as the opening ceremony dragged on, Michael turned off the movie.

Sleep didn't come.

How could Michael rest, confronted by the possibility of as many as 18 races in 8 days and so many people counting on him? Argent Mortgage, PowerBar, Omega, Speedo, and Visa had invested in Michael's dream of matching Mark Spitz and his seven gold medals from 1972. Dick Ebersol, the chairman of NBC Sports, was also holding his breath, as Michael figured prominently in the network's 1,210 hours of Olympic coverage on assorted affiliates. After years of bribery, doping, and judging scandals, the Olympic movement itself needed a fresh and wholesome reminder of its ideals. Besides the institutions and individuals who were relying on Michael, there were the skeptics whom he longed to silence. Nothing had changed since the 2003 World Championships, where Australian coach Don Talbot had pooh-poohed his accomplishments with the observation that swimming greatness was "judged by longevity and doing it at the Olympics."

Michael's time had come.

SATURDAY, AUGUST 14

Elvis Presley asked for a little less conversation, a little more action on the sound system that echoed through OAKA. Four years and 2 days after Michael had earned a berth in the Sydney Olympics, he warmed up in the practice pool at the Olympic Aquatic Center. With officials from FINA and the IOC sporting neckties, blazers, and umbrellas to shield themselves from a sun that had the potential to harm even at 10 a.m., Michael began the most ambitious schedule any Olympic swimmer had ever tackled. The 400 individual medley, his most demanding event, had come at the end of the 2003 World Championships. At the Olympics, it would be his first. Michael wore black jammers, a suit that went from his hips to just above his knees. Leading at every wall, the world record holder won his heat by more than two body lengths and posted the fastest time of the 36 men in the preliminaries, 4 minutes, 13.29 seconds. Showing few aftereffects from the broken foot he had sustained a month earlier, Hungary's Laszlo Cseh won his heat in 4:14.26. Cutting it too close for comfort, American Erik Vendt qualified for the evening's final with sixteen-hundredths of a second to spare.

Michael slowed briefly at the first station in the Mixed Zone, still catching his breath as NBC's Melissa Stark, a Baltimore native, asked him about the start of what had come to be called his "quest." Without stopping again, he moved through the gauntlet of microphones, minicams, and tape recorders that Olympians were required to pass. Michael was in the practice pool when Hoff, the 15-year-old from North Baltimore who was viewed as the future of American female swimming, had an inauspicious Olympic debut. She led her preliminary heat in the women's 400 IM at 250 meters, but faded and finished 10 seconds slower than her personal best, which had been the world's fastest time of the year. Hoff had been predicted to take the silver medal, and when she realized that she wasn't even going to make the final, a wave of nausea made her vomit. Michael had no time to console her. He cooled down, jumped on a shuttle back to the Olympic Village, wolfed down a lunch of pizza and pasta that would be his staple carbohydrate load in Athens, and vainly tried to nap.

The stands at the Olympic pool were half-empty at 7:30 p.m. The sound system's bouzouki music faded and was replaced by fanfare for the 400 IM finalists. Michael was a 100–1 favorite according to one London oddsmaker, but he still possessed no Olympic medals. After the starter held the field for an abnormally long interval, Michael nailed his start with a reaction time of .77. He led by more than a second after the butterfly leg and by 3 after the backstroke, a staggering two body lengths ahead. Cseh closed the gap a bit in the breaststroke, but the Hungarian was racing for silver. Michael finished in 4:08.26, making his first Olympic medal a gold stamped with a world record, joy that was compounded by the trailing action. Vendt, a tough Massachusetts native, had blossomed at the University of Southern California, and pushed Michael to his first world record in the 400 IM. Now he produced his second clutch silver medal in as many Olympics, as he passed Italy's Alessio Boggiatto and then Cseh in the final 50. "Yeah, Vendt," Michael screamed as his teammate dove over three lane markers for an embrace. Borrowing a page from Spitz, Michael raised Vendt's hand, then soaked in applause as he turned to the grandstand on his right and made eye contact with his mother.

After Thorpe repeated as Olympic champion in the 400 freestyle, the event in which he was given a free pass by the Australians, the Aquatic Center quieted. The first American to earn a gold medal at the 2004 Olympics bent forward while the prize was draped onto his shoulders by a sheik from Kuwait. A one-size-fits-all olive wreath that would later slip over the ears of a petite Romanian gymnast was placed on Michael's head. The American flag was raised, flanked by another for Vendt's silver medal and by Hungary's, signifying Cseh's bronze. As a recording of *The Star Spangled Banner* that was heavy on the strings began, Michael was at a loss as to what to do with the wreath on his head. A man removed his hat for the National Anthem, so Michael treated the wreath like a Michigan or Oriole cap, took it from his head, and placed it over his heart. His eyes grew damp, from relief and from the realization that, at long last, he was an Olympic gold medalist.

Michael stripped back down to his Speedo and completed his cool-down, then used his cell phone to call Hilary. He wanted to see his sisters and mother, and the designated meeting spot was along a concourse that ran under the main grandstand and alongside the practice pool. Flanked by Bowman and a doping official, Michael reached the metal fence that separated athletes from spectators, who parted to allow room for the one person he was looking for. As Debbie reached through the fence to touch her son, he leaned forward and placed the gold medal that hung around his neck in her hands.

"Mom," he said. "Look what I did."

Debbie had a flashback to a summer day long ago, when Michael had brought her his very first age-group award. Now the little boy who had cried at Meadowbrook when he didn't get his way made his mother weep.

SUNDAY, AUGUST 15

A judo player who had carried the flag of Iran in the opening ceremony withdrew, ostensibly because he didn't make weight, but in reality because he refused to fight an Israeli. At the Olympic pool, the drumbeats over the men's 200 freestyle quickened, and Michael became mired in a controversy over the 400 freestyle relay.

The morning preliminaries included the 200 freestyle, where Thorpe and van den Hoogenband posted the fastest times and two others were quicker than Michael. In the first heat of the 400 freestyle relay, a South African foursome anchored by Ryk Neethling—who had ended Michael's 37-race win streak in Indianapolis—scared the world record and beat the Americans by nearly 2 seconds. Place was irrelevant, compared with advancement and individual split times. At the U.S. Trials, head coach Eddie Reese had declared that Michael would swim the relay final unless two Americans went 48.3 or better in the Athens preliminary. Neil Walker, with a split of 48.16, gained a spot in the final. Hall went 48.73 on the anchor, short of the standard Reese had determined. The coach

had planned to meet with his staff over lunch to discuss the lineup decision, but minutes after Reese got the morning splits, a USA Swimming
press official made an announcement. Michael and Walker would swim
the relay final in the evening with Jason Lezak and Crocker, who had
gone 1–2 at the Trials in the 100 freestyle.

That evening, van den Hoogenband won the first semifinal of the 200
freestyle and Thorpe beat Michael in the second, but all held something in
reserve for the freestyle relay final. The contentiousness of the session escalated after Japan's Kosuke Kitajima took the gold in the 100 breaststroke,
ahead of Brendan Hansen, who went nearly a second slower than his world
record time at the Trials. Aaron Peirsol, one of Hansen's training partners,
won his semifinal of the 100 backstroke, then accused Kitajima of using a
dolphin kick off the turn, illegal in the breaststroke at the time.

"He (Kitajima) knew what he was doing," Peirsol said in the Mixed
Zone. "It's cheating. Something needs to be done about that. It's ridiculous."

Hansen and Peirsol swam for Reese, and a bad night for the men from
Austin, Texas, was about to get worse. At the Olympic Village, in the
room he shared with Peirsol, an air-conditioning vent blew directly onto
the head of Crocker's bed. In retrospect, Crocker figures that it contributed to his runny nose and sore throat, symptoms of a sinus infection.
Antibiotics had made him sluggish before, so he passed on them this
time, but Crocker still felt disconnected from his body as he prepared to
join the world's best sprinters in swimming's most frenzied event.

Relays require the waiting man on the block to anticipate and react to
an incoming teammate's touch on the wall. While his teammates had been
in dozens of important 400 freestyle relays, Michael was an international
rookie in the event, and asked to lead off, where he wouldn't be required
to take a flying start. Reese and a coaching staff that included Bowman,
Jon Urbanchek, and Dave Salo considered that and other options, before
deciding on an order of Crocker, Michael, Walker, and Lezak.

The U.S. men's basketball team was losing to Puerto Rico by 22 as the
four held hands during introductions. Crocker got a good enough start
and was fifth at the turn, but began to slow at 65 meters. His arms and
legs generated none of their usual power and snap as Michael climbed on
the block in lane five and readied for their exchange. He crouched and

waited some more. To Michael's immediate right, in lane four, South Africa's Roland Schoeman touched first in 48.17, the third-fastest time ever off of a flat 100 start. Men from Italy in lane three, Russia in lane two, and Australia in lane one touched. To Michael's left, the second man from France in seven, the Netherlands in six, and Germany in eight dove in. Finally, Crocker reached the wall in 50.05, dead last and nearly a second slower than he had been at the Trials.

Any edge Michael had was left on his block. Of the 36 men who had the benefit of flying starts, he had the slowest reaction time. He passed the second swimmers from the Netherlands and France, but his split of 48.74 was a half-second slower than the staff had anticipated and slower than the 48.73 Hall had posted in the morning. Walker valiantly moved the Americans up to third with the fastest split of his career, 47.97. Crocker was despondent and Michael seemed in shock as they saw Lezak move up to second, but comprehended that he would never catch Neethling, who punctuated a gold medal with a world record, 3:13.17. van den Hoogenband and the fastest split ever caught Lezak for the silver. If Crocker had matched his Trials form and Michael had nailed his exchange, the United States would have beaten the Netherlands, but it would not have caught the South Africans. The Americans hadn't won the 400 freestyle relay at a major international meet since 1998, but that brought no consolation to a bronze medal that represented their worst Olympic finish ever in the sprint relay.

Crocker was too shaken to speak to reporters in the Mixed Zone, where Michael stopped.

"This is the second time in (Olympic) history we've ever been beaten," he said. "We wanted to do better. These are the four fastest guys we have."

That opinion was not unanimous. Hall had been complaining about Reese's relay strategy since the Trials. He protested with his absence at the Olympic pool that night, while David Arluck, his agent, said that the "momentum created by what Phelps is trying to do led to what was not best for the relay." Even Rowdy Gaines, a USA Swimming official who served as NBC's swim analyst, second-guessed Reese for throwing Michael into a pressurized exchange, saying, "That's a bad spot to put a relay rookie in."

Any chance that Michael had at seven gold medals had hinged on a victory in the 400 freestyle relay. In order to match Spitz and win the $1 million bonus from Speedo, he needed to sweep his six remaining events, which would require upsets in half of them. Michael had watched *Miracle* the night of the opening ceremony. Now he needed one.

MONDAY, AUGUST 16

His relay teammates had to stew for several days, but another full day awaited Michael, who washed his hurt away with the first two rounds of the 200 butterfly and the 200 freestyle final. Michael was the most versatile swimmer ever, and van den Hooogenband was the Olympic champion, but Thorpe owned the world record and eight of history's nine fastest times. He had coolly deflected a question regarding Michael coming on to his turf with the response, "I don't see us as being animals and marking our territory."

A media credential is usually enough to get a reporter into Olympic venues, but additional tickets are required for select events like the opening and closing ceremonies, gymnastics finals, and the most anticipated race swimming had seen in years. Major American daily newspapers that send a half-dozen reporters to the World Series or Super Bowl were allocated one media ticket apiece to the so-called Race of the Century. Some couldn't identify Thorpe or van den Hoogenband, but they wanted to be there to witness the end of the Spitz Watch. Bowman cautioned that this wasn't Seabiscuit challenging War Admiral in 1938, and the crowd of 10,000 understood that it was not a match race. Scalpers doubled their investment, and fans ran in off of rush-hour metro trains as the men paraded out for the night's first final. The spectators dressed in red, white, and blue cheered when Michael, still the only U.S. gold medalist, was introduced in lane three. The fans in orange made a louder noise for van den Hoogenband, the fastest qualifier, in four. Both receptions were drowned out for the man in five, and it wasn't just the people in Australia's green and gold who were behind Thorpe. Athenians and swimmers from other nations wanted to see him take down the bold young American and get revenge on van den Hoogenband.

Michael's reaction time was the best of the three, but he was fourth at the 50 wall, where van den Hoogenband was under world record pace and Thorpe settled into second. Michael was in third at the 100 wall, where their efforts didn't seem to equate to the speed with which they were moving. In the third 50, Klete Keller advanced to fourth, but there was no change in the first three positions. Off the final wall, Thorpe overtook van den Hoogenband, and it was a two-man race. Thorpe touched first, more than a half-second in front of van den Hoogenband. Michael made up a full second on the Dutchman in the final 50, but a 1:45.32 that would have won gold at every previous Olympics was only good for the bronze this time. Thorpe, who told van den Hoogenband, "I guess that makes it one all, and I'll see you again in Beijing," had become the first double gold medalist at the Athens Olympics. Five career golds made him Australia's most decorated Olympian ever.

Michael began the evening with the awareness that he had little chance of winning the 200 freestyle and perpetuating his chase of Spitz's seven golds. He was happy with a personal best and thrilled to be a part of a historic race, but there was no time to process what had just occurred. After the medal ceremony, Michael returned to the practice pool and readied for the semifinals of the 200 butterfly. On approximately 40 minutes' rest, he followed Great Britain's Stephen Parry in the first semifinal, which left him 0–2 for the night. Afterward, he reiterated what he had been saying since the U.S. Trials, "I wanted to race Thorpe before either of us is done," and acknowledged the end of the Spitz Watch.

"I guess you can say the pressure is off."

Was the Speedo bonus a distraction?

"How can you say no to that?"

After three events at the 2004 Olympics, the second-youngest man on the American swim team had a gold medal, two bronze medals, and personal bests in both of his individual events. Michael remained favored to become only the second man to ever win three individual swim events at the Games, but his sense of accomplishment was not conveyed to Americans who got their news from the Associated Press, which offered this assessment of his Olympics after 3 days: "Because his audacious challenge fell short, he could be remembered as something of a failure at the Athens Games."

ALL THAT GLITTERS

ATHENS, AUGUST 2004

Age and a series of injuries had made Lenny Krayzelburg a long shot to make the U.S. Olympic team, but once in Athens, he recaptured much of his old form and made a surprisingly strong run in the 100 backstroke. On the evening of August 16, in between Michael's bronze medal in the 200 freestyle and semifinal of the 200 butterfly, Krayzelburg's comeback missed a medal by two-hundredths of a second. The 28-year-old was subdued when he returned to the Olympic Village, but was determined to put on a good face for his roommate. Instead of finding Michael downcast, however, Krayzelburg found him upbeat and oblivious to the fact that their room had sustained an 0–3 night.

Losing was an experience Michael would not deal with again in Athens.

TUESDAY, AUGUST 17

Olympic swimming stretched over 8 days, and Michael figured to compete on the first 7. This was his only morning without a preliminary, but it held an important development, the ongoing struggles of the man who had provided his primary motivation the previous 13 months. Thirty-six hours after the 400 freestyle relay debacle, Crocker couldn't advance out of the preliminaries of the 100 freestyle. Neither could teammate Jason Lezak, the second-fastest man ever in the event. For the first time, the nation that had produced Johnny Weissmuller and Mark Spitz would not be represented in the semifinals of the oldest and most enduring Olympic sprint, the 100 freestyle, let alone the final.

The morning did end on a reassuring note for the American men, as the foursome of Scott Goldblatt, Ryan Lochte, Dan Ketchum, and Peter Vanderkaay posted the fastest qualifying time in the preliminary heats of the 800 freestyle relay. Goldblatt and Ketchum would come out, and Michael and Klete Keller would go in the final that evening, when the U.S. dynamics would have as much to do with blue and gold as they did red, white, and blue. Michael had plans to enroll at the University of Michigan and represent Club Wolverine. In a matter of days, Bob Bowman and Michael would replace Jon Urbanchek and Keller, respectively, as the Michigan head coach and volunteer assistant. Vanderkaay was midway through his college career at Michigan. Ketchum had just gotten a degree from the university. Lochte went to the University of Florida and was a native of the Sunshine State, but had been training as hard as the Michigan men.

Bowman had come across as boastful with his prediction of a gold medal in what he described as the ultimate test of a nation's swimming fitness. The Australians had been invincible since the 1998 World Championships, when a 14-year-old Ian Thorpe first teamed with Grant Hackett and Michael Klim. They won gold at the Sydney Olympics and lowered their world record again at the 2001 World Championships. At the 2003 worlds, however, the United States had narrowed the gap to 1.67 seconds, and Reese referenced that race and Olympic history during a pep talk. In 1984, the year before Michael was born, the West Germans anchored with the great Michael Gross, but the Americans front-loaded their lineup and had a 3-meter lead when the Albatross entered the pool. Gross rallied, but the U.S. won the gold. Now Reese was channeling the "Grossbusters" and imploring Michael, Lochte, and Vanderkaay, in that order, to forge a substantial lead for Keller, who would go against Thorpe on the anchor.

Michael had the final of the 200 butterfly before that relay, in an evening session that felt daunting and disorienting. The Olympic Aquatic Center had little of the anticipation and electricity that had charged the air 24 hours earlier. Swimming was no longer a hot ticket, and the reporters and photographers who had crammed elbow to elbow to see Michael challenge Thorpe and Pieter van den Hoogenband in the 200 freestyle the previous night went prowling for new stories. The Australians tied the mighty American women's soccer team. What was supposed to be the deepest U.S. women's gymnastics team ever took the silver medal, behind the Romanians.

The Race of the Century and the Spitz Watch were history, but Michael was not.

The 200 butterfly had gone from his signature event, the one that made him a 2000 Olympian and the youngest man ever to set a world record, to a practice afterthought in the winter of 2001–02, when he turned his focus to the three other strokes. A loss to Malchow at the 2002 Pan Pacific Championships had gotten Michael's attention, but a pattern had repeated itself. His goals required diversification, which allowed specialists to eat into his margin of error. Malchow was putting off surgery to repair a torn shoulder muscle, but if Michael faltered, two other veterans were primed. Japan's Takashi Yamamoto had been the runner-up at the 2003 World Championships, and Stephen Parry of Great Britain had edged Michael in the semifinals. That outcome piqued the royal family, as Princess Anne was at the pool to award the medals.

Michael wanted to bury their hopes early. He swam the first 50 meters four-tenths of a second faster than he had during his world record in Barcelona, and led Parry by .65. Michael extended that cushion and remained under world record pace at the 100 wall, but his stroke began to slow in the third 50. Half of his lead on Parry evaporated, and Yamamoto bounced off the final turn and made it a three-man race. With 20 meters left, Yamamoto nearly drew even with Michael, and NBC's Dan Hicks and Rowdy Gaines anxiously noted that the greatest closer in the history of the butterfly was in trouble. Just as he appeared to be faltering, however, Michael applied greater purpose to his next two strokes and restored order. He finished in 1:54.04, .11 off his world record.

Yamamoto became the second-fastest man ever, with a 1:54.56. Parry faded but held on for the bronze medal.

Michael looked exhausted as he studied the scoreboard, then pumped both fists. One by one, the new Olympic champion shook hands with the men who finished second through seventh. Each had improved his lifetime best. Only Michael and the man who finished dead last were unable to lower what swimmers called their PR, personal record. Racing on guts and memory, Malchow appeared nonplussed by his eighth place. The 2000 gold medalist was the last competitor to congratulate Michael. The American cocaptain, Michigan grad, and member of Club Wolverine patted his successor on the butt, and implored Michael to go kick some Australian ass.

How could he possibly be in the moment during the medal ceremony for the 200 butterfly? Princess Anne, an Olympian herself in equestrian, gave Parry and Yamamoto their spoils, then moved to Michael, placing the gold medal around his neck and an olive wreath on his head. Parry, his country's first medalist in Athens, was 27, the shorter man from Japan was 26, and both reveled in the peak of their swimming careers. Michael had just produced another bit of minutiae that only the aficionados appreciated. The 11th man to win an individual medley at the Olympics had just become the first to win gold in a separate stroke. Michael's first two individual events had produced PRs, and he had just turned in his fastest 200 butterfly final. He was supremely prepared, but yearned to shake the annoyance of being at the center of a botched relay. In the previous 48 hours, he had experienced extremes that few athletes encounter in a lifetime, and now there were less than 15 minutes to prepare for the 800 relay. As the National Anthem played in his honor a second time, Michael dropped his nonchalance and cried, like a confused, tired boy. To his left, in the main grandstand, Debbie Phelps dipped into her bottomless reservoir of tears. A dozen rows behind Michael, Fred Phelps puffed out his chest a little further than normal.

The night, like Michael, was young.

He did not appear in a rush to get to the ready room, patiently posing with Yamamoto and Parry for photographers, and stopping to high-five Krayzelburg in the front row of the competitors' section. Michael joined his relay teammates as the women's 200 IM unfolded. Katie Hoff had bounced back from her failure in the 400 IM to get the third seed in the final, but faded to seventh.

The evening air was pleasant as the men's relay teams sauntered onto the deck. The loudest cheer went to Greece, the slowest qualifier in what all understood was a two-nation race for the gold. Michael was matched against Hackett, the same man who had befriended him on his trip to Australia in the spring of 2003. A few months later, at the world championships, Michael had opened the 800 relay with an American record for the 200 freestyle. Twenty-five hours after he had gone 1.24 seconds faster than Hackett in the Olympic final, Michael passed him just before the midway point and poured it on in the final 50, staking the Americans to a lead of 1.01 seconds. Lochte gained a tenth against Klim, and Vanderkaay produced a split that was .37 faster than Nicholas Sprenger.

That meant Keller dove in 1.48 seconds ahead of Thorpe. In the 200 freestyle final the previous night, Thorpe had beaten Keller by 1.42, and the difference as the anchors dove in was the kind of circumstance that bookmakers describe as a "pick 'em," a gray area that made coaches on both sides go limp. Keller had shaved nearly three-quarters of a second off his personal best in the previous night's final, when he finished fourth. If he couldn't deliver a similar effort, the Australians would prevail again.

Thorpe went out boldly and took nearly a second off the gap in the first 50 alone. As Keller's lead shrunk by another tenth in the second 50, the only people who believed in him were his teammates and the American brain trust that admired his cool. Keller was 22, but had racing savvy beyond his years. He had been 3 months out of high school at the 2000 Olympics, when his anchor leg from well off the pace got the U.S. a silver medal in the 800 relay. He had initially gone to the University of Southern California, where Mark Schubert fortified his self-confidence as an anchor swimmer. He had moved on to Ann Arbor, where Urbanchek hardened him some more. Now Keller drew on that background and refused to fold, as he went faster than Thorpe in the third 50. Coming home, Thorpe moved up on Keller's right. The American breathed on his left and couldn't see the greatest middle-distance freestyler ever make one last push as they stretched for the final wall.

Relay teammates must remain behind lane judges. Michael leaned forward, but couldn't see Keller touch just in front of Thorpe. After a half-mile, thirteen hundredths of a second separated the two nations, the second-closest 800 relay finish ever at the Olympics, eclipsed only by the Grossbusters of 1984. The most suspenseful race Michael had ever participated in produced the most demonstrative reaction of his life. Seeing the result certified on the scoreboard, he raised both index fingers to the heavens and let out a long, primal scream. Michael was the first to congratulate Keller. Finding no solace in a split that was his second-fastest ever, Thorpe shook hands with the Americans and walked off dejectedly. It was his first 800 relay loss in international competition. When the day had dawned, Thorpe had been the dominant figure at the Olympic pool, and the entire American contingent in Athens possessed three gold medals. Now Michael had that many himself, and still had three events to go.

As the medalists took their bows, Hilary Phelps made her way to the grandstand railing and tossed a stuffed animal, a bulldog, to her brother, a ritual they had begun at the 2003 World Championships. On several levels, the evening's double was more satisfying than Michael's historic night in Barcelona, when he had set two world records. The whole world was watching now, and the accomplishment was shared. Lochte, Vanderkaay, and Keller climbed into a van for a short drive to the International Press Center, where they made a joint appearance on ESPN. Not that it mattered, since he was incapable of describing his delight at winning two gold medals in one night, but Michael stuck to his protocol. Until he was done swimming, he was not going to sit in a studio and chat, even though it would have been a fine way to pass the time. At 3 a.m. in Athens, when NBC began its primetime telecast for the United States, Michael remained awake. On the eve of his first race, he had been too excited to sleep. Now, he tossed and turned, trying to absorb the best night of his life.

WEDNESDAY, AUGUST 18

Michael figured to have at least seven races left and hoped for eight, so Debbie and his sisters served as proxies for NBC's *Today Show*. Mercifully, little emotional investment was required for his day's work, the first two rounds of the 200 IM, the event in which he was most invincible. Laszlo Cseh, on the mend from a broken foot, was the only competitor among 50 to break 2 minutes in the morning's preliminaries. Michael went 2:00.01 and shook his head as he sipped from a container of Carnation Instant Breakfast en route to the practice pool. He vowed to find a McDonald's as soon as his racing was done. Michael lowered the Olympic record with a 1:58.52 in the semifinals, on an evening when he was an afterthought.

The 100 freestyle final went off without nine-time Olympic medalist Alexander Popov and any Americans. van den Hoogenband repeated, and Thorpe took the bronze, becoming the second man after Michael with medals in three individual events in Athens. In the 200 breaststroke, Japan's Kosuke Kitajima got his second gold medal and Daniel Gyurta, a 15-year-old Hungarian, took the silver over Brendan Hansen, who remained well off the form he had displayed at the U.S. Trials. The session ended with Natalie Coughlin, who didn't swim the 200 freestyle at the Trials, helping the Americans erase the 800 relay world record that the East Germans had set 17 years earlier to the day.

That 1987 record had been the product of a state-sanctioned system that pumped testosterone into adolescent females, and the stench of doping continued to linger over the Olympics. Now Kostas Kenteris and Katerina Thanou, the Greek sprinters who had ducked random drug tests, were stripped of their Olympic credentials. At the site of the ancient Olympics, 180 miles southwest of Athens, track and field held its shot put competitions. Russia's Irina Korzhanenko won the gold, then tested positive for the steroid stanozolol.

On the second floor of the Athens Holiday Inn, the Court of Arbitration of Sport monitored a gymnastics judging controversy that had mistakenly awarded American Paul Hamm a gold medal. The anti-American undercurrent was so strong that NBA commissioner David Stern fretted about fans back in the United States rooting against his all-stars, who were having the nation's worst Olympic basketball tournament ever. Amid all that turmoil, NBC's ratings were increasing. Millions who had tuned in for the Spitz Watch did not turn away once it ended. The results of Michael's finals were known by 2 p.m. on the East Coast, but some

Americans avoided the Internet and tried to build suspense for NBC's tape-delayed coverage in prime time. A resident at an assisted-living facility outside Baltimore preferred to watch alone, in her room, with the door closed.

"I like to watch Michael by myself, so I can scream and cry and nobody sees me," Leoma Davisson, his 85-year-old grandmother, told a reporter. "I'm a very emotional person."

THURSDAY, AUGUST 19

Politics hung over the Olympic pool for much of the day. In the morning, Gary Hall Jr. looked sharp in the preliminaries of the 50 freestyle and claimed that Michael hadn't put in enough practice with the 400 free-style relay. Michael, also part of the other two relays, declined to mention that he had practiced more flying starts than anyone in the American camp. He was more concerned with the preliminaries of the 100 butterfly, which exemplified the conflicting goals of the International Olympic Committee, which wants to identify the elite while encompassing all. Rad Aweisat, a 17-year-old Palestinian who trained in an unheated 25-meter pool, finished in 1:01.60. Andriy Serdinov of Ukraine, who had briefly held the world record at the 2003 World Championships, won heat six in 52.05, a time Michael couldn't better in heat seven. He exited the pool to an odd version of a heavy metal classic, "Smoke on the Water," redone with horns and xylophone. Crocker promptly went 52.03 in heat eight.

Even without the 200 backstroke, the event Michael dropped after the U.S. Trials, his evening was busy enough, as the official timeline showed 31 minutes between the final of the 200 IM and the semifinals of the 100 butterfly. He was invincible in one and Crocker loomed in the other, but the session's first final brought a reminder that form doesn't always hold at the Olympics.

Peirsol attacked the world record he had set at the U.S. Trials, and touched more than 2 seconds in front of Austria's Markus Rogan, seemingly completing a sweep of the backstrokes. A turn judge, however, disqualified Peirsol, which the surfer dude described as "bogus." Was it retaliation for his accusation that Kitajima had cheated in the 100 breaststroke? Had Michael not dropped the 200 backstroke from his program, would the Spitz Watch still be alive? His best was 2 seconds faster than the time that had just gotten Rogan an apparent gold. Any second-guessing over his program was brief and eliminated, however, as Peirsol's disqualification was not accepted, because the turn judge's report was "inadequate and not in the working language of FINA."

That tempest delayed the start of the 200 IM final by 7 minutes, and paranoia was in the air as Michael toweled down his block. Were renegade turn judges scrutinizing everyone, or just the Americans? Michael removed his headphones and resumed his work. With a semifinal in the 100 butterfly to follow, this was not the night to go after his world record, but Michael nonetheless opened with a lead on the butterfly and followed with the fastest split in the backstroke. Four men went faster during the breaststroke, but whatever Michael lost there, he regained on the freestyle, as he concluded the most lopsided 200 IM in Olympic history with a 1:57.14. Lochte, his 800 relay teammate, moved from fifth to the silver medal in the final 50, which finally elicited a smile and fist pump from Michael. How high had he raised the bar? Michael now had history's eight fastest times, but if he hadn't been in the field, it still would have been the most competitive Olympic 200 IM ever. Cseh didn't medal, despite a time that would have won gold at every previous Games.

The bigger picture showed Michael with three individual gold medals in a single Olympics, a plateau only Spitz had reached among male swimmers. With the evening's finals done and thousands filing out of the Olympic pool to get a head start on the march to the OAKA metro station, Michael accepted his fourth gold medal. Already in possession of six olive wreaths, he tossed this one into the grandstand, where his sisters conveyed it to Debbie. As was usually the case, rather than reflect, he had to prepare for another race.

The semifinals of the 100 butterfly were a reprise of the 2003 World Championships, where Serdinov had set a world record, only to see Michael better the new mark 5 minutes later. This time, the Ukrainian took the first semi in 51.74, an Olympic record. The second semi was over at the turn, where Michael trailed by just three-tenths of a second, close enough to easily reel in Crocker. The time was 51.61, Michael's second Olympic record in a span of 42 minutes. That was insignificant compared with the fact that Crocker had yet to regain the speed that had allowed him to defeat Michael at the world championships and U.S. Trials. If Crocker couldn't hold off Michael on 3 days' rest, did he have any chance of beating him in the final? The ramifications extended beyond the 100 butterfly final. The fastest American would also swim in the final of the medley relay, the last event on the Olympic swim schedule. A year after losing out on that honor at the world championships, how badly did Michael want to beat Crocker?

"Big time," he told the press. "Everybody wants to swim in the finals of a relay. I missed out on that last year. I hope to be there."

FRIDAY, AUGUST 20

In Barcelona, the men's medley relay had been a 1-day affair, with the preliminaries coming the morning after Crocker had beaten Michael. At the Olympics, the two rounds of the relay were separated by 32 hours, with the 100 butterfly final in between, which made for torturous decisions on the American lineup for the preliminary. Michael had gone faster in the semifinals. Crocker was the world champion and world record holder, but most important, he had won at the U.S. Trials. As the Trials runner-up in the 100 freestyle, Crocker could also have taken that stroke in the preliminary, but Reese had him rest for the butterfly final.

Michael took the butterfly in the preliminary, where Krayzelburg got a substantial lead on the opening backstroke but Kitajima passed Mark Gangloff on the breaststroke. Michael's reaction time for his flying start was .28, substantially faster than his takeoff on the 400 freestyle relay. He gave Neil Walker a lead, which ballooned on the freestyle. It was most likely Krayzelburg's final international race, and he lingered in the Mixed Zone. The medley relay preliminary was essentially an insurance swim for Michael, since participants in that round got whichever medal their nation's finalists earned. Some purists turned up their noses at what they perceived to be tainted booty, disparaging the work done in relay preliminaries as "morning swims." Michael wanted no such asterisk attached to his medal count. Beat Crocker one more time, and he would be in the medley relay final and presumably atop the medal podium when swimming concluded at the 2004 Olympics.

Less than 5 hours later, Michael and an escort from Larry Buendorf's USOC security staff boarded a bus at the Olympic Village. For the 13th time in 7 days, he made the commute to OAKA, where there was five times the usual commotion. It was the first night of track and field, and 80,000 were converging on the Olympic Stadium. On an evening when Alan Webb, America's great mile hope and former Michigan man, failed to advance out of the preliminaries of the 1,500-meter run, Michael set about securing his place in the Olympic pantheon.

The penultimate session of Olympic swimming began before thousands of empty seats. Kirsty Coventry, who swam collegiately for Auburn, got Zimbabwe's first Olympic gold medal, in the 200 backstroke. The sociological import of a white woman from a troubled African nation taking gold at the Olympics was still sinking in when the finalists for the 100 butterfly emerged from the ready room at 7:38 p.m. and took their places behind their blocks. After beating a subpar Crocker in the semifinals, Michael was no longer the underdog. He was in lane four, the top seed, but as jittery as a man who had won four gold medals in the previous 6 days could be. He swung his arms around his torso and shook his legs more than usual. On the blocks, before the starter called for the swimmers to set, Michael began the ritual that had been his calling card for years, raising his arms above his spine until they made an audible whap, and repeating the motion. It was Michael's 17th race of the Olympics, and the fifth for Crocker, but the seemingly fresher man knew that no one finished a butterfly like his friend and rival. Crocker knew that his only hope was to get out fast and hold on.

Michael's reaction time was nearly as good as Crocker's, but the world record holder located a rhythm he had yet to find in Athens. Crocker went out in 23.59, faster than at the world championships in Barcelona, where he led Michael by .62 at the turn. Crocker hadn't gone out this fast at the Trials, where he led Michael by .75 at the midway mark. Now, Michael was .77 behind and in fifth place at the 50 wall, where he executed a fine turn and used his dolphin kick to quickly pick off Germany's

Thomas Rupprath and Croatia's Duje Draganja. There were 35 meters left, and for the next 25, Michael's comeback stalled. He no longer gained on Serdinov, let alone Crocker, and with 10 meters remaining, appeared destined to earn his third bronze medal.

Peter Carlisle, the final member of Team Phelps, stopped his pacing. Michael's mother, father, sisters, aunts, uncles, and family friends, some of whom had paid nearly $17,000 apiece for two weeks in Greece, were also in the stands, fists clenched. Bob Bowman, the coach whose destiny had been intertwined with Michael's since 1997, sat poolside, squinting to see the finish. Brian Campbell, the massage therapist with more international experience than Michael, was waiting to knead his back muscles once more. Buendorf's security men, ready to assure his safety outside the pool area, lingered nearby. Michael had heard other swimmers poke fun at what they called his "entourage," but now he was as naked and alone as an athlete can be, seemingly beaten in the biggest race of his life.

Moments like this, however, were what Michael loved about his sport. In individual races, there are no alibis. Electronic touchpads measure who gets to the wall first, but there was no way to calibrate the courage and strength that Michael mustered as he attached his name forever to the Athens Olympics.

Crocker was experiencing severe muscle fatigue, and Serdinov was tightening, too, as Michael wound up his 6-foot-7 wingspan and maintained the stroke rate that neither could match. With 2 meters left, he was still stuck in third place. Serdinov was in position to steal the race, but he bobbed too high, a counterproductive vertical motion in a horizontal pursuit. Crocker got caught in midstroke as he floated into the wall, his arms out to the side as they reached for the wall. Both Michael's head and torso were behind Crocker's and his arms were underwater when he completed his final stroke and reached forward with a motion that culminated a decade's worth of planning and perspiration. Eleven-hundredths of a second separated the medalists in one of the greatest blanket finishes Olympic swimming had ever produced in a 100 butterfly. Three dazed men turned to the scoreboard. It had brought Michael bad news in Barcelona, where he assumed he had beaten

Crocker, and now he expected to see another loss as he removed his goggles and registered the results.

```
1. PHELPS MICHAEL USA      51.25
2. CROCKER IAN USA         51.29
3. SERDINOV ANDRIY UKR     51.36
```

Defiance and incredulity mixed on Michael's face as he clenched both fists and raised his arms. He wasn't going home with seven gold medals or a $1 million bonus from Speedo, but he had made Olympic history. He had a fourth individual gold medal, as many as Spitz and double the total any other male swimmer had ever attained in a single Olympics. With his 200 freestyle bronze factored in, Michael had five individual medals, the most impressive haul ever for an Olympic swimmer. He had just become the first man to win swimming gold over three distances, 400, 200, and now 100, but for the moment, all of those distinctions were irrelevant to the fact that he had earned the right to swim one more race. Michael would go in the final of the medley relay, an honor that had eluded him at the 2003 World Championships. The United States had never lost an Olympic medley relay, so he was a veritable lock to earn another gold medal.

"That race is something I dreamed about every single day leading up here," Michael gushed, clad in his jammers and a film of chlorinated water and sweat. "That's exciting. I'm able to be part of the relay, and that's even more exciting."

Michael's satisfaction was in poignant contrast to Crocker. Normally reserved even in victory, he now had a crushing defeat to explain. Crocker had come to Athens expecting to earn three gold medals, but he was leaving with none. A 21-year-old who had had to learn to talk about his feelings while he overcame clinical depression stood in front of strangers and poured out his heart.

"I fought the good fight," said Crocker. "Without Michael's rivalry, I wouldn't hold the world record right now. He pushes me, and pushes a lot of other people as well. Before Michael started swimming the 100 fly, I was only the best in the United States. When he started, I became the world record holder, and that says something."

Michael, Crocker, and Serdinov were dressed in their national warm-ups when Gary Hall Jr. won his second gold meal in the 50 freestyle, beating training partner Draganja by a hundredth of a second. Draganja had finished seventh in the 100 butterfly, and the three medalists admired the Croatian's turnaround before their ceremony under a crescent moon. Michael and Crocker received a standing ovation from their teammates and countrymen, but in the athletes' section, the majority remained seated and only a few applauded. Perhaps envy was at play. No men's national team, including the Australians and the rest of the Americans, matched Michael's four individual golds at the 2004 Olympics. One man, however, identified with him. As Michael walked a victory lap, he made eye contact with Spitz, who placed his thumb against his palm and raised a hand that showed four fingers.

There was too much for Michael to digest as he returned to the practice pool and resumed lowering his lactate to the preferred level. When they finally had a moment alone, Bowman mentioned the scenario that had first been raised a month earlier, at the U.S. training camp at Stanford University.

Bowman: "Well, you got your bonus swim. What do you think that means for Ian?"

Michael: "What do you think?"

Bowman: "You earned that spot, nobody's doing you any favors."

Michael: "Yeah, but Ian isn't gonna get a medal."

Bowman: "You finish swimming down. You don't have to decide just yet."

There was much to weigh. When he had turned professional in the spring, Crocker hired Carlisle, who shared his hometown of Portland, Maine. Octagon was planning a post-Olympic tour for Crocker, Krayzelburg, and Michael. There was also the matter of quid pro quo, since Crocker trained under Reese, the Olympic coach who had stuck his neck out for Michael. All those considerations were secondary to the debt that Michael felt he owed Crocker. For the last 391 days, ever since the shocking reversal at the 2003 World Championships, Crocker had served as Michael's muse, a reminder that he could be beaten. On the cold winter mornings when he didn't want to leave a warm bed, Michael had looked at Crocker's photo, taped to a window in his bedroom. They had known each other since the Sydney Olympics. Crocker had changed from someone to chase to a threat to a friend, one who was going to leave Athens with a silver medal and a bronze that represented failure.

Bowman alerted Carlisle that Michael was considering stepping aside, and the agent readied a statement in the event that occurred. Finally, Michael decided that 17 races in 7 days was enough, and told Bowman that he wanted to give his spot to Crocker. As Michael waited in a corridor for his final press conference at the Olympic pool, Bowman repeatedly drilled him on the words that Carlisle had prepared. Two hours after he had won the 100 butterfly, Michael met the media, joined by Bowman and Reese, who dropped a bombshell in the room.

"Bob and Michael and I talked about the medley relay," Reese said in a measured tone. "Since the race was so close, and Ian's relay takeoff is so much better, Ian is going to do the fly in the medley relay. It's a helluva gesture, and it had to come from him."

The magnanimity had little precedent in the swim community, which was caught off guard by a young man whose competitive greed had been criticized.

"We came into this meet as a team," Michael said, "and we're going to end it as a team."

Fred Phelps was en route to his stateroom on a cruise ship. Debbie was celebrating with family and friends when she received word that Michael was done competing at the 2004 Olympics.

"I didn't walk out of the venue thinking it was his last swim," she said. "I thought I would see him swim the last event of the Olympic Games. It was one of those 'aha!' moments. I've always tried to be one up on Michael. This time he was one up on me. I was blown away."

Seconds after Reese's announcement, Carlisle fielded a call from Rick Reilly of *Sports Illustrated,* then another from an assistant to NBC Sports chairman Dick Ebersol. Carlisle heard Ebersol in the background jokingly shout, "Is there any way we can change his mind?" At the 1972 Olympics, ABC had not warmed to Spitz and gave greater play to Russian gymnast Olga Korbut. NBC, however, had a major investment in Michael, and the network was done waiting for him. It was finally time to sit in a studio and chat with Bob Costas.

SATURDAY, AUGUST 21

If Michael agreed to talk to NBC and an American television audience, he would also have to stop at the Main Press Center and brief the print media once more, but some things could wait. Michael posed for an impromptu photo with some of the kids working the counter, as the McDonald's in the MPC canteen prepared a special order, a bag of Egg McMuffins. He was finishing off another at 12:15 a.m. when he entered the conference hall nearest the USOC press office. Michael acknowledged that Crocker was probably the only teammate he would have stepped aside for, but had difficulty assessing the pressure he had encountered and his place in Olympic history.

"Every single newspaper article," Michael said, "had 'seven gold medals, Mark Spitz.' I still think I'm a normal 19-year-old, but this is different. I think I've changed. I don't even know if I can explain it, to tell you the truth. There's so much going through my mind."

Michael slept in that morning and returned to the Olympic Aquatic Center as a spectator for the first time that evening. Larsen Jensen, the only younger man on the American swim team, gave Hackett a strong challenge in the 1,500 freestyle, the last individual event, but Michael's 400 IM held up as the only world record by a man in an individual event during the 8-day swim meet. The American women took silver in their medley relay, earning Jenny Thompson her 12th Olympic medal, surpassing Spitz's record for a swimmer.

The Australians waved Japanese flags, and Michael was in the front row alongside lane one, on his feet, as Peirsol opened the men's medley relay with a world record on the backstroke leg. Hansen surrendered little ground to Kitajima on the breaststroke, and Crocker, making the most of his second chance, delivered the fastest butterfly leg ever. When Lezak anchored with his fastest freestyle split ever, the Americans had taken nearly a second off the world record and Michael's sixth gold medal was secure. After the medal ceremony, the four Americans who had gone to the podium stopped near the competitors' viewing stand. Two young men who were old rivals hugged.

"Congratulations," Michael said.

"Thank you," said Crocker.

At the 1980 Olympics in Moscow, Aleksandr Dityatin of the Soviet Union had medaled in every gymnastics event, as he earned three gold medals, four silvers, and a bronze. His tally was unaffected by an American boycott, but in a Games in which nearly every nation on earth competed, Michael matched Dityatin's record total of eight medals for one Olympics and doubled his three golds. From Athens in 1896 to Athens again in 2004, approximately 120,000 men and women had competed at the Summer Olympics. None had put on a performance like Michael's.

Before the day was done, Michael would discover that it could be very lonely at the top.

DON'T LOOK BACK

MONTREAL, JULY 2005

Michael Phelps made more history at the 2005 World Championships in Montreal, Canada, where he won five gold medals, one more than he had at the 2003 worlds. On July 26, his victory in the 200 freestyle made him the first man ever to earn titles in four different individual events over a career at FINA's showcase meet. His time, 1:45.20, was a personal best. Two nights later, he became only the second man ever to repeat in the 200 IM at the worlds, as his 1:56.68 was another improvement from the Athens Olympics.

Few were moved by his latest milestones. The majority wanted to know what was wrong with Michael.

Three of his five gold medals in Montreal came in relays, where the United States dominated watered-down fields. Aside from the 200 title, a post-Athens focus on freestyle was a flop, tarnishing the luster that had accompanied his being the first man to attempt five individual events at the Worlds. His two previous international campaigns had been unlike anything the sport had ever seen, but now the hottest swimmer in the world had cooled off. A few weeks past his 20th birthday, was Michael washed up? A young man whose life had been defined by a high-stakes gamble used percentages to explain how his career had lost its momentum, of how the single-mindedness that had driven him between the 2000 and 2004 Olympics had been fragmented by a series of distractions in the previous year.

"Each year between Sydney and Athens, 1,000 decisions were made, and 999 of them were made correctly," Michael said at a July 28 press conference. "This past year, maybe 600 out of 1,000 were the right call. Decisions were made that were not going to improve my swimming. That's why I'm where I am in the swim world."

The Team Phelps manual did not include the word *regret*, but that's what Michael confronted. Privately, he had wrestled with a frightening medical crisis that had the potential to end his career. Publicly, he had to overcome a self-inflicted wound that had damaged his image. He was still learning how to live on his own and with fame, and if there was one lesson Michael had taken from Athens, it was this: Be careful what you wish for.

On the evening of August 21, 2004, after Ian Crocker and the American medley relay secured his sixth gold medal and eighth overall at the Athens Olympics, Michael was ready to celebrate. Family and friends were having one last group dinner in the Plaka, the tourist area beneath the Acropolis. Roommate Lenny Krayzelburg was heading out on the town. Michael wanted to do the same, but Bowman informed him that Larry Buendorf suggested that instead he should remain in the Olympic Village. The USOC's chief security officer was wary of the Games' greatest success story being out on his own in a city where anarchists had long run free. Thirty-two years after Mark Spitz had been rushed from Munich, Germany, and the 1972 Olympics, Michael was sequestered in his suite in the Olympic Village. He passed several hours on a balcony, running up his cell phone bill and occasionally venting his frustration.

"Mom, this is ridiculous," he said to Debbie. "I just gave one of the greatest performances in Olympic history, and I'm in my room, by myself."

Debbie passed the phone to his sisters and then the aunts, uncles, and family friends who had put their lives on hold to support him in Athens. The city is 7 hours ahead of Baltimore, where Matt Townsend and other friends were pleasantly surprised to get calls from Michael. It was after midnight in Athens, and he was packing his bags when Krayzelburg returned and remarked how quickly 4 years had passed since the 2000 Olympics. After swimming had concluded in Sydney, Michael had rushed back to his sophomore year at Towson High School. Bowman told him then that it would be different if they got to Athens, and now it was time to make good on that promise. Besides feeling compelled to give Michael some space, Bowman was eager to start his new job at the University of Michigan.

"I'm going to Michigan," Bowman told Michael. "I told you in Sydney that the next time, you'll be on your own. Well, you're on your own."

The cutting of the cord was abrupt.

"In preparing for Athens, we had crossed every *t* and dotted every *i*, left no stone unturned," Bowman said. "With the exception of the 400 freestyle relay, everything went according to plan. Halfway between the Trials and the Olympics, coaches start to ask, 'When will this be over?' The minute the Olympics are over, we want to go home, we don't want to be around when the kids are having their fun. I don't know if it was naïveté on my part or the thought that I just didn't want to deal with it for a while, but I was at the end of my rope. I thought Michael would have some free time once he was done swimming. I was uncomfortable with how it unfolded, but even if I had wanted to squash the second week in Athens, his sponsors wouldn't have let me."

Despite missing out on the $1 million Speedo bonus, Michael was a very rich 19-year-old. His Speedo contract alone included incentives that brought more than $700,000 for his work in Athens. A gold medal merited $50,000 from USA Swimming and $25,000 from the USOC, so those two bodies combined to reward Michael with another $425,000. USA Swimming and the USOC no longer required his services, but now Speedo and his other sponsors expected the face of the Athens Olympics to appear on their behalf.

The morning after the completion of swimming, Michael checked out of the Olympic Village and into a stateroom on a cruise ship, where *Sports*

Illustrated picked up the bill. En route to that liner in Piraeus, Michael stopped at a tennis club that had been rented by Visa, the credit card company that had introduced him to much of America. The facility had been built for the 1896 Olympics, near the ruins of a temple to Zeus and not far from Syntagma Square, where the Greek parliament met. Against a backdrop of clay courts and mimosa trees, wearing one of his 200-meter gold medals—the Cyrillic lettering was all Greek to him—Michael fielded questions at a formal press conference for the ninth time in 12 days. He blushed when a CBS reporter asked about being a sex symbol.

"All this is a new experience for me," Michael said. "I don't know how to answer that."

To Michael's surprise, a girl from Baltimore whom he had dated off and on had traveled to Athens, along with her mother. The Internet had Jenna Bush and Paris Hilton mentioning Michael. For 8 straight nights, he had been a main storyline on NBC, an ongoing drama that helped the network to record ratings for an Olympics held outside the United States. On August 23, just as the *Today Show* went live on the East Coast, Michael dove off a chartered yacht in the Aegean Sea. In exchange for a studio interview with Michael, a German television network agreed to help with logistics and security later that afternoon, for a chaotic photo shoot beneath the Parthenon. Michael wore a Speedo and all eight of his medals, and the shot and circumstances behind it evoked Spitz, who had been made rich by a German publication in 1972. What had been planned as a quiet family dinner grew when Michael insisted on having all of his friends from Octagon join him at a restaurant in the Plaka.

A day later, Islamic extremists took credit for the crash of two planes in Russia, and Athens was shaken by an earthquake that hit 4.5 on the Richter scale. Michael attended a Speedo function in the afternoon and a *Sports Illustrated* party at night. In the VIP section, Michael met NBA commissioner David Stern and hung out with Alice Mills, the Australian record holder in the 200 IM. He was done competing, and relaxed with a 21st-century cocktail, vodka and an energy drink. On August 25, 2,000 paying customers, Michael, and some contemporaries listened to Dannii Minogue sing at a beach party thrown by MTV and Speedo. Windsurfer Gal Fridman earned Israel's first gold medal and vowed to take it to the Tel Aviv memorial to the 11 who had been slain in Munich in 1972. Paul Hamm, the American who had benefited from a judging error, refused a request from the International Gymnastics Federation to return his gold medal. A day later, on August 26, the USOC asked President Bush's reelection campaign to pull a television advertisement that showed the flags of Afghanistan and Iraq, with the following voiceover: "Freedom is spreading throughout the world like a sunrise. And this Olympics there will be two more free nations. And two fewer terrorist regimes." The athlete in the spot was a swimmer. That night, Michael cheered the U.S. women as they won soccer's gold medal match.

Michael slept in until 12:30 p.m. on August 27, when Athens police used teargas to repel a crowd of some 1,000 protesting the pending arrival of Secretary of State Colin Powell, who eventually canceled his trip. Along with Krayzelburg and Erik Vendt, Michael saw the U.S. men's basketball team lose badly in a semifinal against Argentina. That same day, Marion Jones was involved in a failed baton exchange in the 400 relay and left Athens without a medal. During that same session at the Olympic Stadium, Morocco's Hicham el Guerrouj became the first man to complete a sweep of the 1,500- and 5,000-meter runs since Paavo Nurmi in 1924.

The host nation won six gold medals at the Athens Olympics. That matched Michael, who doubled the total of Canada, Poland, Turkey, and Spain. All medalists had to submit to drug testing, so Michael also led the Olympics in samples submitted. Three gold medalists and a record seven in all were caught cheating. A Hungarian hammer thrower supplied urine samples from different people, and a Greek weight lifter blamed spiked orange juice for his high level of testosterone. Kostas Kenteris and Katerina Thanou, the banned Greek sprinters, were linked to the Balco scandal. In the 7 months prior to Athens, Michael and Ian Thorpe had been the only athletes randomly tested four times by FINA. It would randomly test Michael once the rest of the year. In December 2004 alone, FINA conducted three random tests of Thorpe, who had criticized antidoping efforts as halfhearted.

Having opened on a Friday the 13th, the Athens Olympics closed under a full moon on Sunday, August 29. Three miles from the finish of the men's marathon, a defrocked Roman Catholic priest from Ireland attempted to tackle the Brazilian front-runner. Jacques Rogge, the president of the International Olympic Committee, ignored that security lapse and congratulated the host nation, saying "Dear Greek friends, you have won." At least there had been no acts of terrorism. Basketball veteran Dawn Staley hoisted the American flag at the closing. Michael hugged hundreds, and the Australian papers ran a shot of him embracing Mills. Before he marched onto the infield, NBC's Lewis Johnson asked for one last comment from Athens.

"I just want to go home and sleep," Michael told America.

Rest would be a long time coming.

A few hours later, Michael took a flight to London, then another to Orlando, Florida. On the same day that he landed on a commemorative Wheaties box, Michael began a monthlong, cross-country bus tour that was a joint venture of Disney and Octagon. The Swim with the Stars tour began at Disneyworld and concluded at Disneyland in Anaheim, California. It covered nearly 7,000 miles as Michael, Crocker, and Krayzelburg swam exhibitions and signed autographs at 15 pools. They hit Atlanta, then Long Island and Manhattan, where a gossip columnist reported that Michael passed along his phone number to Jenna Bush's publicist at a nightclub.

Forty years after the Beatles played Baltimore, the tour hit Michael's hometown. He had given the region a welcomed summer diversion from the Orioles, who finally snapped a 12-game losing streak on the day of the Closing Ceremony. Politicians and cameramen in the dark about his itinerary flocked to Pete's Grille, his old breakfast stop, where he did not show. As "Someday My Prince Will Come" pumped out of the sound system, Michael appeared on the Loyola College pool deck. The stands were filled with children from Riverside Elementary School, where he had been a regular visitor. That night, the tour visited the University of Maryland pool. A day later, on September 11, Baltimore County honored its favorite son with what it called the "Phelpstival." A road leading to Towson High was renamed Michael Phelps Way. Three years after the 9/11 bombings, Gerry Brewster, one of his ninth-grade teachers, led a moment of silence. A crowd of 10,000 lined York Road during a parade to the county courthouse, where local, state, and national office holders read proclamations and presented keepsakes to Michael. Seemingly on cue, Robert Ehrlich, the Republican governor of Maryland, yawned at the introduction of Martin O'Malley, the Democratic mayor of Baltimore City. The rising stars in their respective parties were already gearing up for a 2006 gubernatorial campaign. U.S. Senator Barbara Mikulski directed a bizarre taunt at Beijing, the host of the 2008 Olympics: "We know those Chinese will eat their eggrolls when you get there."

The bus made its way to campus pools at Penn State University and Ohio State, then a recreation center in Chicago. Michael missed the longest leg, 920 miles to Dallas, to make an appearance at the Ryder Cup in suburban Detroit, a short drive from Ann Arbor. The golf competition was televised by NBC and backed by Argent Mortgage, one of Michael's sponsors. He enjoyed a long visit with Larry Brown, who had gone from coaching the NBA champion Pistons to overseeing the most disappointing Olympic basketball team ever. Michael rejoined the tour in Dallas and resumed his rolling poker game with Crocker and Krayzelburg. Leaving Dallas, they motored 780 miles to Denver, then 530 to Salt Lake City, and 850 more to Seattle. The bus had once been the mobile home for magician David Copperfield. It was outfitted with sleeping quarters, arcade games, and PlayStation 2 consoles. The road and electronics were nothing new, unlike the lack of supervision. For the first time in his life, Michael didn't have his mother or coach telling him what to do.

"No Mom, and no Bob," Michael said. "Being away from Bob was actually weirder. When I'm at a meet, I really don't get to see my mom, but from the time I was 12, I had never spent more than 48 hours away from Bob."

Krayzelburg turned 29 on the 170-mile leg from Seattle down to Portland. The veteran had put off a third shoulder surgery to race in Athens, where Crocker had experienced his untimely poor health. Peter Carlisle, Michael's agent, suffered from exhaustion at the Opening Ceremony. Heat stress forced Gary Giles, among the family friends who went to Athens, to miss Michael's gold medal in the 200 IM. Debbie was emotionally spent as she returned to her administrative post with the Baltimore County schools. Analyzing Michael's races had been the most draining assignment Rowdy Gaines had ever had with NBC. Michael seemed to be the only person who hadn't been laid low by the Olympics, but trouble loomed in Oregon.

Sensitive to back pain since 1999, Michael felt something sharp on his lower right side during an exhibition at the Mount Hood Community

College Aquatic Center. It flared again during a freestyle start. Masking his pain, he gingerly emerged from the pool and headed to a ready room.

"This isn't good," Michael told Morgan Boys, an Octagon advance person. "There's pain on my right side, and it shouldn't be there, because that was supposed to be an easy swim. I don't feel right. Something isn't right."

Crocker and Krayzelburg calmed Michael as the bus began a 600-mile leg down to Sacramento. The pain subsided, but he obsessed about the back problems that had halted his sister Whitney's career. Challenging Aaron Peirsol at the U.S. Trials or Thorpe at the Olympics was a lark compared to this uncertainty. Michael was no longer the king of the Olympics, but an insecure, uncertain teenager. He was in tears, not because of physical pain, but fear of the unknown. The tour concluded in Anaheim, where Debbie and Bowman met him. After Michael had a reassuring response to a session in Tustin with two physical therapists who had helped Kaitlin Sandeno win three medals in Athens, it was assumed that his condition was the product of 6 weeks without training and a month on a bus.

"The tour was a great idea, but the next time, we're going by jet," Michael said. "It was great getting to know Ian and Lenny better, but it was a long month, a really long month. It was fun at the start, but then I really started feeling like crap."

The Swim with the Stars tour closed on October 5. En route from Disneyland to John Wayne Airport, Michael alerted Debbie and Bowman that their car was being followed. At the airport, two men and a woman emerged from the trailing vehicle and attempted to force their way into Michael's car. The most familiar was the stalking swim fan, the same taxi driver who had wanted to get close before and after the U.S. Trials 3 months earlier. Bowman confronted the man, who was detained by airport security as coach and athlete took a flight to Indianapolis. Debbie took a different one to Baltimore, and the incident added more anxiety to an already difficult farewell.

Michael was inclined to withdraw from FINA's world short-course championships, which were scheduled to capitalize on post-Athens buzz, but Argent Mortgage was a primary sponsor and he felt it his duty to compete. On October 7, the meet opened at Conseco Fieldhouse, and

Michael won the 200 freestyle with an American record time. His back tightened, however, and he withdrew from the next morning's preliminaries of the 400 IM. After consulting with a physician from USA Swimming, Michael withdrew from the meet and returned to Baltimore on the morning of October 9. A session that afternoon with Scott Heinlein, his physical therapist, nearly doubled Michael's range of motion, but Peter Rowe, his personal physician, scheduled an examination with Andy Cosgarea, an orthopedic surgeon and the director of Sports Medicine at The Johns Hopkins Hospital. Like Rowe, Cosgarea was a North Baltimore Aquatic Club parent.

Cosgarea studied a magnetic resonance image (MRI) of Michael's back and found evidence of damage in and around the L4 and L5 vertebra, what he would describe to laypeople as "low back pain due to repetitive hyperextension." The MRI showed evidence of a stress reaction and a spondylolysis, a defect in the pars interarticularis section of the vertebral arch, a condition that occurs most frequently among young athletes. A vertebra could slip over the one below it, compressing nerves in the spinal canal and causing pain. Compounding Michael's alarm, his pain originated in the same vertebra where Whitney had suffered a stress fracture and a herniated disc, respectively. With no major meets on the horizon, caution was advised, and Michael was ordered to limit his training to 20 minutes of freestyle per day and to wear a back brace outside the pool.

"The only thing I knew for sure was that this was just what Whitney had gone through," Michael said. "That was the low point of my swimming career. I was scared. I didn't know what was going to happen. If my Mom and Bob were worried, I didn't notice, because I was freaking out on my own. When Dr. Cosgarea recommended rest, that's not what I wanted to hear. I wanted to get back in the pool, return to my regular routine. It was like going through physical withdrawal. You have something that's a part of your life for 12 years, every day, and then someone says back off for 8 weeks? I didn't know what to do with myself. I laid around our house in Rodgers Forge, ate, watched TV, and slept. I was jealous of the guys at Michigan, who were back in the water. I was down. I was not energized or excited about anything."

Michael got his first real taste of Michigan culture on October 30, when he attended the Wolverines' triple-overtime football victory over Michigan State in Ann Arbor. Post-Athens obligations had delayed his enrollment in the college, and now he was an idle teen in search of a diversion. The adrenaline rush he had been on for nearly a year magnified his boredom.

Townsend, Michael's best friend, had studied at Salisbury University, and on November 4, they took a road trip to that town on the Eastern Shore of Maryland. Once in Salisbury, Michael had two beers and a shot of alcohol at an off-campus get-together, where he left Townsend and headed out with some new friends. A few blocks away, he drove his 2005 Land Rover through a stop sign, in plain view of a Maryland State Police patrol car. During questioning, Michael mentioned that his father had been a state trooper for 30 years. The officer responded that he knew who Michael was. Asked to take a Breathalyzer test to determine his blood alcohol content, Michael's measured at 0.08, the exact minimum for driving under the influence of alcohol in Maryland. He was also charged with driving while impaired, violation of a license restriction— the state's legal drinking age is 21—and failure to obey a traffic control device. Four weeks to the day after Michael had withdrawn from the world championships, he was released from the state police barracks in Salisbury at 1 a.m.

Too disgraced to explain his arrest to his mother or coach, Michael telephoned Carlisle. His parents and Bowman were disappointed but supportive. It was a Friday, and they took the weekend to assess the situation and weigh his options. Any notion that Michael's arrest would remain private was naïve, but he attempted to go about his business as usual. He remained an honorary captain of the Baltimore Ravens at their November 7 Sunday night game against the Cleveland Browns. Michael could have contested the charges, but on November 8, after weighing that option and others, he decided to admit that he had made a mistake and telephoned writers for *USA Today,* the *Washington Post,* the *Baltimore Sun,* the Associated Press, and ESPN.

"You can hope that situations like the one I faced go away, but unless you're an average Joe, that's not a realistic option," Michael said in retrospect. "I made a serious mistake, and I needed to man up to what I had done. For 8 years, my life had been so structured. I had little or no freedom. When I finally got some, I grabbed too much. Things can change in the blink of an eye. One minute you're on top of the world, feeling so good, and the next you're experiencing the exact opposite, in the pits. That was the worst month of my life, but just when you think things can't get any worse, you find out that they can."

Michael had good genes, was raised in a swimming family, and followed his sisters into one of America's premier clubs. He had come of age in an era that fueled his ambition, and had been teamed with an iconoclastic coach who ignored the accepted limits of an endurance athlete. For 7 years, nearly every decision that had been made by Michael or for him had been weighed with Olympic greatness in mind. If any of those choices or circumstances had not turned in his favor, it's doubtful that Michael would have accomplished what he had in Athens. There, he had been compared to the Greek god Poseidon, who lorded over the sea, but now he related to Ikaros, who had flown too close to the sun and tumbled to the ground. It seemed as if his golden touch had turned cold, as if he was overdrawn at the bank of Olympic karma.

He immediately made a public appearance and spoke out against drinking and driving, but most days were spent stewing in embarrassment and isolation, wondering what else could go wrong. He watched his television in disbelief on November 19, as the Indiana Pacers were involved in a brawl in Detroit. It resulted in a 25-game suspension for Jermaine O'Neal, whose No. 7 jersey had been given to Michael by Larry Bird during an April Fools' Day promotional appearance.

On December 6, a second MRI of Michael's back showed more definitive evidence of a stress fracture on both sides of the L4 vertebra. Three options were outlined. He could stop training for 6 months; train through the pain and risk further degeneration to several back discs; or undergo surgical repair, screws and a bone graft that would mean a postoperative recovery of 3 months with no swimming. As Cosgarea and Rowe received third and fourth opinions from leading orthopedic surgeons, Michael and the other members of Team Phelps mulled the unspoken fourth option, that he might never swim at an elite level again.

"It had taken us a while for Whitney to hang up her suit," Debbie said. "If Michael calls tomorrow and says 'I'm done, I can't do this anymore,' all I can say is 'heck of a job.' To do this, day in and day out, how much can the body take?"

Bowman alternated between worst-case scenarios and the sense that it was much ado about nothing. Other world-class athletes, like Steve Nash, the 2004–05 NBA Most Valuable Player, soldiered on through conditions similar to Michael's. Bowman asked Rowe to get an opinion from Scott Rodeo, an orthopedic surgeon who had qualified for the NCAA swim championships during his undergraduate days at Stanford and been the U.S. swim team physician at the 2003 World Championships and 2004 Olympics. Rodeo had helped elite athletes endure back pain, and knew Michael. After studying his history, Rodeo recommended that it would be safe for Michael to resume training, albeit with a reduced load.

"When it was suggested that Michael take 6 months off, it might as well have been a death sentence for him, so I wanted another opinion," Bowman said. "We were all walking around like he was made of eggshells, wondering if he'll be able to move 8 years down the road, but the injuries to his back were so minute, and what we found after a few days of inactivity was that Michael became symptom-free. It got to the point where he was going to go for it, or it was never going to happen."

That angst mounted as Michael waited to complete the purchase of a house in Ann Arbor. He spent late November and early December in Bowman's home, where their nerves frayed more than ever.

Bowman: "Are you eating enough? Are you sleeping enough?"

Michael: "Stop treating me like a kid. I can't stand this anymore. I'm going to leave."

Bowman: "Fine. Don't let the door hit you on the way out."

Michael: "Good. I'm going back to Baltimore."

When he called home to break that news to his mother, Debbie told Michael to slow down, think rationally, and to make a mental list of the pros and cons of leaving Ann Arbor and returning to Baltimore. He mulled his situation for a few hours and returned to practice that afternoon, tardy but in no way contrite.

"I was fed up living with Bob," Michael said. "I felt like a 12-year-old, like he was trying to make decisions for me. It was like nothing had changed. I had to get out on my own."

Days later, Michael signed the settlement papers on a four-story townhouse in an upscale development near campus. Before Debbie could help him furnish, he slept on an air mattress supplied by a Michigan assistant coach. On December 29, Michael was a humbled figure as he walked past a bank of TV minicams and entered Salisbury District Court to plead guilty to driving while impaired. Given his clean record, dozens of written testimonials to his character, and the fact that he had represented his country with courage, distinction, and honor at the world's biggest sporting event, his plea bargain was fairly routine. The state dropped its other charges against Michael, who was granted probation before judgment and ordered to pay $305 in fines and court costs, to speak at three local schools on the perils of drinking and driving, and to attend a meeting of Mothers Against Drunk Driving.

He then jetted across the country to Southern California, to resume his place as a volunteer assistant coach with the University of Michigan and a member of Club Wolverine. Bowman had taken the teams to a meet at Soka University, a fledgling liberal arts college with a Buddhist influence a short drive south of Long Beach, site of the U.S. Trials. Bowman ordered an 11 p.m. curfew on December 31, 2004, and it was already January 1 back in Baltimore when Michael called family and friends to say Happy New Year. The first meet of a long, momentous Olympic year had come at Auburn University in Alabama, where Michael had unwound playing arcade games with teammates as young as 13. Now it closed on a quiet, equally innocent note.

A week after Michael's arrest had been made public, USA Swimming held a $1,000-per-seat fundraiser in Manhattan. Eleven "Living Legends" were the presenters, and Michael received his Male Swimmer of the Year award from Spitz. The USOC went on to name Michael its Sportsman of the Year, but the 2004 Sullivan Award went to Hamm, and *Sports Illustrated* gave its Sportsman of the Year Award to the Boston Red Sox. Michael's arrest didn't enhance his chances at the prestigious *SI* honor, but Spitz and his seven golds didn't win it in 1972, either.

Bowman fretted that Michael's sponsors would drop him. None did. After his arrest, Michael avoided unwanted scrutiny by spending a night at his father's home and felt the eyes of the world on him at a rest stop in Ohio, but even if the arrest had never happened, he would have had difficulty adjusting to being a public figure.

"I had no idea that it was ever going to get that big," Michael said. "It was weird, but fun, although there are times you want to be an average person. I read a story about (New England Patriots quarterback) Tom Brady. He can't go to the grocery store or movies in Boston, because he's so big. You go out to eat, there may be times you have to stop for autographs, but in the end, that's not a very big sacrifice. I wouldn't trade that for the alternative."

Carlisle told Michael that his fans had a right to be angry, but that most would forgive him.

"There is no class in how to handle fame," Carlisle said. "I don't think you can prepare a kid for that, any better than you can prepare someone for parenthood. Listen to Michael Jordan and Tiger Woods discussing their adjustment to the realization that they would never have another anonymous moment. It's the one thing they can't adequately express, how great it is to be a star and how simultaneously hard it can be."

Michel Eyquem de Montaigne observed that fame and serenity do not mix. Michael had never heard of the 16th-century French essayist, but he was familiar with the words of Eminem, whose "Till I Collapse" had provided inspiration from Barcelona to Athens. Michael was driven to win gold medals, not become a celebrity. He had no idea how to define his place in the world; even the supreme effort that resulted in his feat at the Athens Olympics remained inexplicable.

"I don't know, I just got in and swam," Michael responded, when asked how he accomplished what he did in Athens. "It was a combination of me growing up, and not wanting to lose. I was taught to dream big. If you don't, you're going to fall back."

Bowman has a degree in child psychology and has spent nearly a decade with Michael, but there are some things he doesn't want to know.

"There are all kinds of psychological tests that we can give athletes, but I don't want to get into the specifics of Michael's performance mentality," said Bowman, whose interest in the horseracing business is growing. "I don't want to mess with it. Once you take a thoroughbred to the starting gate and he's okay, you don't do it again. You don't want to mess with stuff that's natural."

Only one member of Team Phelps was dismayed by Michael's disinterest in recounting his performance in Athens. Debbie was eager to learn what her son had thought of it all, but Michael is still not given to intro-spection, perhaps in step with the influence of Bowman and Carlisle.

Bowman, who had hired Carlisle as *his* agent after the Olympics, was all of 39 in Athens. Driving from Baltimore to Ann Arbor afterward, he wouldn't even spare a single afternoon, as he abandoned his plan to stop in Western Pennsylvania and tour Fallingwater, a landmark structure designed by Frank Lloyd Wright. Carlisle missed the burial of his grand-mother to go to Barcelona in 2003, and dealt with the loss of two other members of his immediate family in the run-up to Athens. Late in 2004, as Michael dealt with his assorted crises, Carlisle began to negotiate for him the most lucrative sponsorship deal ever for an Olympic athlete.

"I don't have the luxury of digesting the significance of what Michael has done," Carlisle said. "My obligation is to make the best of it and protect against the worst of it. If I quit doing that, and sat on the beach and looked at the horizon, then I wouldn't be doing my job."

At the North Baltimore Aquatic Club's fundraiser in May 2004, Michael successfully bid $5,000 for a week at a vacation home in Jackson Hole, Wyoming. Well into 2005, he had no idea when he would use it. He was concerned not with taking a vacation, but with regaining his form, branching out into freestyle, and acclimating himself to Michigan.

He got the "M" logo tattooed on his left hip, balancing the Olympic rings on his right. He purchased a gas grill and learned how to live with-out steamed crabs, a Chesapeake Bay delicacy. In his first semester as a college student, Michael assumed a light load in the classroom and the pool. In late March, he returned to an old stomping ground, Indianapo-lis, for USA Swimming's qualifying meet for the 2005 World Champion-ships. Michael won the 200 IM, as expected, but it was a surprise when he caught Crocker in the 100 butterfly and upset Jason Lezak in the 100 freestyle.

"What it came down to," said Rowe, his personal physician, "is that Michael did his usual superhuman recovery."

On April 11, Michael returned to Baltimore to serve as a hometown judge at the Miss USA pageant. One week later, he was in Salisbury, speaking to high schoolers, who were not much younger, about their prom pledge not to drink and drive. May took Michael and Speedo Inter-national's other elite athletes to Monte Carlo. In June, rather than take a bus, Michael jetted between appearances at Swim with the Stars camps in Atlanta, Denver, and San Jose. At the Santa Clara International Invitational that month, Michael's lactate reading was so high after a third-place finish in the 100 freestyle, Bowman declined to tell him the count.

Four days later, Michael turned 20 in Ann Arbor, where he had a fairly routine disagreement with Bowman at a morning practice. What made it atypical was that a camera crew, hired by Carlisle for a documentary on Michael and Crocker, recorded it all. Ordered to work on his relay starts, Michael dismissed Bowman, blew off his warmdown, and said, "What's one more bad decision?" He reported late for the afternoon practice, "just to piss Bob off."

On July 6, the IOC chose London over Paris, New York, and other bid cities to host the 2012 Olympics. A day later, Islamic terrorists detonated four bombs in the London subway system, killing 55 in the worst attack on British soil since World War II. Softball and baseball were voted out of the Olympics, as IOC president Jacques Rogge noted that not only does baseball not send its best athletes, its leagues "perform in an environment where doping controls are not what we have in the Olympic world."

That very day, Orioles first baseman Rafael Palmeiro took part in a teleconference at the invitation of a U.S. Congressional task force on sports doping. Unbeknownst to Congress, Palmeiro had tested positive for a steroid 2 months earlier, and the newest member of baseball's 3,000 hits and 500 home runs club was about to serve a 10-game suspension. (The doping war continued to evolve. Kicker Vencill, the cautionary tale of a swimmer, completed his 2-year doping suspension and received a $578,000 settlement from the manufacturer that produced the tainted supplement that had caused him to test positive for a steroid in the first place. Before the year was out, Balco's Victor Conte would be sentenced to 4 months in prison in a plea bargain over his role in supplying banned substances to athletes, a group that allegedly included Barry Bonds and Marion Jones.)

Two weeks later, Michael was in Montreal for the 2005 World Championships. The year had begun with FINA citing budgetary concerns and organizational mismanagement as rationale to strip the meet from Canada's largest city. After the chief of the local organizing effort committed suicide, FINA sheepishly returned the meet to Montreal.

Athens had gone an estimated $3.2 billion over its projected $5.5 billion budget, and Montreal's Olympic Park was an older monument to Olympic waste. Built for the 1976 Games, its defining feature, a retractable roof, wasn't begun until September 1985, when Michael was 3 months old. After decades of blasé support, the stadium had lost its primary tenant when its Major League Baseball team moved to Washington, D.C., for the 2005 season. An American football field covered the stadium floor, which in 2001 had filled in as the fictitious "Baltimore Forum" in *The Sum of All Fears,* a movie based on a Tom Clancy thriller.

Michael attended his very own premiere on July 22, when Carlisle debuted the documentary *Unfiltered.* In the 75-minute film, Michael is seen visiting with the girl he took to his high school prom. At the premier, he accompanied Elsa Larson, a Michigan swimmer. Two days later, he began the most daunting schedule a man had ever attempted at the world championships, but with little of the attention he had gotten in Athens. Among family and friends, only Debbie, his sister Hilary, and Larson made the trip. Whitney had begun a new job in the office of Heinlein, the physical therapist who had worked wonders on Michael. Both Jamie Barone and Kevin Clements, Michael's training partners leading up to Athens, had taken coaching jobs on the East Coast. Marianne Limpert, who had trained at the NBAC in an ill-fated attempt to make a fourth Canadian Olympic team, was on hand to do commentary for local television. The only live TV coverage in the United States was on a regional cable network that reached 15 million homes, and the meet did not warrant staff reporters from either the *New York Times* or *USA Today.* Michael had fought to elevate swimming's status, but on the first day of swimming, he was glad that the meet attracted little media interest.

A hot spell had broken and a breeze cooled the temporary open-air venue at Parc Jean-Drapeau on Ile Saint Helene, an island in the St. Lawrence River. It was a great contrast to the last two summers, which had peaked in steamy Mediterranean locales. In his first international race in the long-course format since his consummately professional effort in the

Athens 100 butterfly final, Michael raced like a rookie in his preliminary of the 400 freestyle. Third at the final turn, he was unable to shift into the gear that had made him such a formidable closer, and faded to seventh. He finished in 3:50.53, nearly 4 seconds slower than his personal best and almost 6 seconds behind Grant Hackett. As he processed that scoreboard news, Michael closed his eyes and shook his head in disbelief. He was the 18th fastest of the 57 men entered and didn't come close to advancing to the final, a new and unpleasant experience that he remains clueless to explain.

That evening, Michael helped the American men win the 400 freestyle relay at an international meet for the first time since 1998. Two nights later, on July 26, with Thorpe taking the year off and Pieter van den Hoogenband of the Netherlands recovering from surgery, Michael scored a resounding win in the 200 freestyle that made his failure in the 400 free all the more puzzling. He was ahead of Thorpe's world-record pace at the midway mark, faltered a bit on the last turn, and showed his lack of conditioning in the final 50, but nonetheless took a tenth of a second off his American record and beat Hackett by nearly a second.

One night later, Michael went 48.93 in the semifinals of the 100 freestyle, another personal best, but it would be his last of the year. On July 28, he finished seventh in the final, more than a half-second out of the medal hunt. The night was hardly a failure, as he returned an hour later and dominated the deepest 200 IM field ever, one that saw Hungary's Laszlo Cseh and American Ryan Lochte become only the second and third men under 1:58. The next evening, Michael was the youngest member of the victorious 800 freestyle relay. July 30 brought another memorable 100 butterfly, but this time he was more than a second behind Crocker's world record of 50.40. How far had their sport advanced? Crocker went nearly a second faster than Spitz had gone in the 100 *freestyle* at the 1972 Olympics.

The meet closed on July 31, when 16-year-old Katie Hoff, Michael's replacement as star-in-residence at the NBAC, added to the club's hundreds of national age-group records with her second world title and a meet record in the 400 IM. Crocker swam in the final of the medley relay, while Michael was relegated to the preliminary. He won five gold medals and a silver, a haul that would have been the high point in the career of all but a handful of men, but it was a disappointment by his standards. The fifth and sixth individual world titles of his career had brought him even with Thorpe, but Hackett's sweep of the 400, 800, and 1,500 freestyles made him the all-time leader with seven. Michael fed primarily off what was left of the fitness he took to Athens. The previous year had included little more than half of his customary annual mileage, but that was of little solace.

"I'm not where I want to be right now," Michael said after the loss to Crocker. "This world championships has sort of been a big wake-up call. It hasn't been a normal year for me. The only thing I can do is use this as motivation."

That evening, Bowman and Carlisle discussed a reordering of Michael's priorities. The coach felt that his athlete was overextended. If Michael was going to continue to develop his potential, Bowman said, it was imperative that he spend more time at the University of Michigan pool and less promoting his sponsors.

Before that could be done, however, Michael had a rather important commitment to fulfill.

EPILOGUE

BEIJING, AUGUST 2005

Michael wore a perturbed expression on the first day of August, as he passed time at Dorval, the Montreal International Airport. The dominant figure on the United States swim team, never mind the most successful athlete at the Athens Olympics, had drawn a middle seat in the coach section on a cross-continental flight to Los Angeles and the 2005 Duel in the Pool.

A day later, Michael won both individual medleys, the 200 butterfly, and finally got to team with Ian Crocker on a medley relay as the American men enjoyed another rout of Australia. USA Swimming's Summer Nationals began the next day at that same pool in Irvine, where titles in the 200 butterfly and 200 freestyle gave Michael 27 for his career, the most by a man since 1945. It left him 11 shy of Johnny Weissmuller's record 38. Club Wolverine won the team title and the 400 freestyle relay, where Michael split faster than Roland Schocman, the great South African sprinter.

After nearly 2 straight weeks of racing, most world-class swimmers would have demanded rest and relaxation, but Michael had stopped being average a long time ago.

Matsunichi, an electronics manufacturer based in Hong Kong, had signed Michael to a sponsorship contract in March 2005. What was reported to be the single most lucrative sponsorship deal ever for a traditional Olympic athlete will pay Michael $1 million annually through 2008 and introduce him to the largest market on earth. When the men from his father's generation missed a putt, they consoled themselves with the knowledge that a billion Chinese didn't care. Now the nation had closer to 1.3 billion, and its isolationist history was giving way to epochal economic change. The People's Republic of China had not entered the United Nations until 1971, and the International Olympic Committee was among the institutions that had ostracized the nation in favor of Taiwan. Mainland China wasn't welcomed into the IOC for good until 1979. It gained more official approval in 2001, when China joined the World Trade Organization and Beijing was awarded the 2008 Olympics.

Michael got his first taste of the burgeoning economic superpower on August 12, when he landed in Hong Kong on a promotional tour arranged by Matsunichi. He discovered a city that seemed like Manhattan on steroids. The neon and skyscrapers overwhelmed his senses, and Michael kept having experiences that could have been scripted by Lance Acord, the director of his Visa "Lap" commercial. Acord had worked on *Lost in Translation,* an offbeat Bill Murray film about an American celebrity trying to find his bearings in Tokyo. Michael had a surreal moment of his own when he emerged from a taxi and needed a good 30 seconds to see that he was the butterflyer on a billboard for Omega watches.

In Athens, after his mother and sisters had been introduced at a reception, they found themselves swarmed by photo-snapping members of the Beijing organizing committee. He was prepared for a similarly zealous reception, but found the newspaper and television reporters in China unfailingly polite and respectful. Members of the American media did not bow during introductions. There was more ritual at a lavish dinner with the chairman of Matsunichi. The traditional dishes included eel gills, jellyfish heads, and a salad made of flower petals, but Michael took an immediate liking to Peking Duck.

Day two in Hong Kong was marked by a typhoon, a stroll through one of the world's busiest intersections, and the launch of his Matsunichi commercial on Chinese television. The next morning, Michael jetted to Beijing and checked into the Hotel Kerry, a few blocks east of Tiananmen Square, an enduring symbol of Chinese political oppression. He had been 3 years old in May 1989, when protesters were brutally shot down there.

On August 14, a year to the day after Michael had won his first gold medal in Athens, Matsunichi officials escorted him north to the National Aquatics Center, the 17,000-seat venue that will host Olympic swimming in 2008. It sits at the very heart of the Olympic Green, what OAKA was to Athens and Olympic Park was to Sydney. Given the air pollution in Beijing, Olympic Green seems a misnomer, but the title is meant to symbolize a commitment to clean the environment. In contrast to Athens, the IOC had told the Beijing organizers to slow their preparations. Like much of the city, the Olympic Green was very much a construction site, and security officials declined Matsunichi's request to have the star of the last Olympics check out where he planned to medal some more.

Michael was a seasoned world traveler but had rarely had time to do any serious sightseeing. When Grant Hackett had served as his Australian host in the spring of 2003, Michael had been enthralled by the Gold Coast and vowed to one day explore the Great Barrier Reef. In Athens, Michael had posed with his eight medals beneath the Parthenon, but he was too freshly famous to tour it without being mobbed by the general public.

There was much he had missed, but on his last full day in Beijing, Michael ignored the inclement weather and made the most of a trip north of Beijing. It was pouring rain when the car that had chauffeured Michael, Peter Carlisle, and Octagon press officer David Schwab pulled up to a visitors' entry near the Great Wall of China. Carlisle and Schwab are adventurous types, but it had been a hard 4 days. They would have been content with a quick photo opportunity, but Michael had other ideas.

"Let's go," he announced. "We're here. We might as well really see this thing."

Debbie is a power walker, and her son, armed in a raincoat, set a brisk pace for the group during a 75-minute walk to and along the Wall.

It was another 75 minutes on the return back to their car, but Michael seemed energized. He plans to return to the city several times before the next Summer Olympics open on August 8, 2008. He will always be linked to Athens, but Beijing could be the city where Michael separates himself from every previous Olympian. Spitz, Finnish distance runner Paavo Nurmi, sprinter Carl Lewis, and Soviet gymnast Larysa Latynina earned nine gold medals in their Olympic careers. No one has ever won 10. Michael won six in Athens, and his career goal for Beijing is clear.

"I know what I want to do," Michael said. "If it happens, great. If I become the most decorated Olympian, I do. I'm going through life, doing something I love."

On August 18, Michael, Carlisle, and Schwab completed their long journey back to the States. During a layover in San Francisco, Michael heard the news that Eminem had canceled a 10-show tour of Europe, citing exhaustion. The artist who had written and performed "Till I Collapse," the song Michael used to psyche himself up from Barcelona to Athens, had done just that.

Michael took a brief, Baltimore-based break before he returned to Ann Arbor, where a second attempt to settle down unfolded much smoother than the first. His townhouse gradually turned into a home. The basement game room featured a poster-size blowup of Michael landing a mock punch on the chin of Muhammad Ali. The residents included a kitten named Sydney and Dan Ketchum, one of the Michigan men who had helped the United States win gold in the 800 freestyle relay in Athens. Ketchum needed a place to stay as he finished his engineering studies at Michigan, and rented a room from Michael in the fall semester. Michael took a light course load but grew more comfortable with college and his new surroundings.

After his arrest, Bowman had observed that Michael didn't really fit in anywhere, that he would never be just another member of Club Wolverine or an average Michigan student. Michael had lived a fishbowl existence, but now he was in an extremely big pond, one of the nation's best college athletic programs. He loved it when the secretary in the kinesiology department called him Joe. Maybe Michael was the only undergraduate driving his own 2006 BMW 750 onto campus, but as a volunteer assistant coach, he did not have his own parking space at the

Michigan pool. Michael walked to games at Michigan's 107,000-seat football stadium, and said "Go Blue" when he accepted an ESPY for his performances in Athens. He pulled for his Wolverines but didn't forget his roots, which showed when the Indianapolis Colts made their annual exit from the NFL playoffs.

"The one thing I won't sit for," he said, making a point about the migration of National Football League franchises, "is when someone in the Midwest says 'the Ravens are really the Browns.' Well, if you're going to say that, then the Colts belong in Baltimore. I know they left before I was ever born, but I was raised right."

While other activities blossomed into spectator sports, his own showed modest gains. In the year after Athens, observers noted a spike in boys mimicking Michael and wearing jammers at meets, and USA Swimming added more than 16,000 to its rolls. It was a 7 percent increase in membership, a boost, but not as big as the one the governing body had seen after the 1992 Olympics, which only reinforced Michael's desire to spread the word about swimming.

"Whoever said life is going to be fair?" he said. "Just because we're never going to be as big as football or basketball doesn't mean you give up. That's why I've given so much time and effort as I can to promote the sport."

Michael said he was "broadening his horizons, reading the business section in the paper, not just the sports." He traded e-mails with Troy Pusateri, the NBAC swimmer who long ago had dubbed him "Little Phelps" and was now doing security work in Afghanistan. Driving around Ann Arbor, Michael was more apt to listen to an acoustic mix CD than rap.

Did people remember that he was still only 20 years old?

"Sometimes, they don't," he said. "I'll have facial hair before an event or a public appearance, and someone will tell me that I have to shave it off. . . . I was walking back from the Big House (the Michigan football stadium) after a game, and struck up a conversation with a stranger. He said he graduated from Michigan in 1985. I told him that was the year I was born."

With all of the demands that were placed on him, did Michael feel that he had a normal childhood, that he was allowed to be a kid growing up?

"I think so. I think I was allowed to be a kid," he said. "The accomplishments I had in Athens and the mistakes I made afterward, that all matured me, but in some ways, I'm still a big kid, and I'll probably be like that when I'm 30. It's like the Toys R Us commercial: I don't want to grow up."

At the same time he wants to expand interest in swimming, Michael longs to play celebrity poker on television. Jon Urbanchek, the longtime Michigan coach who had handed his program over to Bowman, said, "I hope Michael never loses that smirk on his face."

Much occurred to make Michael ponder the passage of time. He would attend the 2006 Winter Olympics in Torino, Italy. Katie Hoff followed his lead, as she turned professional at age 16, hired Carlisle, and signed a 10-year endorsement contract with Speedo. The NBAC has already produced the fastest all-around swimmer ever; now it intends to do the same for women. Michael's new swimming circle would be shaken by the accidental death of Eric Namesnik, a 35-year-old former Wolverine who won Olympic silver in 1992 and 1996 and was Urbanchek's heir apparent until the university sought Bowman. Michael was better prepared for the passing of Leoma Davisson, the only grandparent he had ever known. He lost that bond but became an uncle, as Whitney gave birth in 2006 to a daughter, Taylor. The year before, when Fred discovered that Whitney wanted both him and Michael to walk her down the aisle, he balked and did not attend. The two Phelps men maintain a chilly relationship.

"I grew up without a father," Fred said. "It's the last thing in the world I wanted my son to do."

Debbie busied herself with a plum assignment: She'll be the principal when Baltimore County's first new middle school in decades opens its doors in August 2006.

While emotional or physical distance separated Michael from his family, he began his ninth year of swimming for Bowman. The bookshelf in Bowman's office includes Gerry Spence's *How to Argue and Win Every Time,* and one photo of coach and athlete, taken at the 2000 Olympic Trials. Is Michael surprised that they're still together?

"No, we both want the same thing," he said. "Bob wants me to swim faster, and I want to swim faster. The venting we do, that's good, it just shows that neither of us is scared of the other."

Weary of having Michael proceed cautiously because of his back condition but wanting to add variety to his regimen, Bowman introduced some new methods. There was no weight room back in Baltimore, but now Michael was pumping iron, albeit with the distance men, only twice a week. Three mornings a week in the preseason, there were conditioning runs of 3 miles.

At 6:15 on a starlit September morning, the lanky guy with the surprisingly smooth gait near the head of the pack on State Street was Michael. He veered left into campus and cooled down on Ferry Field, the Michigan track, where a plaque commemorates the day in 1935 when Ohio State's Jesse Owens set four world records at the Big Ten championships. The opposite straight is flanked by the Michigan Union, where Johnny Weissmuller had some landmark races. One building down, at the Don Canham Natatorium, swimmers from Michigan and Club Wolverine set out to beat Michael during intervals. They included Olympic relay teammates Klete Keller and Peter Vanderkaay, and, thanks in part to Michael's notoriety, a strong class of freshmen. In 2006, Erik Vendt joined the group.

Bowman burned to make Michigan a regular NCAA contender and have Michael shore up the foundation of his fitness.

"We need to make a deposit," Bowman said, using a banking metaphor. "We had already taken a lot out for Athens, and all we've done from Athens to now is withdraw some more. The account is a bit low. Michael is nowhere near the aerobic shape he was in 2003, but he's stronger and his technique is better. His freestyle has improved significantly. In Athens, he had an unnecessary movement in his right hand. It's not there anymore."

The sense that Michael was regaining his fitness was reinforced when he busted his fastest 300 backstroke ever, but he still lacked the focus that had allowed him to make history in each of the previous five years. To make that point, Bowman cleared his morning calendar the very next day, September 20, for a frank discussion with Michael. The coach no longer had the time or inclination to hold the young athlete's hand and nag about nutrition and rest. The time had come for Michael to take stewardship of his career, and his legacy.

"I know," Michael said later that day, "what I have to do to start the second part of my life."

"It was the most productive, adult meeting we've ever had," Bowman said. "I laid out some things, and Michael nodded at everything I had to say. I have dozens of other swimmers besides him. He has a lot more responsibility in the areas of his life that affect performance. He has to take charge. I can't, his mom can't, Peter Carlisle can't. He understands that if he wants to remain the best on the planet, and if he wants free rein from me and his mom, he has to be more in control."

That afternoon, Michael returned to the pool for his second workout of the day. On the far wall, mounted high, alongside the diving platform, was a small, electronic scoreboard. As Michael finished practice, it read:

1052.09.12.05

The signage above was in the colors of the flag of the People's Republic of China, a red background decorated with yellow script that read "Countdown to Beijing."

1052 days, 9 hours, 12 minutes, 5 seconds.

That's how long Michael had until the start of the 2008 Olympics.

ACKNOWLEDGMENTS

A black-and-white set was good enough for Jackie Gleason and John Unitas. Valery Brumel and Wilma Rudolph, however, were another matter. On a July night in 1961, my father brought the first color television into our home, for a more vivid look at the *ABC Wide World of Sports* telecast of a track and field meet between the United States and the Soviet Union. It was in front of that television that I became enthralled with the Summer Olympics. Classmates knew Bob Hayes as a wide receiver for the Dallas Cowboys. I remembered him as the "World's Fastest Human" from the 1964 Games in Tokyo. Four years later, in 1968, my father and I marveled over Bob Beamon, Lee Evans, and Bill Toomey slicing through the thin Mexico City air. In 1972, we watched silently as Jim McKay told us of the horror unfolding in Munich. Four years after that, along with my brother, Tim, then and now a supporter of my writing, we planned a family trip to the Montreal Olympics. Health issues forced my father to remain home. Ed Zaruba, a friend of mine, took his place, and is still telling me to get over marathon king Frank Shorter being dethroned by an East German who ended up being exposed as a doping cheat.

The apple does not fall far from the tree. In July 1984, a portion of the money my wife, Mary, and I received as wedding gifts went to the only state-of-the-art television we have ever owned. The Los Angeles

Olympics were starting in a few days. A dishwasher lost out to Carl Lewis and Daley Thompson.

I wish my father were alive, so I could tell him about the events and places he inspired me to see. In January 2000, days after I had decided to cut back on my travel as a college sports reporter with *The Baltimore Sun*, I received an opportunity that I thought had passed me by. Molly Dunham Glassman, my editor at the time, offered me the assignment of covering the 2000 Olympics in Sydney, Australia. Molly believed in me, for which I remain grateful.

Mary, my wife, understood my fascination with the Games, and encouraged me to go back out on the road that I had just exited. As always, she makes it a wonderful life.

That family road trip to the 1976 Olympics began with the first session of swimming I had ever observed. I would not witness another until August 2000, at the U.S. Olympic Trials in Indianapolis, as the Summer Olympics beat reporter for *The Sun*. At the start of that assignment, I asked Murray Stephens if he had anyone at the North Baltimore Aquatic Club I should keep an eye on. Murray briefed me on a 14-year-old, Michael Phelps. I was ignorant to the ways of swimming when Bob Bowman allowed me to pull up a chair at the Meadowbrook Aquatic and Fitness Center. He answered my questions, debated some of my conclusions, and made me stop thinking like a civilian. Besides Bowman and Stephens, Paul Yetter, Cathy Lears, John Cadigan, Michael Brooks, and Scott Armstrong were among the NBAC coaches who pointed me in the right direction. Jamie Barone, Kevin Clements, and Marianne Limpert were generous with their time.

At the 2000 Olympics in Sydney, Australia, I leaned on John Eisenberg, Bill Glauber, and John Makely, coworkers at *The Sun*. I followed Michael at every meet he competed in from the 2003 World Championships in Barcelona to the Athens Olympics, and some of the themes that are in *Amazing Pace* were first explored in a series of articles in *The Sun* called *The Road to Athens*. Sam Davis, Randy Harvey, Bill Marimow, and Tim Franklin found the resources for a unique assignment. Jean Packard aided my research. Ray Frager offered a gentle editing touch. In Athens, Randy, Karl Ferron, Candi Thomson, Laura Vecsey, and John Cherwa helped me do my job.

Eisenberg has been my guide into the book world. He shared his expertise and his agent, Scott Waxman. Farley Chase of the Waxman Agency did a man's job completing a complex deal. Heidi Rodale was equally determined to get it done. Emily Williams and Susan Hindman made astute editing suggestions.

I am particularly grateful to those who volunteered to make my manuscript better. Brad Snyder scrutinized every word, and motivated me to reorganize and rewrite. Nicole Jeffrey, the authority on Ian Thorpe, helped with the chapter on Australia. Elliott Almond gave clarity to the doping chapter. Dr. Peter Rowe explained Michael's medical history. Greg Eggert checked my facts.

Before there was a book deal, John Craig, Vahe Gregorian, Mark Hyman, Rick Maese, Ken Rosenthal, and Ted Simendinger offered encouragment. Mike Ruane was great company on the Michael beat. Eric Adelson, Almond, Jo-Ann Barnas, Brian Cazeneuve, Chris Clarey, Wayne Coffey, Lisa Dillman, Phil Hersh, Jeffrey, Tim Layden, Craig Lord, Vicki Michaelis, Mike Sokolove, and Phil Whitten made pertinent observations of Michael in their work that aided my own. Mike DeArmond and Skip Myslenski tried to keep me sane at the Long Beach chapter of the Algonquin Round Table.

Rowdy Gaines, Everett Uchiyama, Mike Unger, Genadijus Sokolovas, and Chuck Wielgus of USA Swimming offered their insight, and Larry Herr, Nick Wallin, and Deb Whitney of that organization patiently answered my inquiries. Mary Wagner, Tarrah Smith Pollaro, and Sara Hunninghake of USA Swimming's media services department kept their cool when I lost mine. Whatever the continent, Bob Condron and Bill Hancock of the U.S. Olympic Committee make me feel welcome. Chris DeBlasio knew where to find me. Nick Thierry of FINA was a most valuable resource. The Web sites of FINA, USA Swimming, and *Swimming World* magazine were daily stops on the Michael beat.

Paul Bergen, Beth Botsford-Vencill, Cecil Colwin, Peter Daland, Gary Hall Jr., Scott Heinlein, Tom Himes, John Naber, Stu Isaac, John Leonard, David Marsh, Anita Nall, Dave Salo, Don Schollander, Jon Urbanchek, and Kicker Vencill returned my calls. Eddie Reese let me hang out at the University of Texas. In Australia, Grant Hackett and Don Talbot made time for me. Ian Crocker, Tom Dolan, and Lenny

Krayzelburg are thoughtful men who provided a unique perspective of Michael. On more than one occasion, Mark Spitz answered his telephone, apologized for not having the time, then stayed on the line for more than an hour.

Frank Morgan and David Pessin furthered my understanding of Michael's move into the professional ranks. *Amazing Pace* would not have been possible without the assistance of Peter Carlisle. Morgan Boys, Kathy Connors, Sean Foley, Drew Johnson, David Schwab and—most important—Marissa Gagnon are other Octagon employees who aided my work.

Michael's parents and sisters allowed me to peer into their lives. Debbie was always eager and willing to explain vital details of her son's development. Fred took me to the Tri-Towns. Hilary was always patient, and Whitney was most forthcoming. B.J. and Krista Davisson and Darlene Blaney, other members of Michael's extended family, made me feel at ease. Gerry Brewster is a great booster, of Michael and my work.

I thank the Olympic gods for producing Michael Phelps on my watch.

Most of all, thanks to Michael.

SOURCES

Chambliss, Daniel F. *Champions: The Making of Olympic Swimmers.* New York: William Morrow and Company, Inc. 1988.

Colwin, Cecil M. *Breakthrough Swimming.* Champaign, Illinois: Human Kinetics Publishers. 2002.

Fortin, Francois. *Sports: The Complete Visual Reference.* Westport, Connecticut: Firefly Books Ltd. 2000.

Grimsley, Will, ed. *The Sports Immortals: 50 of Sports' All-Time Greats As Selected by the Sports Staff of The Associated Press.* Englewood Cliffs, New Jersey: Prentice-Hall, Inc. 1972.

Kerper, Barrie, ed. *Athens: The Collected Traveler.* New York: Random House, Inc. 2004.

Lear, Chris. *Sub 4:00: Alan Webb and the Quest for the Fastest Mile.* Emmaus, Pennsylvania: Rodale Inc. 2003.

McKay, Jim. *My Wide World.* New York: Macmillan Publishing Co., Inc. 1973.

Miller, Geoffrey. *Behind the Olympic Rings*. Lynn, Massachusetts: H. O. Zinman Inc. 1979.

Mohindra, Vandana. *China: Eyewitness Travel Guides*. London: Dorling Kindersley Limited. 2005.

Mullen, P. H. *Gold in the Water: The True Story of Ordinary Men and Their Extraordinary Dream of Olympic Glory*. New York: St. Martin's Press. 2001.

Parrish, Marc. *Paths to the Olympics. Maize and Blue to Olympic Gold*. Detroit, Michigan: Colemar Press. 1997.

Phelps, Michael with Cazeneuve, Brian. *Michael Phelps: Beneath the Surface*. Champaign, Illinois: Sports Publishing L.L.C. 2004.

Voy, Robert, M.D. *Drugs, Sport, and Politics*. Champaign, Illinois: Leisure Press. 1991.

Wallechinsky, David. *The Complete Book of the Summer Olympics: Athens 2004 Edition*. Wilmington, Delaware: Sport Media Publishing, Inc. 2004.

INDEX

Spring National Championships, 12, 53, 63, 85–86, 94–97, 100, 110
Stephens, Murray, 30–34, 37–38, 63, 91, 121–22, 129, 152
Steroids, 134–35
Stewart, Melvin, 18
Summer National Championships, 30, 35–36, 39–41, 43–44, 48, 63, 91–93, 111
Super Bowl XXXVIII, 82–83
Swimming. *See also specific competitions*
  demographics of, 78
  history of competitive, 45–46
  marketing, 78–79
  Olympic program and, 87–89
  pedophile issue and, 107
  Phelps's (Michael) impact on, 227
  second-class status of, 72, 76–77
Swim with the Stars tour, 208–10
Szabo, Dominic, 144

T

Talbot, Don, 23, 178
Teeter, Susan, 51
Televised sports, 72, 77
Thanou, Katerina, 177, 191, 207
THG, 132
Thomas, Petria, 56
Thompson, Jenny, 66, 103, 123, 165, 200
Thorpe, Christina, 46
Thorpe, Ian
  agent of, 54
  Australian Trials and, 115
  coaches of, 46, 55
  Commonwealth Games and, 23
  fame of, 49–50, 55
  fluid and nutrition intake of, 128
  mother of, 25
  nickname of, 47
  Olympic Game participation of, 46, 50–52, 179, 183, 189
  Pan Pacific Championships and, 54, 108
  Phelps (Michael) and, 44, 46–47, 53–54, 93–94, 108, 169, 173, 183, 221
  physique of, 46
  press and, 142, 144
  sister of, 46
  Spitz (Mark) and, 56
  Summer National Championships and, 43–44

swimming technique of, 47–48
World Championships and, 24, 53, 186
year off and, 220
Thorpe, Jim, 59
Thorpe, Margaret, 25
Torres, Dara, 49, 130
Townsend, Matt, 7, 205, 212
Tucker, Scott, 94

U

Urbanchek, Jon, 48–49, 67, 121, 186, 228
U.S. Anti-Doping Agency (USADA), 130, 137
U.S. Olympic Training Center, 69

V

van den Hoogenband, Pieter, 50, 52–53, 94, 180–84, 191, 220
Vencill, Kicker, 129–30, 132, 136, 218
Vendt, Erik, 51, 92, 138, 178–79, 207
Viren, Lasse, 135
Visa, 80, 82–83, 151, 153, 176

W

Walker, Neil, 36, 95, 180, 182, 194
Wax, Charles, 6
Webb, Alan, 66
Weber, Bruce, 171
Weinberg, Moshe, 105
Weissmuller, Johnny, 4, 41, 59, 88, 223
Women in sports, 5, 87–88
World Anti-Doping Code, 131
World Championships, 16, 23–28, 39, 46, 47, 53–54, 74, 86, 108, 120, 123, 144, 186, 190, 203–4, 217–21

Y

Yamamoto, Takashi, 187–88
Yetter, Paul, 39

Z

Zeiger, Joanna, 118–19